THINGS CATHOLICS
ARE ASKED ABOUT

BOOKS ON CATHOLIC APOLOGETICS
BY FATHER SCOTT

———

GOD AND MYSELF
THE CREDENTIALS OF CHRISTIANITY
RELIGION AND COMMON SENSE
CHRIST OR CHAOS
THE HAND OF GOD
YOU AND YOURS
CONVENT LIFE
THINGS CATHOLICS ARE ASKED ABOUT
THE DIVINE COUNSELLOR
THE VIRGIN BIRTH

THINGS
CATHOLICS ARE ASKED
ABOUT

BY

MARTIN J. SCOTT, S.J.

TWENTY-SECOND THOUSAND

NEW YORK

P. J. KENEDY & SONS

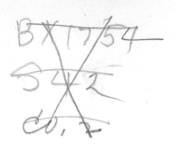

Imprimi Potest:

LAURENCE J. KELLY, S.J.

Præpositus Prov. Marylandiæ Neo-Eboracensis

Nihil Obstat:

ARTHUR J. SCANLAN, S.T.D.

Censor Librorum

Imprimatur:

✠ PATRICK CARDINAL HAYES

Archbishop New York

NEW YORK,
    MARCH 17, 1927.

TO

JAMES A. FLAHERTY

SUPREME KNIGHT
KNIGHTS OF COLUMBUS
WHOSE LIFE AND CHARACTER ARE AN INCENTIVE
TO LOYALTY TO GOD AND COUNTRY
THIS VOLUME IS DEDICATED
WITH THE ESTEEM OF THE AUTHOR

FOREWORD

Outside the Catholic Church there is at present very great interest in things Catholic. Sincere people of other denominations are dissatisfied with the vagueness and uncertainty of their creeds and the worldly character of their churches. Sensational preaching may make a preacher popular, but does not satisfy the yearning of the religious soul for the things of the spirit. Hence, many earnest people, thoroughly dissatisfied with religion as they find it, but who nevertheless realize the needs of the spiritual life, are turning to the Catholic Church with its certainty of creed and its sacramental solace and support.

Ordinarily these people do not come in contact with the Catholic clergy, but they do associate with Catholics in business and society. The present volume is intended to furnish a ready and satisfactory answer to the inquiries commonly made with regard to Catholic belief and practice. Catholics who are able to give a convincing reason for their faith are a light unto those who are groping after the truth.

Busy pastors will find this volume a serviceable book to hand to those who seek instruction in our holy religion. Catholics generally will find it a storehouse of information for themselves, and also for the enlightenment of others.

CONTENTS

CONTENTS

THINGS CATHOLICS ARE ASKED ABOUT

CHAPTER I

THE CHURCH AND NON-CATHOLIC INQUIRERS

A GENTLEMAN said to me, some time ago, "Father, why is your Church so narrow with regard to divorce? Do you not realize that your marriage doctrine keeps a good many people from your religion?" My reply was that people said the very same thing to Christ in His day. I then went on to show him that the Catholic Church is no narrower or broader than her Founder, Jesus Christ. His Church may no more alter His teaching than a judge may alter the Constitution, or a decision of the United States Supreme Court.

I further explained to him that the Church's teaching on marriage did not originate with her, but with her Founder. Furthermore I showed him that the Catholic Church originated no doctrine, but only taught what Christ commissioned her to teach. I proceeded to say that from the beginning the Catholic Church has been the depository and guardian of Christ's teaching. That is why she never changes. And that is why the churches change which are not His. Truth never changes. Christ was Truth. The Church which is His teaches what He taught, and that is why her doctrine on marriage is what it is. It is God's own. As many rejected Christ, Truth itself, because His teachings did not accord with their views, so they reject His Church because she does not teach what they want to believe. But on the great day it is Christ's standard that will prevail, not the world's.

After I had developed this point at some length, he replied, "That is all news to me. Why doesn't the Church explain her position to the public? People have an entirely different view of the matter." Before proceeding I may say that as a result of this and similar conversations, this gentleman has become a Catholic.

There is no doubt at all that when the Church's position on any matter is made clear to those outside they either become Catholics or at least drop their hostility to her. Most people are fair-minded and when they have the facts of the case judge reasonably. The trouble to-day with regard to the Church is that those outside have not the facts. They have plenty of supposed facts, which is worse than having none at all, but of facts they have only distortions.

How is this situation to be remedied? You may say by suggesting books which will set them right. But they will not read books, especially Catholic books. What is to be done? The very best thing is to use the opportunities of personal intercourse to give correct notions of the Church and her teaching. Nearly all persons whom I have received into the Church, have approached the matter of conversion as the result of a chance conversation they had with a Catholic friend or acquaintance.

When known for what it is in reality there is nothing in the world so appealing and convincing as the Catholic Church. The difficulty is that many Catholics do not know how to express themselves with regard to their religion. Of course this is not to be wondered at. Many people know a thing well enough for their own needs and satisfaction but are not able to convey their knowledge to others. This holds in every department of life. Many good and patriotic citizens of the United States know enough about the Constitution to appreciate, reverence and uphold it, yet are not able to explain it to the satisfaction of others. It is easy to understand a thing but not easy to put the matter in a way to make others understand it. However, the average intelligent Catholic should be sufficiently instructed in the Faith to be able to convey a fairly accurate idea of it to those outside.

Frequently a non-Catholic has said to me, "Father, what is the matter with your people? I often ask them why they do this or that, why they believe such and such a doctrine, and they put me off with a shrug of the shoulders." I replied that often the reason was shyness, or a suspicion that they were being asked out of malice. I also added that many people cannot explain what is perfectly clear to themselves. This I made evident by the fact that only a few persons out of a hundred can give a rational explanation of the political party to which they belong, yet they have their own good understanding of it. To know a thing and to be able to impart the knowledge of it are two very different things.

Yet if one is really interested in something one will endeavor to know enough about it to interest others. We Catholics are vitally interested in our religion. We know that nearly all the hostility to us and our Church comes from bigotry based on misunderstanding, for the most part. Out of self-protection, not to say loyalty, we should equip ourselves to meet all ordinary comers in matters pertaining to our Faith. We should have a conversational knowledge of the main points of difference between ourselves and others. If every Catholic gentleman could give a satisfactory explanation of his belief and practice he would be doing real service to his religion.

Catholics should be crusaders of Christ. In the days of knighthood the staunchest defenders of the throne were those valiant men who formed the bodyguard of the king on the battlefield and in every place of danger. These knights gloried in the defense of the realm. Educated Catholics should be a chosen body of loyal sons of holy Mother Church. They are, for the most part, professional or business men or skilled craftsmen. As a body they are above the ordinary intelligence. They are doing splendid work for Church and State in social and civil activities. Many, too, are spreading abroad right notions of religion and morality. But altogether too few are doing the personal work for God and His Church which they could do if they made themselves well-informed on Catholic matters and used their opportunities to enlighten inquirers.

It is with a view to aid in this particular that in the present volume I hope to present topics of paramount importance, and to set them forth in such a way that Catholics will be well-informed on them and able to inform others. There is only one thing the Catholic Church fears—ignorance. She welcomes all the light that can be thrown on her. But it must be white light. Too often she is seen under the colored light of bigotry, and in that guise she may repel rather than attract. But in herself she is so beautiful, her teaching is so sublime and logical that the greatest minds in every age have been captivated by her. Surely when we see an intellectual giant like Newman bow down in submission to her we may know that she does not quail before the most rigid investigation. And when, in our own day, we behold a master-mind like Chesterton's acknowledging her divine character we need not fear that the assaults of lesser minds will harm her. It is not for her we fear, for she has the guarantee of God Himself, but it is for ourselves, lest we fail in what we owe her.

To-day people outside the Church are hungry for the things of the spirit. Their own churches give them stone for bread. They have a longing for something more than the unsatisfying things of earth. They find life empty. The end of a day brings them nothing really worth while. They would welcome our blessed religion if they knew it for what it is. Most of them have drifted into materialism or indifferentism, and they are dispirited. The Catholic Church answers every cry of the soul, as we know. She satisfies the loftiest aspirations of the human mind. She needs only to be known to be loved. We can help make her known. Our lives are the best portraits of her, if we are true to her. After our lives, our conversation, our information tactfully and correctly conveyed, will do most to bring her into the affections of those who are now estranged from her.

With this in view I shall endeavor to treat various essential subjects in a simple and understandable way, which will, I trust, enable my readers to meet the questions which are at times put to them by inquiring non-Catholics. Hardly a day passes without some of us being asked questions about our Faith. In the office, on the street, in the shop, religious topics not infrequently occupy the principal place in conversation. It is astonishing to note the rapt attention one receives if on such occasions one can say something to the point. The matter of fact is that deep down in every man's heart there is a yearning for knowledge about the soul and God and the hereafter.

The Catholic religion has definite information on all these matters. Moreover, a well-informed Catholic has also the answer to the perplexing problems of daily life. The Church is simply the continuation of Christ's mission to mankind. He taught us the way to live for our peace here and our eternal welfare hereafter. He has given the reply, at least in principle, to every question of life. His Church is His mouthpiece. If we want to know what God thinks of marriage or of any other issue of life we may go to her for the information. After all, it is God's judgment on these matters that counts. Sometimes a patient declines to consult a physician with regard to an ailment for fear of learning the truth. But it is better to know the truth, even though it be undesirable, than to walk on in darkness and fall over a precipice.

The truths of religion are not for our passing pleasure, but for our permanent peace. Christ came on earth not to give us the fading joys of time, but the everlasting joy of life with Him. He did not come to give us anything which man of his own power could obtain, but what was above the power of man to achieve. He came to give us a share in divine life. All His teaching was to help us to become partakers of the divine nature. That is the end of religion, to make us children of God, members of the divine family. His Church was established not to make us rich, nor to give us honor, nor to make us long-lived, but to make us children of God. A Catholic who is well-informed has the true knowledge of life.

In considering the teaching of the Church we must always bear in mind that she has in view not merely the welfare of this brief life but of the life which knows no end. A father often makes regulations for a child, which the child, seeing only present interests, considers unnecessary restraints. But the father sees the future, and knows that later on his child will bless him for those salutary restraints. Our Father in heaven is solicitous mainly for our eternal well-being. His commandments are for our lasting blessedness. And every man in his innermost nature feels that this is so. That is why the Catholic Faith, when rightly explained, satisfies the most exacting inquirer.

God is the Author of Catholic Faith and also the Author of human nature. It is only distorted human nature that can find Catholic truth, rightly explained, at variance with human aspirations. It is with the hope of presenting to the reader the truths of Catholicism in their real significance that I undertake the present volume. A Catholic, rightly informed, is an asset to Church and State.

CHAPTER II

FAITH

OUTSIDE the Catholic Church there is, for the most part, a more or less confused idea of what faith is. Even among Catholics, who, generally speaking, have a right understanding of faith, there are some who, if asked by a non-Catholic to explain what faith is, would be at a loss to do so satisfactorily. It may be said that it is a lack of the right understanding of faith that is responsible for many of the prevalent erroneous notions concerning religion. Some people think that revealed religion is a subject for their personal approval or disapproval. Hence they render a verdict on what they will accept or reject. They fail to realize that revealed religion, such as is the religion of Christ, is a communication from God to man. Man has a right to learn if the communication is from God. But once he knows that it is from God, his duty is to accept it, not to pass judgment on it with a view to acceptance or rejection. The very meaning of the word revelation signifies a showing, or a manifestation of something. Divine revelation means the showing of something by God, directly or indirectly. The fact that God makes known something is proof that what He makes known is true, since God can neither deceive nor be deceived.

Faith, therefore, means believing what God declares to us, not because we understand it, nor because we approve it, but simply because God, who speaks, is Truth itself, who can neither be in error nor declare what is erroneous. From the fact that we admit revelation we admit that God has declared something to us.

As said previously, revelation means a showing of something. It signifies the drawing aside of a veil, to let us see what is beyond it. Divine revelation means the drawing aside of the divine veil and showing us something about God, which otherwise we should not know.

We may know God in a degree from His work in the universe, and by the process of reasoning. But this is a very limited knowledge. "And hardly do we guess aright at things that are upon earth, and with labor do we find the things that are before us. But the things that are in heaven who shall search out? And who shall know Thy thought except Thou give wisdom and send Thy Holy Spirit from above?" (Wisd. ix. 16, 17).

By revelation God gave us knowledge of things beyond our capacity to learn by ourselves, enlightening us on divine things. Hence it is that St. Paul, referring to his mission, says: "My speech and my preaching was not in the persuasive words of human wisdom, but in the showing of the Spirit and power." And again he says: "I give you to understand that the Gospel which was preached by me is not according to man: for neither did I receive it of man, nor did I learn it, but by the revelation of Jesus Christ."

Our divine Lord Himself plainly states the fact of revelation: "No man hath seen God at any time. The Only Begotten Son, who is in the bosom of the Father, He hath declared Him." Faith, therefore, means believing what divine revelation declares to us. In faith our belief does not rest on our comprehension or understanding of what is revealed, but on the veracity of God who reveals. It may be said that this is clear and quite evident, but how are we to know that God has revealed something or that it is precisely what He revealed? This is the main point of the whole matter. Any one may say he has a revelation from above, but how are we to know if he really has such a revelation? If a monarch sends an ambassador with a communication to his subjects or to another ruler, the ambassador presents credentials, which attest that he is the accredited representative of the monarch. So with regard to revelation. Jesus Christ declared that He was the Only-Begotten Son of God, and moreover that His mission to mankind was to reveal divine truths and to direct mankind to eternal life. He proclaimed that He was God, and that His mission was divine. Realizing that divine credentials were necessary to confirm His claims, He proceeded to give them, presenting divine deeds, known as miracles, which were God's seal on His mission. A miracle is God's sign language, approving some person or thing. God could not permit a divine deed to be performed to uphold a false person or mission. A divine deed cannot be done without God's help, and this He could not give to aid falsehood.

God is Truth. Hence when the Jews were astounded at Christ's claim He said, "If you do not believe Me, at least believe the works that I do, they give testimony of Me." He then proceeded to do what only God could do. By His own power He gave sight to the blind, made the lame walk, healed the leper, raised the dead, foretold the future, and commanded nature. He thus established His right to speak as God and to be believed as God. Having in this way presented His divine credentials, He revealed to us certain things about God and our future destiny which we should never have been able to acquire by human effort. He drew aside the veil of divinity, to a certain extent, giving us a view of God and His attributes and of the relationship between Him and ourselves.

He told us that God is not only the Creator, who made all things out of nothing, but that He is also our Father. Furthermore He informed us that God so loved us as to give His Only-Begotten Son for our salvation. He declared also that if we live as He ordains we may become children of God, partakers of the divine nature, members of the divine family. "To as many as receive Him He gives the power to become the sons of God." But He also states that God is to judge all mankind, and that they who do not live as He ordains will be banished forever from His presence. These and many other things revelation teaches us.

Furthermore, Christ, having established His divine claim, founded a Church to perpetuate His mission, and endowed this Church with divine guarantees. By the same divine power, by which He manifested God to mankind, He guaranteed that His Church should teach truth only. In fact He did this to such a degree that He proclaimed that His Church taught with the same authority as Himself: "He who hears you hears Me" He said of it.

The meaning, therefore, of faith is that what revelation teaches, and what the Church teaches, must be believed by us as firmly as if God in person addressed us. Faith is not a high probability nor a strong persuasion, but a firm conviction. And this conviction is not based on the fact that the matter of belief is comprehended by us, nor on evidence in its behalf, nor on its reasonable appeal to us, but solely on the veracity of the one who reveals, namely God, who can neither deceive nor be deceived.

The Incarnation, for example, is not understood by any mortal intelligence. The Incarnation means that God became man. How this was accomplished we do not know. But revelation states that God the Son, the Second Person of the Trinity, became man. We believe it, and if necessary would die for our belief, not because we understand this mystery, but because God has revealed it to us.

It is the same with the Blessed Eucharist. No one understands how, by the words of consecration, the bread and wine become the Body and Blood of Christ. There is no evidence of this change, and moreover it is entirely beyond our comprehension, yet we believe it on the word of God. That is faith, believing not on the testimony of the senses, not on evidence, not on understanding, but on the veracity of God. It is the highest honor we can pay God, for by our belief we sacrifice our highest faculty, our judgment, on the altar of His veracity.

Of such importance is this worship of faith that Scripture declares that "without Faith it is impossible to please God." Almighty God Himself sets such high value on it as to say, "I will espouse thee to Me in faith." From this it is evident what an essential feature of religion is faith. We can pay no greater honor to our fellow man than to believe him, even when he tells us what we can neither understand nor prove. If you have evidence for belief in a statement you are obliged to yield consent, since evidence compels assent. God wants us to trust Him and to believe in Him simply because He is God. If He revealed only what met with our comprehension or approval there would be little or no credit in our believing. But when, as in the mysteries of Faith, we believe without evidence, and without comprehending, but solely on God's word, we are truly paying Him an honor which is most worthy of Him, and most acceptable to Him.

An illustration of human faith may help us to understand better the nature of divine Faith. Let us take the historical fact of the discovery of America by Columbus. Columbus believed that there was a land west of Europe. No one had ever seen that land. As far as human observation could determine, the Atlantic Ocean was the western border of the world. But the astronomical studies of Columbus, together with his close observation of natural phenomena, led him to believe that there was land west of the Atlantic. Finally he became firmly convinced of the existence of land beyond the ocean by the nature of certain driftwood washed ashore. This was entirely different from anything known to Europeans. Columbus concluded that it could come only from some land west of Europe. He had such firm faith in his conclusion that he devoted his life's efforts to the discovery of this land. On what was the conviction of Columbus based? No one told him of the existence of America, no one had known of it. His conviction was based on reasoning. Strange and unknown wood indicated a strange and unknown land. This, together with his previous belief that the earth was round, made him conclude the existence of a land beyond the sea. That was the basis of his belief. But those who embarked with him on his voyage of discovery, on what did their belief rest? They were incapable of appreciating the astronomical argument, and they had not seen the strange driftwood which had so much impressed Columbus. Their belief in a far-off land in the Atlantic rested on their confidence in Columbus. They had faith in him. They knew him to be a learned man, a skilful navigator, and especially a man of careful and conservative character. Hence they trusted their lives to his venture. Accordingly they set sail with him, with what results we know. Having discovered America, Columbus and his crew had personal knowledge of a new world. Their knowledge was based on actual evidence. On their return to Europe they published their discovery to the astonished Europeans. The court of Spain and the people believed in the new land. On what did their belief rest? Not on evidence. They had not seen the new country. On what then? On the word of Columbus and the crew, corroborated by the evidence which was brought from the newly discovered country.

Our knowledge of things, therefore, may be acquired either by personal experience or by the testimony of others. Most of our knowledge depends on the testimony of others. All our knowledge of history depends on human testimony. Even the knowledge of so recent an event as our War of Independence, 1776, rests on faith in human testimony. No man now living witnessed that war. We have faith in those who recorded it, and on this faith our knowledge rests. Most of our knowledge depends on faith in others. Up to a certain age we take nearly everything on the word of our parents. Afterwards we take for granted as true what our teachers and text-books impart to us. Later on in life we put faith in our employers, physicians, lawyers and associates. Life would be impossible, and knowledge almost nil, unless we put faith in human testimony and human nature.

Of course our faith in people may occasionally receive a rude shock. But that is proof that such an experience was unexpected, out of the ordinary, and contrary to the rule. Hence, exceptions are said to prove the rule. If, therefore, mankind depends so much on faith for knowledge and for well-being, we should not be surprised that faith is an important element in our relationship with God. And if we put faith in human testimony, we should be more ready to place faith in divine testimony. God is the Creator of man. He is entitled to our trust and confidence much more than fallible man. Hence the apostle says: "If we receive the testimony of men, the testimony of God is greater" (I John v. 9). And again he declares: "He that believeth in the Son of God hath the testimony of God in himself."

God is a spirit. No mortal man has ever seen God, as God. We have seen Him in some of His effects; His power shown in the elements of nature, His goodness and beauty manifested in creation, His knowledge and greatness as displayed in the firmament. Finally we have beheld His love and His mercy by the revelation of Himself in the person of Jesus Christ, the God-Man. Christ is called in Scripture the Word. "In the beginning was the Word, and the Word was with God, and the Word was God . . . and the Word was made flesh and dwelt amongst us." With man, a word is the manifestation of the invisible mind. So Christ, the Word, is the visible manifestation of the invisible God. "No man hath seen God at any time: the Only-Begotten Son, who is in the bosom of the Father, He hath declared Him" (John i. 18).

The mercy and tenderness and love of Jesus for mankind are the manifestations of God's love and mercy and tenderness. Christ performed His divine deeds in order to show that He was indeed God. Since He spoke with the authority of God, and claimed the allegiance due to God and commanded that He be worshipped as God, He necessarily had to present the credentials of God. And this He did, not only by His personality, but also, and especially, by His miracles, the divine seal on His mission. Hence St. John in concluding his Gospel says: "Many other signs also did Jesus in the sight of His disciples, which are not written in this book. But these are written that you may believe that Jesus is the Christ, the Son of ·God, and that believing you may have life in His Name."

Faith, therefore, in Christ means the absolute belief in what He taught because He has taught it. "God so loved the world as to give His Only-Begotten Son, that whosoever believeth in Him may not perish, but may have life everlasting" (John iii. 16). Faith, let me repeat, is not evidence, it is not the conclusion of a process of reasoning, it is not a logical inference, but it is simply the absolute belief in divine revelation because it is divine. We may employ all our faculties in order to make sure that there has been a divine revelation. But once we admit revelation to be a fact our duty is belief, not debate. And let it be said emphatically that if there has been no divine revelation Christianity is the greatest fraud ever perpetrated on mankind. But if there has been a divine revelation it is to be accepted in its entirety and with the firmest belief. There is no room for question or doubt once God has spoken. That is why Catholic faith is so strong and so absolute. There can be no wavering or hesitation, no ifs or ands or buts when revelation has declared a thing. Hence faith means the firm assent of the will to what revelation teaches. Faith is not selective, it does not permit one to accept part and reject part of what is revealed. If any part of revelation is false it is all false, since nothing containing even the slightest error can be from God. Rather it should be said that it is not revelation if it is not all true.

Hence to admit revelation at all is to acknowledge that God has spoken, and consequently our duty is to accept His manifestation humbly and gratefully and absolutely. To say that we will not accept what we cannot understand is to dictate to God, and to limit Him in His relations with His own creatures. If a subject were to do that to his sovereign it would be impertinence and grossly offensive. If a soldier were to do that to his commander-in-chief it would be insubordination and severely punishable. God is Sovereign of creation and the Ruler of mankind. He gave us our reason, which we are so proud of, and we may be sure that having given it to us He will not want us to use it unreasonably. The whole matter of revelation resolves itself to this, has there or has there not been a revelation from on high? If there has not been such a revelation the sooner we reject Christianity the better. If there has been such a revelation, it is as true as God, and our part is to accept it in its entirety and to live by it. To believe certain parts of divine revelation and reject others is to insult God. To sit in judgment on God's communication and accept what accords with our views is not believing in God, but putting God on trial for His prudence and veracity. He is the best judge of what to reveal and of the advisability of revealing it.

Faith is a virtue. Like every virtue it must be tested. If God revealed to us only what we approved of we should not be practicing faith, but censorship. And that is what many people are now doing in the name of religion. Instead of believing in God they are censoring God. They are willing to believe that God is love, but not that He is just, and a punisher of the wicked. They are willing to believe in heaven, but not in hell. In other words they believe in themselves, not in God. Faith is not that. Faith is the firm belief in what God declares because He declares it.

Being a supernatural virtue it requires God's grace for its reception and practise. But God's grace is at hand for all those who have good will and do their part to correspond with grace. Revelation has as good credentials as any fact of history. The Gospels are among the most authentic documents of mankind. The greatest scholars of all creeds are agreed that the Gospels are genuine history. The Christ of the Gospels is a historic personage. His miracles are His credentials. If we reject revelation we must reject Christ and regard Him as an impostor. They who do that must be prepared to do so when they face God in judgment. But if revelation be accepted, every part of it must be believed, believed so firmly that if need be we would die for our belief. That is the faith of the saints, the faith of the martyrs, the faith of the hundreds of millions who in every generation have lived in accordance with revelation, and were prepared to die for it. Christ is the Light of the world. His revelation is the beacon to eternal life. Blessed indeed are they who are guided by this light, for it leads them to the very house of God, and to membership in the family of God.

In conclusion let it be understood that a chain is no stronger than its weakest link. If any part of revelation be not true it is not divine revelation at all. If, therefore, we believe in revelation we believe it entirely and absolutely. Christ did not propose His doctrine for debate, but imposed it for our acceptance, as God alone can do. Hence His Church, which He constituted to be His voice to mankind, speaks with His authority and with His certainty. His Church is part of divine revelation, and the vehicle of conveying revelation to mankind. Faith, therefore, is the firm belief in all that revelation teaches, because it is God's communication to mankind. Faith is not selective, permitting us to accept certain things and to reject others. We must accept revelation in its entirety or reject it altogether. In accepting revelation we are simply hearkening to God. We need not fear to go astray following that Voice.

CHAPTER III

THE DIVINITY OF CHRIST

THE twenty-fifth of December records the birth of Christ. We call the day Christmas, which means Christ's Mass. For on that day Mass is celebrated in commemoration of the birth of the divine Babe at Bethlehem.

It was a strange way for the Creator to come into His own world. Human wisdom would dictate a more glorious entry. Only God could stoop so low as to be born in a stable amid animals. No mere man, who was master of his own condition, would make his first appearance on the world stage as a helpless babe and as a rejected stranger. "He was in the world, and the world was made by Him, and the world knew Him not. He came unto His own, and His own received Him not." None but God could inaugurate the greatest undertaking in the world in such an unseemly way. Christ is the dividing point of history. We date our years before or after Christ. He is also the dividing point of man for all men are either with Him or against Him. It is thus seen that Christ is the most important personality in the world. He has even now more followers, who are devoted lovers, than any monarch that ever lived, no matter how powerful or beloved.

Napoleon was once complimented on the devotion of his people to him. He replied: "Do not speak to me of loyalty and devotion. There is One who died on a cross nearly two thousand years ago who has had, and now has, more ardent lovers than any monarch that ever lived. There are millions to-day who are ready to lay down their lives for the Crucified, millions to-day are living for Him and toiling for Him in every part of the world. No King was ever served so faithfully and generously as He who said, 'My kingdom is not of this world,' and whose crown was of thorns, and whose throne was the cross."

To man's way of thinking Christ chose poor means of establishing His kingdom. But the wisdom of the world is folly, and the foolishness of the cross wisdom. To-day Christ is the dominant factor of life, and His kingdom numbers loyal adherents from every nation on the globe. The two greatest and most joyous festivals of civilization are those which commemorate His birth and His resurrection. Christmas and Easter are living tributes to the influence of Jesus Christ in the world. The great personages of antiquity are but names. Alexander and Caesar, with all their power and pomp, are but memories. Who, to-day, would die for Caesar or Alexander? Literally, millions would gladly die for Christ. In every century, from the beginning of Christianity, the followers of Christ have endured calumny, confiscation of property, imprisonment, torture and death for His Name. None but God could inspire such loyalty so continuously and so long.

Even if Christ never worked a miracle, we have in this age-long devotion to Him a perpetual miracle, and a proof that He was what He proclaimed Himself to be, the Son of God. All that is really worth while in civilization to-day is the result of Christ in the world. The sages of old and the wise men of various epochs have left their impress on certain nations and periods, but Christ has left His impress on mankind the world over and for all time. We can not be indifferent to Christ. Men love Him or hate Him. He foretold it. "He who is not with Me is against Me." And so it has been during all the ages. Christ has been passionately loved and violently hated in every age.

It is so to-day. While millions live for Christ and are ready to die for Him, other millions blaspheme Him and diabolically oppose Him. The world hates Christ because He does not cater to it. The world would love Christ if He gave it what it wanted. It wants to be a law to itself, to make self-indulgence the principle of life. But Christ came to give us something more than what this world at its best can give. "To as many as receive Him He gives the power to become the sons of God."

He left heaven and became man in order that man might become, in a sense, divine. The world is opposed to Christ because its principles are directly opposite to His. The world sets up this life as man's goal. Christ proclaims that this life is probation, and that the grave is not the goal but starting-point of man. Between the followers of these two antagonistic standards there must always be inevitable opposition. Which is right, Christ or the world? That is the great question. The greatest.

If Christ is God there can be no question as to who is right. Hence it is that the most vital matter for each individual is his attitude toward Christ and his relation to Christ. If Christ is God, He is to be honored as God, believed in as God, served as God. Is He God? The high priest put that question to Christ personally and heard the answer, "I am." For that response He was accused of blasphemy and adjudged guilty of death. He was led to Pilate, falsely charged with making Himself king. Pilate asked Him "Art Thou a King?" Christ answered "I am, but My kingdom is not of this world." Pilate found no fault in Him, yet to satisfy His accusers he sentenced Him to death after proclaiming Him innocent.

This is the only case in the annals of justice where the judge, after solemnly proclaiming the accused innocent, nevertheless sentenced him to death. Christ was crucified for proclaiming that He was God. He meant that He was God in the true sense. He was so understood by His accusers, otherwise He would not have been accused of blasphemy, the penalty of which was death. Was Christ what He claimed to be? He gave the best proof that He was when He died for His statement. Men do not die for a lie. Christ solemnly proclaimed that He was God and died for so proclaiming. Are we to believe Him?

The greatest opponents of Christ's divinity declare that He is the one perfect being that has ever been in this world. They affirm that His is the best balanced mind known to mankind. They acclaim Him the most exalted and virtuous personage that history records.

This perfect being, distinguished for soundest intellect and most exalted virtue, solemnly declared He was God, and sealed His testimony with His Blood. Since this perfect being can not be a deceiver or a victim of delusion, it follows from the admission of His opponents that Christ is God. This perfect being would not lie, nor would He be under an insane delusion. Christ proclaimed He was God. If He was not God He was either an impostor or a madman. But all admit He was the most upright person that ever lived, and also the sanest. His very opponents, during His lifetime, were forced to admit His exalted sanctity and His marvelous mentality. "Which one of you can accuse Me of sin?" was His challenge to them, and they were forced to hold silence. Again they said, referring to His mentality, "Never spake man as this man speaks." Of all mankind He alone could point to Himself as a model of conduct. "Learn of Me, who am meek and humble of heart." Moreover, He proclaimed Himself the standard of truth. "I am the Light of the world." "I am the Way, the Truth, and the Life." What arrogance and what insanity if He were not God! But holy as was Christ, and mentally perfect, His divinity rests on something more than His word. Christ knew that in affirming He was God He was making a most astounding claim. The Jews had such reverence for God that they never pronounced His name, uttering, instead, a substitute, "Adonai." It was this great, Almighty Being that Christ affirmed Himself to be. No wonder the Jews were amazed at His claims, and resisted them. Christ, who knew their exalted idea of God, made every allowance for their slowness to believe in Him. He realized the magnitude of His claims and the need of substantiating them. Accordingly He said to them that they had a right to demand of Him corroboration of His word. Hence He proceeded to confirm His statement, as a scientist would, by evidence.

"If you do not believe Me, at least believe the works which I do, they give testimony of Me." His miracles were the evidence He furnished for His claim. Any man could say he was God. But no one who was not God could do the things which God alone can do. Christ gave sight to the blind, made the cripple walk, cleansed the leper, cured the deaf, raised the dead to life. He commanded nature as only the Lord of nature could do, bidding the storm to cease and the elements to subside. The winds and the waves obeyed Him.

On a certain occasion "they came to Him bringing one sick of the palsy, who was carried by four. And when they could not offer him unto Him for the multitude, they uncovered the roof where He was; and opening it, they let down the bed wherein the man sick of the palsy lay. And when Jesus had seen their faith, He saith to the sick of the palsy: Son, thy sins are forgiven thee. And there were some of the scribes sitting there, and thinking in their hearts: Why doth this man speak thus? He blasphemeth. Who can forgive sins, but God only? Which Jesus presently knowing in His spirit, that they so thought within themselves, saith to them: Why think you these things in your hearts? Which is easier, to say to the sick of the palsy: Thy sins are forgiven thee; or to say: Arise, take up thy bed, and walk? But that you may know that the Son of man hath power on earth to forgive sins, (He saith to the sick of the palsy), I say to thee: Arise, take up thy bed, and go into thy house. And immediately he arose; and taking up his bed, went his way in the sight of all, so that all wondered and glorified God, saying: We never saw the like" (Mark ii. 3-12).

On this occasion Christ gave conclusive evidence that He was God. He admitted that only God could forgive sin, and then proceeded to show that He had forgiven sin and that consequently He was God. If one person says to another, "Thy sins are forgiven thee," there is no evidence that sin is forgiven. But Christ, in order to show that He actually forgave sin when He pronounced the words of forgiveness, did something which proved that His words were power, and that they accomplished what they signified.

Any one could say to the paralytic, "Thy sins are forgiven thee," but only God could say to the prostrate man, "Arise and walk." In order to show that His words of forgiveness effected what was spiritual and invisible, He wrought, by a mere word, the instantaneous cure of an incurable paralytic, which was something visible to all. It was as if He had said, "That you may know that I am God and have power to forgive sin I shall heal, by a word, this paralytic. If My word gives him immediate restoration to soundness of body you will know that My word also has remitted his sins." Then turning to the expectant paralytic He spoke the word of power, the word of God: Arise! The cripple leapt to his feet at the word of the Creator. Christ had, indeed, forgiven sin.

Christ was God. "In the beginning was the Word, and the Word was with God, and the Word was God, all things were made by Him, . . . and the Word was made flesh and dwelt amongst us."

The perfect being, Christ, whose mentality and holiness were unapproachable, not only declared He was God, but confirmed His declaration by the deeds of God. His whole public life was a record of divine deeds. Hence He said to the Jews: "If you do not believe Me, believe the works which I do; they give testimony of Me." The last and greatest miracle of Christ was wrought as a direct and final confirmation of His divinity. Just before He raised Lazarus from the dead He declared that He was going to do it in proof that His mission was from God Almighty. "That they may know that Thou hast sent Me." After declaring that it was to be a corroboration of the truth of His claims, He turned to the tomb wherein lay the dead Lazarus, dead now four days, and already beginning to corrupt, and with a commanding voice, exclaimed, "Lazarus come forth!" The corpse leapt to life at the summons of the Creator, and Jesus gave to Martha and Mary their beloved brother, now fully and instantly restored to them.

It was after this miracle, which was witnessed by a large concourse of prominent Jews, that the people acclaimed Christ the Messias, and on His way to Jerusalem met Him in large numbers, waving palms and leading Him in procession to the holy city. This alarmed the Jewish leaders, who were opposed to Jesus as darkness is to light, and they planned to put Him to death. They were convinced but not converted, as happens with many to-day. Members of the Jewish council had witnessed the miracle and reported it, with the result that instead of being converted the council became hardened in their opposition and malice. Instead of being converted they became perverted, and plotted false accusation and death against Jesus, and also the murder of Lazarus, the living evidence of the divine power of Jesus.

"Many therefore of the Jews, who were come to Mary and Martha, and had seen the things that Jesus did, believed in Him. But some of them went to the Pharisees, and told them the things that Jesus had done. The chief priests therefore, and the Pharisees, gathered a council and said: What do we, for this man doth many miracles? If we let Him alone so, all will believe in Him; and the Romans will come, and take away our place and nation. But one of them named Caiphas, being the high priest that year, said to them: You know nothing. Neither do you consider that it is expedient for you that one man should die for the people, and that the whole nation perish not. And this he spoke not of himself: but being the high priest of that year, he prophesied that Jesus should die for the nation. And not only for the nation, but to gather together in one the children of God, that were dispersed. From that day therefore they devised to put him to death . . . But the chief priests thought to kill Lazarus also: Because many of the Jews, by reason of him, went away, and believed in Jesus. And on the next day a great multitude that was come to the festival day, when they had heard that Jesus was coming to Jerusalem, took branches of palm trees, and went forth to meet Him, and cried: Hosanna, blessed is He that cometh in the name of the Lord, the King of Israel" (John xi. 45-53—xii. 10-13).

The Jews did not deny the miracles of Jesus. They could not with the evidence before them. But having begun an evil course they would not turn aside from it. It led them, in the end, to deliberate calumny and murder. It may be asked why the Scribes and Pharisees rejected Christ in view of the evidence of His miracles. The same question may be asked to-day. Thousands have seen unquestionable miracles at Lourdes. Zola, having witnessed a marvelous cure wrought there, declared he would not believe if he saw a thousand such cures. If belief entailed no change of life many would believe. But one can not believe in Christ without living as Christ prescribes. That is the obstacle, frequently.

Evidence that would persuade and convince in other matters is disregarded when there is question of Christ. But Christ is God. He declared He was God, and confirmed His declaration by deeds which God alone could perform. Miracles are God's mark, putting the seal of divine approval on the person and mission of the one who performs them. Since Christ wrought miracles He gave evidence that His mission was from above. The Gospels, which record Christ's mission, are the most genuine and authentic documents of history. This is the judgment of the best scholars of the world.

To sum up—Christ, the one perfect person, intellectually and morally, that this world has known, solemnly declared He was God, in the true sense, and died for His statement. Moreover He confirmed His word by divine deeds, and throughout His life assumed the prerogatives of God, forgiving sin, setting Himself up as Judge of the living and the dead, and declaring that in all things He was equal to the Father. Besides, the Church which He established is in the world to-day, and is extended to every nation and people, the Light of the world, the true way of peace and the guide to eternal life. The Son of God became man in order that man might become, in a sense, divine. Christ did not come upon earth to give us fame or riches or a long life. He had none of these things Himself. He came to give us life—real life, a share in His own eternal life. He came to us in weakness and love. He came thus to win our love, knowing that if we love Him we will serve Him. Christ was God's gift to mankind. "God so loved the world as to give His only Son."

God wants our gift in return, the gift of an upright life for love of Him. Then when Christ comes in power and glory and justice we shall be glad to meet Him, knowing that He will be our reward exceeding great. Christ's birth as man is our birth as the children of God. Through the Babe of Bethlehem we have received the wonderful inheritance by which we "may become partakers of the divine nature" (2 Pet. i. 4). No wonder that Christ means so much to mankind.

CHAPTER IV

THE RESURRECTION

IF THERE be no future life the bottom drops out of Christianity. If there be no future life Bolshevists are right in assailing Christianity. If there be no future life Socialists are justified in their opposition to Christianity. The very basis of Christianity is immortality. Take that away and the whole Christian edifice topples. The resurrection was the main argument of the Apostles for the truth of the religion of Christ. St. Paul declared that if Christ be not risen from the dead, Christian faith is shipwreck of life. The life and mission of Christ were meaningless unless there is a life beyond. He did not come to give man riches, or long life, or honors, or comfort, or anything that this world can give. He had none of these things Himself, although He might have had them all. He came to give us life. Not this present life, which is rather a living death, but life everlasting and glorious.

This present life is a steady march to the grave. We begin to die as soon as we are born. Hardly have we drawn our first breath when doctor and nurse are called in to ward off disease, accident, or death. Every day brings us one step nearer to the inevitable grave. Christ said: "I have come to give you life." He was speaking to those who already had life, otherwise His words were vain, but not the life which He came to give. The life that He promises to those who serve Him is a share in His own eternal and blessed life, that life which knows no end, no anxiety, no pain, no sorrow, no desire unfulfilled. "They that shall be accounted worthy . . . of the resurrection from the dead . . . neither can they die any more, for they are equal to the angels and are the children of God" (Luke xx. 35, 36).

24

Man's destiny is to share the life of God. That is the key to life. We have not here a lasting city, but seek one which is to come. This life is preparation. Life is probation and the grave is not the goal but starting point of man's real destiny. Hence Christ proclaims, "What doth it profit a man if he gain the whole world and suffer the loss of his own soul?" In comparison with the life beyond, nothing in this life matters, except as a means of securing that blessed eternal life. Hence Christ, who knows, proclaimed that if need be we should sacrifice life itself for that other life. "He who loses his life for My sake shall find it." Life is the supreme sacrifice. Yet even this sacrifice is imperative if it be necessary to ensure eternal life.

The whole body of Christ's teaching rests on the certainty of immortality. Christian virtue calls constantly for the denial of what this world prizes most. Man desires to have his own way, to do his own will, to be his own master. Christ bids us look up to God in heaven and say, "Thy will be done." Man desires personal gratification, and the world caters to his passions. Christ preaches the doctrine of the cross. And so all the way through. Christ and the world are antagonistic. That is why the world hated Him and put Him to death. The Jews would have accepted Christ if He gave them what they wanted, worldly power and glory. He came to give them something more than that. But because they had to receive His gift in humility, being proud and self-willed, they rejected Him. They not only rejected Him, they crucified Him. They not only crucified Him, but did so criminally, by false witnesses and false charges. His is the only case on record of a person being judicially proclaimed innocent yet condemned to die as a criminal. Christ foretold His crucifixion. He also foretold His resurrection. The Jews knew of this prophecy. Hence they went to Pilate for a guard to prevent any interference with the tomb of Jesus. On the third day after the crucifixion Christ rose from the dead as foretold. The resurrection was not only Christ's greatest miracle, but it was also a very definite prophecy fulfilled. On the third day, precisely as foretold, while the tomb was guarded by the Roman soldiers, the best soldiers in the world, the huge stone of the tomb was rolled aside, and amidst a brilliancy which momentarily blinded the guards, and threw them in terror to the earth, Christ rose triumphantly from the grave.

Christ made the greatest claims ever made by any one in this world. He declared that He was Almighty God. He knew the magnitude of His claims, and the need of substantiating them. That was why He was so patient with His hearers, and made every allowance for them. The Jews held Jehovah in such reverence that they never directly mentioned His name. Yet here was one, in appearance like themselves, proclaiming that He was Jehovah. Christ, therefore, proceeded to confirm His claims by performing deeds which Jehovah alone could do. By His own power and in His own Name He gave sight to the blind, cleansed the leper, made the cripple walk, commanded the elements, and raised the dead. In presence of these divine deeds He said: "If you do not believe Me at least believe the works which I do, they give testimony of Me." As a result the people at large believed in Him, as we see from the multitude that proclaimed Him the Messias after He had raised Lazarus from the dead. This alarmed the Jewish leaders, who called a council and said: "What do we, for this man doth many miracles? If we let Him alone so, all will believe in Him" (John xi. 47, 48).

The Jewish leaders were looking for a glorious Messias. They confused the prophecies of His first coming in humility with His final coming in glory. Their wish being father to the thought, they blinded themselves against the evidence Christ gave them. They were convinced of His miraculous deeds, as is evident, but they were not converted. They did not see, because they chose to remain blind. Finally, Christ, when directly appealed to for proof positive of His divinity, gave His resurrection as the great confirmation of His divine claims. As said previously, the Jews knew of this prophecy and took every precaution to prevent its fulfillment. But all their precautions only served to make more certain the fact of the resurrection. If Christ is God the resurrection is the most natural thing in the world. If He were not God the resurrection is incomprehensible, nay, an impossibility. The evidence for the resurrection is the best that has ever been presented for a fact of history. First of all, the Gospels which narrate it are the most genuine and authentic documents of mankind. This is the verdict of the most learned men in the world to-day. If we distrust the Gospel narrative we must reject every record of the past. The resurrection is better attested than any achievement of Julius Caesar. There are more and better monuments to Christ's resurrection than there are to the victories of Caesar. The greatest monument to the resurrection is the Church of Christ, which rests on the resurrection as its foundation. To bring about the worship of one crucified as a malefactor by order of a Roman governor, was an impossibility without divine aid. The resurrection was the sign from heaven attesting the divinity of Jesus Christ. The Apostles based their mission solely on the resurrection. St. Paul, addressing his hearers, said: "If Christ be not risen again, then is our preaching vain, and your faith is also vain; yea, and we are found false witnesses of God . . . If in this life only we have hope in Christ; we are of all men most miserable. But now Christ is risen from the dead" (1 Cor. xv. 14, 19,20).

This was the burden of the preaching of all the Apostles, as we may see by reading the Acts of the New Testament. After St. Peter's first sermon, which was on the resurrection, three thousand converts to Christianity were made in the very city and among the people who had witnessed the crucifixion. When we consider the nature of Christ's religion, it will be seen, that unless the resurrection were a fact, its establishment as the dominant religion of the civilized world could never have been effected. A complete moral and social transformation of the world, such as that brought about by Christianity, demands an explanation. The resurrection is the explanation. Christ's resurrection was proof of a future life as well as proof of His divinity. It was the sign from heaven, confirming as true the teaching and mission of Christ. It thus came about that those who accepted the religion of Jesus Christ not only believed in a future life, but also believed that that future life was to be happy or miserable according as this present life was virtuous or vicious. The converts to Christianity, while living in this world, did not live mainly for it, but for that life beyond which was to be unending. This made them not only avoid the wickedness which prevailed but inspired them to that virtuous conduct which won the world's admiration. Realizing that the world with its vanity was a passing thing, they regarded themselves as pilgrims on the way to their true and everlasting home. This realization of a blessed life beyond for all those who lived as Christ prescribed, brought hope and peace to a despairing people. It gave a new outlook on life to the slave—and over half the world was in slavery—who, though in human bondage, knew that he was the brother of Christ and destined to share the eternal life of God.

To those who were in poverty or illness or misfortune it was guarantee that the ills of this life could be the means of purchasing an everlasting life of blessedness. And thus it came about eventually that the Rome of the Caesars became the Rome of the Popes, and the pagan Roman empire became Christendom. All this was the result of belief in the resurrection. Some people are apt to think that only in these latter times has there been close examination into facts. They forget that the period when the resurrection occurred, and was preached, was the most sceptical in history. Never before or since was there keener analysis of human thought and events. That period is known in history as the golden age of literature. Philosophers, scientists, historians and statesmen flourished then, whose writings have been found worthy of preservation even down to our own day. Consequently, the resurrection had to present evidence capable of the closest scrutiny in order to gain belief. The religion of Christ was utterly unlike and opposed to the dominant religion of the age. Unless its main credential, the resurrection, bore the clearest marks of genuineness, the religion founded on it would never have supplanted the congenial cult of paganism.

Paganism flattered man and pandered to his passions. Christianity humbled man and curbed his passions. Unless the resurrection were a fact, the austere creed of Christ could never have triumphed over the pleasant and easy-going state-religion of the haughty Romans. Yet triumph it did, and the throne of Caesar became the throne of Christ's Vicar, and Christianity became the religion of civilization.

The establishment of Christianity without the resurrection, says

St. Augustine, would be a greater miracle than the resurrection itself. As well expect a delicate lily to grow on the asphalt pavement, as for the spiritual and austere religion of Christ to take root in pagan soil, unless by divine power. The divine power was the resurrection of Christ, a fact so incontestable, that it was never denied even by the Jews. They endeavored to stop the Apostles preaching the resurrection, but never denied that it occurred. It may be asked how could they fail to be convinced of Christ's mission if they acknowledged the resurrection? I ask how could they fail to acknowledge Christ's mission after His resurrection of Lazarus, who was dead and buried? After the resurrection of Lazarus they held a council, admitted the resurrection, and seeing all the people turning to Jesus, planned to kill Him, and also to kill Lazarus, the living witness of His divine power (John xi. 45-53 and xii, 9-11).

The Jewish leaders were convinced but not converted. Their hearts were evil. Proof of it is that they deliberately plotted murder, a double murder, in order to do away with Christ and Lazarus, and thus hold their supremacy over the people. They hated Christ because He disclosed their hypocrisy and flayed their vices. Those bent on an evil course do not stop at anything. By intrigue and propaganda they finally brought Christ to an ignominious death. They thought, then, that all was over with Christ, that they had triumphed. But it was the beginning of His victory. Like the grain of wheat cast into the earth and which dies before springing into new and multiplied life, Christ, after expiring on the cross and being entombed in the earth, rose gloriously, and became, by His resurrection, the source of eternal life to all those who believe in Him and live by Him. Now, two thousand years after His enemies pronounced the end of Him and His mission, He is living in the hearts of hundreds of millions of subjects throughout the entire world, in every nation and in every land known to man.

The death and resurrection of Christ accomplished what His teaching and labors and miracles did not effect. All these prepared the way. It was the resurrection which made effective in the lives of men the doctrine which He taught while among men. Up to the time of Christ there was, it is true, a universal belief in a future life.

But it was not, except in certain cases, of a character to influence conduct effectively. Christ's resurrection demonstrated not only a future life, but also the truth of what He taught about it. A future life in itself means merely future existence. But Christ taught that future life would be eternally happy or eternally miserable according to man's good or bad conduct in this life. That it was, which made it difficult for the resurrection to gain belief among men. If believing in the resurrection entailed no consequences, it would be easy to explain why such a consoling doctrine as the resurrection should win the favor and consent of mankind. But since believing in the resurrection implied living in accordance with the austere morality of the Gospel, the resurrection was submitted to the severest tests ever applied to any fact among mankind. That thousands in the very city of the resurrection embraced the religion of the resurrection on the very first day it was preached is compelling evidence of its reality. And when we reflect that nearly all those who became followers of the Crucified, not only embraced a life of exalted virtue, but were also persecuted by imprisonment, exile, and death, it becomes evident that the basis of their faith, the resurrection, must have presented the strongest possible credentials for its genuineness.

Apart from the teaching of revelation, there are abundant reasons that there is a future life. Philosophy teaches that whatever pertains to man everywhere and at all times is natural to him, that is, inherent in his nature. Speech, for example, is natural to man. There may be individuals or groups here or there who have not the faculty of speech, but these are the exception and prove the rule. Whatever is natural to man has the Creator for its author, and is given to man for a purpose. The appetite for food is a natural craving for nourishment, implanted in nature by the Creator in order that man might sustain life. Every natural appetite of man has something corresponding to it which is its object, and which is intended to satisfy it. There is a craving in man as intense and universal as that for food. It is the yearning for happiness. If you analyze your actions of a day or month or year you will find that, either consciously or unconsciously, you were always seeking to satisfy a craving for happiness in one way or another. You might have been mistaken in what makes for happiness, but there is no mistake that happiness was your object. There is nothing in this life that satisfies man's instinctive quest for happiness. Unless, therefore, there be a future life where this natural appetite will find its object, the Creator has given us an appetite in vain, which would be contrary to divine wisdom. It follows, therefore, that there is a future life where happiness, meaning peace, rest, contentment, and the fulfilling of natural cravings, may find its object. There is no permanent happiness in this life. The most fortunate of mankind are in uncertainty always. Accident, death, the possibility of reverses, ever threaten peace and security. No matter what we have we want something else. What we most desire, when attained, loses its value. Finally disease or accident awaits each one of us to usher us to the grave. Such an ending does not correspond to that natural craving for permanent happiness which is inherent in man, which has God for its author, and which has an object somewhere which answers to its call. That object is not here, hence it is hereafter, hence there is a future life. Another reason which postulates a future life is based on justice. God is certainly as just as the creatures He made. All our justice has its source and origin in the Creator. He must possess eminently whatever sentiments of justice He gave mankind, since no one can give what he has not. It is a matter of experience that justice does not reign in this life. Might, cunning, and various other phases of force or cleverness often displace justice among mankind. Frequently the clever wicked triumph over the good. Might often takes the place of right. Unless there be a future life where justice is vindicated we must conclude that God is indifferent to justice, or rather that He favors the unjust, who so often lord it over the just, and in certain cases prosper to the end, while their victims perish miserably. Unless we are prepared to admit that the wisdom and power shown by God in the creation of the world are absent in its governance, we must conclude that there is a future life where Providence will justify its ways. A third motive for belief in a future life is the fact that belief in it is as extensive as the human race. There has never been a race or tribe of men anywhere or at any time that did not believe in a future life. This belief is not based on education or environment or any circumstance of life, but is as universal as mankind. Whatever is thus common to all mankind is natural to man and has its origin in the author of nature, hence can not be false. There may be various forms of this belief in a future life, some of them debasing, but the fact of belief in future existence among all mankind, in one form or another, is incontestable. This does not mean that individuals or groups here or there may not be found who deny future existence. These exceptions only serve to confirm the general truth of the statement. However, all the reasons assigned for a future life, although logical and weighty, did not influence human conduct at large, until the resurrection of Christ convinced man of the absolute certainty of a life beyond the grave. The resurrection of Christ was not merely His own resurrection from the grave, but a pledge of ours. "I am the Resurrection and the Life: He that believeth in Me, although he be dead, shall live" (John xi. 25). It was in accordance with this pledge of Christ that the Apostle St. Paul declared: "If the spirit of Him that raised up Jesus from the dead dwell in you, He that raised up Jesus from the dead shall quicken also your mortal bodies, because of His spirit that dwelleth in you" (Rom. viii. 11). All indeed shall rise from the dead, but not all to the same destiny. "The hour cometh wherein all that are in the graves shall hear the voice of the Son of God—and they that have done good things shall come forth into the resurrection of life; but they that have done evil unto the resurrection of judgment" (John v. 28, 29).

The important thing is, therefore, not future life, which is inevitable, but the character of future life—which will depend on what we make it. That is what gives the resurrection of Christ its tremendous significance. It is a personal matter for each one of us, and a vital matter, eternally vital. Easter commemorates the resurrection. It is the greatest festival of Christendom. It changed the day of worship from the Sabbath (Saturday) of the Old Law to Sunday of the New. Every Sunday recalls the resurrection, but Easter recalls it impressively. What a wonderful thing it is that Jesus Christ is the only person among mankind whose entrance into the world and departure from it are commemorated twenty centuries afterwards! Christmas and Easter, the two most joyous and consequential celebrations of mankind, recall the birth of Christ and the resurrection of Chirst. A belief enduring two thousand years among the most advanced nations of the world, and now professed throughout Christendom, and celebrated as a world-holiday must rest on the foundation of fact. To every man trying to do right the resurrection is the greatest incentive, and the greatest source of strength, peace, and joy.

CHAPTER V

MIRACLES

THERE is a bitter controversy going on at present among non-Catholic Christians. It centers about the Virgin Birth of Christ and His resurrection. But these two points of controversy are only test cases of a matter that is rocking Protestantism to its foundations. Underlying this controversy, which has thrown the evangelical churches into two irreconcilable camps, is the subject of *miracles*. Modernists deny the possibility of miracles; Fundamentals uphold the miraculous.

Recently Bishop Brown of the Episcopal Church gave as his reason for denying the Virgin Birth that it was contrary to biology and hence impossible. He was charged with heresy, brought to trial and found guilty. The Modernists of his church upheld him, declaring that the dogma of the Virgin Birth was based on miracle, and that miracle was an impossibility.

Last year the controversy between Fundamentalists and Modernists grew so bitter that conservative men on both sides feared that it would disrupt the Church. Wise counsel prevailing, oil was poured on the troubled waters and for a time the storm subsided. But it is for a time only. The difference between the two parties is so essential that it is impossible for them to continue long in the same Church. One side affirms what the other side flatly denies and the matter in question is vital to both sides. Let it be said at the outset that Christianity is a supernatural religion. Supernatural signs were as necessary for the establishment of Christ's religion as air is for a human being. Christ made supernatural claims. It was necessary for Him to present supernatural credentials.

Christ Himself is the greatest miracle. Christ without miracles would be a greater miracle than any recorded in the Gospel. Instead of being surprised at miracles concerning Christ and Christianity, we should be surprised if there had been none. St. Augustine declared that the establishment of Christianity without miracles would be a greater miracle than the resurrection.

Christ came with a message to mankind which He declared to be from Almighty God. This message was of such a character that it imposed, in many respects, on those who accepted it a reversal of preceding ideas, a change in the outlook of life, a new and difficult code of morals, and the acceptance of a body of doctrine much of which was beyond the intelligence of man to understand, and which was to be received without any intrinsic proof. Christ came at one of the most intellectual periods in the history of mankind. He addressed Himself to the most conservative, critical, and hostile people that this world has known. He proclaimed that He was Jehovah, the Creator of heaven and earth, the Judge of the living and the dead.

Instead of marvelling that miracles were in order we should marvel if they were not. Christ came as a supernatural Being, presenting supernatural truths, enjoining a life in accordance with His teaching. It was simply impossible for such a one to get a hearing unless He presented supernatural confirmation of Himself and His mission.

Even with His miracles the Jews, for the most part, rejected Him. But they never denied His miracles. In their desperation they said that He effected His wondrous deeds through Satan. If He had not done miracles the Jews would not have been so hard-pressed in their opposition to Him.

They never denied His supernatural works. They could not. It would have been their easiest and best way to discredit Him. Instead, they planned deliberate murder, namely, to do away with Lazarus, the living evidence of Christ's power over the dead. Lazarus was dead and buried. Four days he had lain in the tomb. His body, it would seem, had begun to corrupt, for Martha said to Jesus "he stinketh." At the voice of Jesus this corpse leapt to life. This was in the presence of a large assembly of distinguished people, friends of Lazarus, who had come from Jerusalem to Bethany to offer their condolences to his sisters, Martha and Mary. After this, the Jews believed in Christ. Great multitudes acclaimed Him the Messias. They followed Him in thousands to Jerusalem.

The Scribes and Pharisees and leaders of the people, beholding this, were in consternation. They were convinced of the power of Jesus, but were not converted. A man may be convinced, yet hold out against conversion because he does not want to be converted. These leaders were perverted. They did not want to see, hence they remained blind. Worse than blind. In their rage at seeing the triumph of Jesus, and knowing that His triumph was their downfall, they deliberately plotted to kill Lazarus. Mark it well—they did not deny His resurrection. But being evil men and committed to an evil course, they would not be turned aside. Before Christ performed this miracle He said aloud, before the circle of bystanders, that He was to do it in proof of His divine mission: "That they may know that Thou hast sent Me." The leaders knew this. Some of them were there. But because they were not looking for truth their passions blinded them, as happens with many to-day. Their reaction to Christ's display of divine power was to meet in council and decide on the death of Lazarus and to plot the death of Christ also. Christ knew perfectly well that unless He presented divine credentials He could not be accepted. Hence He said to the Jews, time and again, "If you do not believe Me, believe the works which I do; they give testimony of Me." Miracles were one of the seals of divinity on Christ's mission.

At this late day, after Christ's religion has triumphed over the paganism of the Roman empire, and after two thousand years of Christian civilization, to call in question miracles, is to propose a greater miracle than any recorded in the Bible. The establishment of Christianity without supernatural credentials would be as impossible as Niagara without water. Christianity meant the reversal of man's attitude toward life and the hereafter. It offered man no earthly inducement, but rather the contrary. The early Christians were imprisoned, scourged, exiled, and put to death by frightful tortures. And all this for confessing that Christ was God and practicing His religion. Their main ground for belief was His word combined with His character and divine deeds. They firmly believed that He was God, and that consequently His promises were true, mainly because of the supernatural proofs He offered, among which were miracles.

Christ came as the Son of God. He revealed truths above the capacity of man to comprehend. He legislated for all mankind. He simply had to show divine power in order to have His mission credited. But opponents of the miraculous contend that a miracle is contrary to the laws of nature, and hence an impossibility.

But who made nature and who gave nature her laws? All material nature is under law. It always acts in the same way under the same circumstances. Nothing material can bind itself. Who obliges nature to abide by these laws? A law supposes a lawgiver. Nature, therefore, has a Lawgiver. God, in creating the world, did not abandon control of it. He is still Ruler of the world. We are accustomed to look upon God as we do upon ourselves. With God there is no past or future but all is present. A traveler going along a highway can see just so far before and behind. The part behind is past; the part before is future. But an aviator in an aeroplane with the aid of a powerful field glass can see the highway, perhaps from beginning to end. It is all present to him.

In some such way God sees from eternity to eternity. Foreseeing everything, He so arranged all things from the beginning that in the course of time they would take place according to His plans. Consequently a miracle is not a violation of nature's law. It may be an effect produced without the application of natural forces at all, or the application of nature's law in a way possible alone to the Author and Ruler of nature. An example will make this latter clear. An inventor can so arrange the mechanism of his machine that to the astonishment of onlookers it does the unexpected at specified times. To the bystanders this seems to be accidental, or a hitch in the mechanism. To the inventor it is only an application of forces under his control.

If a civil engineer should go to South Africa where there was a mountain to be removed to make way for a railroad, the inhabitants would say that the thing was impossible. They might allege that if a hundred thousand men were engaged on the work it would take a hundred years to do it, or more, since the mountain was solid rock. The engineer would reply that he could level it in a year with a few hundred men. To them that would be a miracle. But to him who knew the power of dynamite and engines of excavation the thing would be only the application of nature's laws in a way unknown to the savage mind.

No comparison is altogether correct when God is in question. But in some such way God may act when there is a miracle. There is no violation of nature's law, but the application of forces by the Author and Ruler of nature in a way possible to God only. Nature's law is the expression of God's will in creation. God does not violate nature's laws by a miracle. He simply gives a sign that the Creator of the world is at work. Hence a miracle is, as it were, God's language. That is why Christ appealed to His miracles in proof that God was His Father, and that His mission was from heaven. By performing a miracle Christ was demonstrating that God was approving Him and corroborating Him. The Apostle Peter in the very first sermon after Christ's resurrection appealed to Christ's miracles as proof that Christ was what He claimed to be. "Ye men of Israel, hear these words: Jesus of Nazareth, a man approved of God among you, by miracles, and wonders and signs, which God did by Him, in the midst of you, as you also know."

You see he is speaking to those who were among them that witnessed Christ's miracles. In consequence of this first sermon thousands became followers of Jesus in the very city where He was crucified.

How explain the worship of the Crucified and the adoption of His lofty and severe code of morals unless He gave supernatural signs in proof of His mission? Christianity is based on miracles and other supernatural signs. Without these its establishment is the greatest of all miracles. Modernists who deny miracles should be consistent, and abandon Christianity altogether. To uphold and preach a supernatural religion and at the same time deny the supernatural is neither logical nor scientific. If Christianity is not supernatural it is nothing; rather, it is a fraud. Its message is supernatural, its motives are supernatural, its incentives are supernatural. It bids men to live mainly for eternal life. It counts as naught this world unless it be a means to the world beyond. It tells us that although we must live in this world we must not live for it. "What doth it profit a man if he gain the whole world and suffer the loss of his own soul?" If Christianity is not authoritative it is no more than a system of ethics or the teachings of a sage. Without authority to bind conscience, religion is merely directive and optional. Christ's religion was a command. He talked as God, acted as God, legislated as God. Unless He wrought supernatural wonders He never could have reached, authoritatively, the consciences of the millions who worshiped Him and died for Him. Unless we are convinced that the religion of Christ binds us the same as if God Almighty in person spoke to us, we are not Christians. Let us be done with this trifling with Christ and His religion. If He be not God He was an impostor and Christianity a sham. But an impostor and a sham do not last for two thousand years and give to mankind the most wonderful benefits ever conferred on the world, Christian civilization and Christian ideals.

If miracle is impossible, so is Christ, so is Christianity. But Christ is a fact, and Christianity is a fact. Miracle, too, is a fact. Do away with miracle and you must tear out every page of the Gospel. Do away with miracle and you make of Christ nothing but a sage, whose counsels may be accepted or rejected at will.

If Christ was not God His words are the most insane pronouncements that ever came from a disordered brain. And He was not God if miracles are impossible. Miracles were one of the proofs that He Himself gave that He was God. Reject miracles and you not only discredit Christ as God but as man also. For if miracles are impossible Christ was either an impostor or insane.

What sane person unless He was really God could make the statements that Christ was continually making? He said: "I am the Light of the world." "I am the resurrection and the life; he that believeth in Me, although he be dead, shall live." "I am the Way, the Truth and the Life; no man cometh to the Father but by Me." "All power is given to Me in heaven and in earth." "Going, therefore, teach ye all nations, teaching them to observe all things whatsoever I have commanded you: and behold I am with you all days, even to the consummation of the world." "He that loseth his life for My sake shall find it." "As the Father raiseth up the dead and giveth life, so the Son also giveth life to whom He will, that all may honor the Son as they honor the Father."

Christ asserts that He has all the power of God Almighty and claims the honor due to God alone. What blasphemy or insanity unless He was indeed God! But if miracles are impossible He was not God. Christ Himself realized the extraordinary nature of the claims He was making, and the need of their divine confirmation. When they accused Him of blasphemy because He said He was God He replied: "Do you say to Me, Thou blasphemest, because I said I am the Son of God? If I do not the works of My Father, believe Me not. But if I do, though you will not believe Me, believe the works; that you may know and believe that the Father is in Me and I in the Father."

Nothing could be plainer than that. Christ distinctly appeals to His miracles, and declares that they attest His divine claims. This means that if miracles are impossible Christ was a blasphemer. They, therefore, who are logical and consistent must admit miracles or classify Christ as a blasphemer. Christ Himself invited that issue. He openly based His claims on miracles and challenged His opponents on that ground. They who deny miracles proclaim Christ an impostor and Christianity a fraud. But God said of Christ, "This is My beloved Son, in whom I am well pleased: hear ye Him." And Christ said of His Church, "He who hears you hears Me."

Miracles are a fact because Christ is a fact. Miracles are a fact because Christianity is a fact. Modernists are trying to do the impossible, to retain Christianity and deny miracles. Modernism is the last stage of Protestantism. The great Protest which began in the sixteenth century has ended by protesting the supernatural itself. It is now, therefore, back to paganism or Catholicity.

CHAPTER VI

WHY DON'T CATHOLICS THINK FOR THEMSELVES?

THEY do. The greatest thinkers in the world have been Catholics. Recently I received a letter from a gentleman who was contemplating becoming a Catholic, but who was held back by what he had heard about Catholics being driven or herded. He said that a man should not renounce, for any creed, the intelligence that God gave him. He said that he had been authoritatively informed that Catholics let others do their thinking for them. He instanced divorce and birth-control, vital matters on which the great body of Catholics had no say whatever.

I replied to him that because the people of the United States had no say in a matter once the United States Supreme Court handed down a decision with regard to it, did not imply that they were herded, nor that they had renounced their intelligence. I further informed him that in his state of mind he could not become a Catholic if he wanted to. I told him that he misunderstood fundamentally the nature of the Catholic Church if he believed that it was an institution subject to error or revision. Briefly I put before him just what the Church is. Let me sum it up as follows.

Like Christ Himself, the Church of Christ wants man to use his intelligence to investigate her credibility. She claims to be the voice of God in the world, to speak on matters of faith and morality with the finality of God. If her claims are not true she should not receive our allegiance. If her claims are true she speaks with divine guarantee and cannot mislead. To listen to her and to be guided by her is no more surrendering intelligence or being herded than it is for people to submit to vaccination. Millions of people submit to vaccination every year because they have faith in the credibility of those who advocate it. They first ascertain, by intellectual investigation, or by what they consider credible report, that

41

the medical authorities are trustworthy. Once they have faith in them they are reasonable in submitting to them, even if they understand little or nothing about what is prescribed. Not one man in a million who takes a prescription to a druggist understands anything about it, yet he accepts it confidently. In so doing he does not surrender his intelligence, but makes a wise use of it, for he reasons that it is reasonable to trust to one who is an authority or specialist in a matter.

The Church is designated by Christ Himself His authority on earth in matters of faith and morals. The Church can no more teach error with regard to doctrine or morality than could Christ Himself when He was among us.

Now the whole matter reduces itself to this: Is the Catholic Church the Church established by Christ, and guaranteed by Him never to teach error? If so she is to be regarded with the same reverence and trust in matters of faith and morals as Christ Himself. We are free to use our intelligence to the utmost limit to ascertain if the Catholic Church is the true Church of God. Let me say in passing that if she is not, no Church is, and Christianity is false, and all revealed religion is an imposition.

The greatest thinkers in the world have been Catholics. Augustine and Aquinas tower like giants above the world's intellectual celebrities. In our own generation we have seen men like Newman and Manning and Chesterton yielding their intellectual conviction to the claims of Catholicity. Pasteur, the greatest scientist of modern times, found it no abuse of intelligence to adhere firmly to the teaching of the Catholic Church. Foch, the greatest of present-day military geniuses, a man not only of ideas but of action, glories in submitting with child-like trust to the teaching of the Church. Pasteur and Foch were not herded. They were not forced into believing. They used their God-given reason to learn that the Church was the institution established by Christ to continue His ministry to mankind to the end of the world. Christ said to His Church, "He who hears you hears Me." In submitting to the Church, therefore, man makes a wise use of his intelligence, reasoning that God's guaranteed representative is to be reverenced and obeyed. That is the whole matter of religion in a nutshell. Either the Catholic Church is as true as God, or she has no reason for existence. Now, if she is the voice of God, there is no betrayal of reason in being submissive to her, for it is highly reasonable to be guided by Him who gave us our reason, and who can neither deceive nor be deceived.

When the Church speaks she is not giving out doctrine of her own invention but is declaring the truth which Christ commanded her to proclaim. The Church did not originate the doctrine of hell or of the Eucharist or of the Trinity or of the indissolubility of marriage. Christ Himself proclaimed these truths, and solemnly commissioned His Church to teach them to all mankind to the end of time. All men do not listen to the Church. All men did not listen to Christ. That does not make Him or His Church the less true. Some people do not listen to the orders of physicians, who prescribe a certain diet and regime for their ailments. That does not mean that the prescription was not right nor will it save the patients from the ravages of the disease. It all comes back to this, and is as simple as two plus two make four: was Christ God and did He establish a Church guaranteeing it against error? If He did, Catholics are the most reasonable people in the world for believing in the Church and living by her guidance. If He did not so establish and guarantee a Church, then away with all churches, away with revelation, away with Christianity altogether. But we know that Christ, the Son of God, founded a Church, that He promised to be with her always, guiding and protecting her against error. And we know that there is only one Church that goes back directly to Christ, one Church alone that claims to speak with His authority, one Church only which even claims to be unerring and incapable of error, and that is the Catholic Church. In submitting to her Catholics are not herded or driven, but divinely guided. We pay large fees to a physican or lawyer for professional advice. We do not consider that we are surrendering our intelligence in thus submitting to expert counsel and direction. Yet physician and lawyer may be mistaken. In matters of faith and morals the Church cannot be mistaken.

Just what do we mean by faith and morals? By faith we mean the truth which we are to believe, and by morals we mean our way of living, our code of conduct. The Church cannot err in teaching us what we are to believe, or in prescribing what is right or wrong in conduct. When I say the Church, I mean of course the Church speaking authoritatively, magisterially. A priest is not the Church, nor is a bishop or cardinal. Not even the Pope is the Church, except when he speaks *"ex cathedra,"* that is "from the throne." This he does when, as the Vicar of Christ, he proclaims a doctrine of faith or morals which he intends to be a pronouncement, binding on the faith and conscience of the whole Church. Some people outside the Church fancy that the Pope is doing nothing but exercising his power by making infallible statements every day. The Pope never speaks *"ex cathedra"* except to make clear some point of faith or morals which is called in question. Even thus he does not say anything new or of his own opinion, but merely states what has been Catholic doctrine in the matter from the beginning.

There has been nothing added to Catholic doctrine since the days of the Apostles. They received the deposit of faith from Christ, and were divinely inspired by the Holy Ghost. They simply transmitted to their successors what Christ committed to them. No Pope or Council has added any new doctrine to this deposit of faith. All they have done was to state the true significance of it, or any part of it, thus giving the infallible interpretation of the Church when circumstances required it. Our Supreme Court acts somewhat in the same way with regard to the Constitution of the United States, clarifying any article which may need interpretation. The Pope, even when he does not speak *"ex cathedra,"* is listened to with the greatest reverence by the faithful, and if he speaks authoritatively commands obedience. In matters not concerned with faith or morals or when he speaks as a private individual his pronouncements are those of a learned and holy man, but not infallible, not binding on the faithful. But once the Church speaks authoritatively it is the voice of God. To listen to and be guided by the voice of God is no abuse of reason, but its best use. History is proof of this. No individual or nation has ever pursued a wrong course by obeying the Church of Christ. On the contrary, nations and individuals have brought themselves to ruin by going counter to her teaching.

A Catholic is wonderfully blessed in that he need never be in doubt about the great issues of life. Outside the Church people are in constant apprehension with regard to right conduct. Is it right to divorce and re-marry? Is it right to practice birth-control? Is it right to have recourse to abortion? Is it right to practice craniotomy? And so on. A Catholic knows what God's will is in these matters. And since God's will is the greatest thing in life, a Catholic is truly fortunate. After all, it is God's judgment which in the end will prevail. Some may say that it is better not to be informed on such matters, because then one would be unrestricted. As well say that it would be better not to be informed of tainted meat. What is wrong is wrong. God has not legislated to hamper man, but to make him free with the freedom that is salutary. If a mother orders a child to keep away from a smallpox area it is not to restrict but to save the child. God's Commandments are for our eternal welfare, and any light thrown upon them is for our eventual good. All that the Church does is to make clear what God wants of us. She is called holy Mother Church, because like a mother she is solicitous for our real and permanent welfare.

A good mother is not one who gratifies the whims and inclinations of her children, but one who looks ahead to their lasting welfare, and guides and rules them accordingly. The Church, our holy Mother, seeks to rear us, her children here, to be in eternity the children of God. A wise mother looks to the future manhood and womanhood of her children and denies them many passing indulgences for their permanent advantage. If man were made for this life only he might shape his conduct accordingly. But we have not here a lasting city. We are wayfarers to our eternal home, pilgrims to the everlasting country. No pleasure, no self-indulgence on the way, should turn us aside to the paths that lead to misery. The Church is God's appointed guide, who takes us by the hand, not to curtail our freedom, but to lead us to eternal liberty, as the children of our Father in heaven.

CHAPTER VII

IS ONE RELIGION AS GOOD AS ANOTHER?

CATHOLICS often hear it said by those outside the faith that one religion is as good as another. This is sometimes put in another form: "All roads lead to Rome." One reason why the Church meets with opposition is that she claims to be the only true Church. Is one religion as good as another? Evidently those who founded new religious denominations did not think so. If one religion was as good as another there was no reason for the establishment of the various Protestant denominations we see to-day. Every new religious sect is an admission that one religion is not as good as another. The hundreds of sects among the non-Catholic Christians is a declaration that the Church they left was not as good as the Church they inaugurated. Nor can it be said that the reason for establishing a new denomination was simply because the old was personally unsuited to those who left it. The reason for establishing the new was not because of mere unsuitableness, but because the old was objected to doctrinally. But this is not the point. At most it shows that non-Catholics contradict themselves when they say that one religion is as good as another.

In considering this question we must distinguish between a creed and the believer in a creed. A creed may be wrong but a believer in it may be very sincere. A creed may be condemned without condemning its adherents. An example will illustrate this. One man may be opposed in politics to another without being personally opposed to the other. A Democrat may assail the Republican party and at the same time esteem and respect an individual Republican. Two men may be close friends and yet belong to opposite political parties. They may mutually condemn the party of the other, assailing its principles and denouncing its policies, but at the same time esteeming each other. One may condemn a particular political party's policy and principles, and notwithstanding, admire and praise individuals of that party.

So, in considering this matter of the various religions and their claims, we consider the religion only, not its members. It is possible to analyze and examine into and evaluate a religious creed. It is impossible for man to analyze and pass judgment on the individual conscience. God alone sees and understands the individual human heart. Judgment is His. But man may pass judgment on the truth or error of a proposition. If a statement is self-contradictory or contradicts a known truth, or is at variance with known data it is false, and man may so declare it.

If one religion was as good as another there was no reason for Christ to establish the Christian religion. If the pagan religion was as good as the Christian there was no need of the Apostles and the early Christians shedding their blood to establish Christianity. If one religion is as good as another the fetish worship of the African savage is as good as the Christian worship of the true God.

We may condemn idol worship without condemning the poor idolater. We may condemn that worship which sacrifices human life to grotesque idols without condemning the pitiful adherents of the worship. And so we may declare false certain religions of to-day because they are false. If a religion is false it is not as good as the true religion. It is possible for a man to get on a wrong train and eventually reach his destination. But that does not make the train the right one. It is possible for a man to receive wrong directions and yet arrive in course of time at his due place. But that does not make the direction right. Some people go wrong with right directions and others go right with wrong directions. Cardinal Newman hit this off when he said that many Catholics were worse than their religion while Protestants in many cases were better than their religion. After all, religion does not physically oblige any one to follow it. It simply points out the right way and gives aid to walk in it. It can happen that a member of the true religion may lead a bad life and lose his soul, while a member of a false religion may, by living up to conscience, save his soul. That does not make the false religion true, nor the true religion false.

An exceptional person may in any department of life rise above the level of the principles and conduct of his fellows. But religion concerns not merely exceptional cases but mankind generally. And generally a false religion will direct its adherents wrongly, and the true religion will direct its followers right.

Is it true, therefore, to say that one religion is as good as another? No more than to say that a false guide is as good as a true guide. If any one religion in the world is true, every religion which differs from it is false. That is as clear and plain as that two plus two make four. Now, there is only one religion in the world which even claims to be exclusively true, and that is the Catholic. Every other religion states that it is advancing toward the truth, or that there is no fixed truth, or that it is more true than some other creed. The Catholic Church, if right, constitutes all the others wrong. That is one reason of opposition to her.

But she is the only Church that claims to be the truth, the whole truth, and nothing but the truth. The other Churches do not even claim that they have the truth; they admit that the Churches which differ from them are as good as their own. It may be said that they differ only in incidentals. But this is not so, by any means. They differ fundamentally and essentially. Now I think it will be admitted that if the Catholic Church can be proved to be true, it will follow that the others which differ from her are false, and that a false religion is not as good as the true religion, and that consequently one religion is not as good as another.

To prove that the Catholic Church is true it is only necessary to show that Christ founded a Church and that the Catholic is that Church. It is clear that if Christ established a Church, it was true, since He was God. It is evident also that He established a Church, otherwise the various Churches would not claim to be the one established by Him. But is the Catholic the Church founded by Him, and is it alone the Church He established? A whole book might be written on this matter, but in the limit I have set myself for the treatment of the subject I shall be brief. Nevertheless I shall present a proof which any jury of unprejudiced minds would accept. A brief argument is as convincing as a long one, and often more clinching. The proof that the Catholic Church is the one established by Jesus Christ is that for centuries after Christ it was the only Church of Christ known in the world. Even some heretics in those centuries called themselves Catholics, so true is it that the Catholic Church was the recognized Church of Christ. If Christ established a Church it existed as a visible organization because it had to preach and administer the sacraments, etc., all of which required a visible ministry.

Non-Catholics admit this much. They say, however, that after the first few centuries the Church gradually fell into error and that the Reformation re-established the true Christian Church. Two things are against this. The first is that Christ in founding His Church proclaimed that He would always be with it and that it should never teach error. If the only Church in the world which for centuries was acknowledged by Christians to be the Church of Christ fell into error, Christ's guarantee was false. If His guarantee was false He was false, therefore not God, therefore all Christianity is an imposture, and the sooner it is branded false the better.

Moreover, the re-constructed religions of the reformers do not claim that they have the truth, the whole truth, nothing but the truth. But no Church is Christ's which is not the whole Truth. Christ declared that He was the *Way*, the *Truth*, and the *Life*. His Church cannot be partly true and partly false. No Church on earth claims to be exclusively true except the Catholic. How can a Church which is not entirely true be the Church of the absolutely true Christ? By their own admission, therefore, the non-Catholic Churches stand out as not being those of Christ. To say that a Church which is not Christ's is as good as the Church of Christ is to say that falsehood is as good as truth.

To sum up briefly: Christ was God. He established a Church. This Church He guaranteed against error. The only Church in the world which claims not to err is the Catholic Church. Therefore, the Catholic Church is the Church of Christ. Therefore, one Church is not as good as another, because there is one Church which is Christ's which cannot err, and which stands out by itself as the sole true Church. A man in a rowboat may be able to cross the Atlantic. So a man regardless of creed may be able to know the truth and to live by it. But no man would trust himself

to a rowboat for a transatlantic voyage if one of our modern steam-
ships were available for passage.

The Church of Christ is the vessel guaranteed by God to conduct
all who voyage in it to the haven of everlasting life and joy.
No one who voyages in this vessel need fear shipwreck if he remain
aboard. It is only by abandoning the vessel that he can be lost.
No one can make him leave the ship but himself. But one thing
can cause him to leave, and that is to disobey orders. In that
case the security of the vessel will not avail him.

God gives every human being the grace necessary for salvation.
He founded His Church as the appointed means of guiding and
helping man to salvation. While it is possible for those outside the
Church who are in good faith and who live up to a right conscience
to be saved, they nevertheless find themselves tossed hither and
thither on a sea of doubt, they lack the helps and guidance afforded
by the true Church, and too often lose heart and give up the effort
of combating the world, the flesh, and the devil. In the true
Church of Christ there is no doubt, her children are not looking
for the truth, they have it, they have sure guidance in all the
vicissitudes of life, if they fall they find a helping hand to aid
them to rise, and if they are weak they find strength in the sacraments of grace. They have that peace which certainty gives, that
peace which the world cannot give nor take away. No—one
religion is not as good as another. Not when one religion and
one only is established and guaranteed against error by Jesus Christ,
the Son of God.

CHAPTER VIII

DOES IT MATTER WHAT WE BELIEVE?

WE often hear it said that it does not matter much what we believe, but rather what we do. Yet what we do depends mainly on what we believe. If you believe that a bank is going to fail, you will draw out your money. If you believe that a man is dishonest, you will not invest in his enterprise. If you believe that a certain field contains oil, you will be glad to buy it at a reasonable price.

Not only individuals, but government and business shape their action by what they believe. The Monroe Doctrine has affected the policy and action of the federal government for many years and in many crises.

Merchants are guided in the management of their business by their belief in certain business principles. To uphold these principles, they at times suffer considerable loss, but they know that in the end it is more than worth while. Every merchant of standing believes that his reputation for reliability is one of his best assets. To maintain the public's belief in his integrity, he will cheerfully sustain any temporary loss.

In point of fact, life, generally, is just what our beliefs are. We may not live up to our beliefs, but certainly we never live beyond them.

An anarchist assassinates because he believes in assassination as a remedy for social ills. A Socialist aims at destroying religion because he believes or claims to believe that man has no career beyond this earth. What would shock a man of right principles glorifies a man of wrong principles.

It is true that human frailty frequently keeps one on a lower plane than one's ideals and principles, but it remains true, nevertheless, that a man ordinarily does not rise above his ideals. Ideals are nothing but highly admired beliefs. The heroes of mankind are they who, having lofty ideals, whether of patriotism, courage, or generosity, have lived up to them.

Religion has heroes as well as country. The saints are the heroes of Christianity. The saints are the knights of Christ. The saints are those followers of Christ who had as ideals Christ Himself and aimed to live worthily of Him. All Christians are followers of Christ. All Christians must be actuated by the principles of Christ, who has said: "He who is not with Me is against Me." We are with Christ when we live by His principles. We are living by His principles when our conduct is based on belief in His doctrine.

Catholic principles are the principles of Jesus Christ. Catholic principles are the directions of God to mankind on the road of mortal life to the blessed domain of immortality. Catholic principles are the guide-posts set by God Himself along the journey from time to eternity. Catholic principles are a divine leadership conducting man to a blessed destiny.

As in business and government it matters much what our beliefs are, so does it with regard to religion. Our religious belief shapes our life. If a Catholic lived up to Catholic belief he would be an ideal man. As man, father, husband, or citizen, he would be all that is best. There is not a single Catholic doctrine that has ever misled mankind. The reason is because God, who is the Author of human nature, is also the Author of Catholic belief. Whenever you hear of a Catholic who has done wrong, you may know that it was not because of Catholic belief, but against it.

Let us look at a few Catholic beliefs and see for ourselves their effect on conduct.

The Incarnation teaches me that Jesus Christ, the Son of Almighty God, became man, and suffered and died in order to save my immortal soul. Do I believe this? If I do, it means that I must hold my soul to be of very great value. It means that if Christ valued it so highly as to give His life for it, I ought certainly to value it above my life.

Hence, rather than lose my soul, I will submit to every conceivable loss. But one thing can cause me to lose my soul, sin.

Therefore rather than sin, I shall, like the martyrs, sacrifice property, liberty, or life. In doing so, Christ's words will come home to me: "He who loses his life for My sake shall find it."

It was because Sir Thomas More valued his soul aright that he suffered himself to be beheaded rather than do wrong even for his king. Sir Thomas More was the most celebrated and honored man in the realm of Henry VIII. His power was next to that of the king himself. He had everything except the crown. Henry, knowing the weight of his influence with the people, hoped that if he could get the approval of More for his divorce, the whole kingdom would acquiesce. Accordingly he employed every means in his power to get his Chancellor to approve of the divorce. He heaped new honors on him, made all sorts of promises to him, and in every way possible sought to win him over. Finally, when promises and favors failed, he employed threats. He threw More into prison and threatened him with death.

But always the Chancellor remained firm. The king sent various persons to him to persuade him, but to no avail. The king himself visited him and accused him of stubbornness and ingratitude. More's reply was: "My Lord King, I have but one life; it is very dear to me, but I would gladly yield it any time for your Majesty. If I had two souls I would gladly give one for you, but as I have but one, it belongs to God, who purchased it by His passion and death. Rather than lose my soul, I am ready to lose my life. But all else, Sire, that I have is at your command."

Henry, knowing the high esteem in which More was held, hesitated to order him to the block. He tried one last device before committing official murder. More had a daughter Margaret whom he loved as seldom father loves child. Her love for him was as great as his for her. There is nothing in human annals more tender than More's love for his daughter Margaret.

The king had her sent to her father in prison to prevail on him to come over to his side on the divorce. In tears Margaret pleaded with her beloved father. Only a loving parent can understand the anguish of More under this ordeal.

Finally he said to her: "Well, daughter, suppose I do go over to the King, what then?" "Oh, father," she replied, "he would restore all your honors. Again you would be the first personage in the realm." "And how long, daughter, would I enjoy these honors?" "For years and years. You are young yet. We should have many happy years together in comfort and honor." "How many, daughter?" "Twenty, forty, maybe more." "And after that, daughter?" She made no reply. Instead, tears blinded her as she sobbed, "You are right, darling father. Eternity is too great a price to pay for even the greatest worldly pleasure and honor."

The next day Sir Thomas More was led to the scaffold. Before placing his head on the block, he indulged in pleasantry with the executioner. Running his finger over the edge of the axe he said: "It's a sharp remedy, but a cure for all human ills." The next moment he calmly placed his head on the block, telling the axe-man to take good aim and make a clean job of it. The axe fell, and the noblest head in England was severed from its body. The axe fell, and More beheld the countenance of Christ and heard His words of welcome to eternal life and bliss. More had confessed Christ before men. Christ now confessed him before His heavenly Father.

It does not take more than one truth of faith properly realized to make a saint. Any one of the great fundamental beliefs of Catholicity will safely guide a man along the path of life. Some of these beliefs are Judgment, Heaven, Hell, the Eucharist, the Passion of Christ, the Church as God's Voice in the world, the Sacraments.

Father De Smet, an Indian missionary, relates that it was his custom to visit the various tribes of his mission, one after the other. It usually took him two years to cover the field. After instructing a tribe, he baptized those properly prepared and the infants, and administered holy communion to the adults. On leaving he selected the one best qualified to act in his place, whose duty it was to assemble the tribe for morning and evening prayers and for special service on Sunday.

Returning to a certain tribe, after an absence of two years, he began by hearing the confessions of those who were to receive holy communion at Mass the next day. Having heard all who presented themselves, he noticed that the one whom he had put in charge of the mission did not come to confession. After a time he went in search of him. Coming across him he said, "My good man, I have been waiting for you to go to confession." The Indian replied, "I am not going to confession, Father." He said this reverently, but firmly. The priest was shocked. In a distressed voice he inquired: "How is this—you, who should set a good example, refuse to do your duty?" To which the Indian replied, "There is no need of going to confession." But, on beholding the consternation in the countenance of the missionary, he added, "Did you not tell us, Father, that Jesus Christ, the Son of God, suffered a cruel death on the cross for me?" "Yes, my child, I did." "And did you not say that He suffered because of my sins?" "I did, my child." "Well, Father, if an Indian suffered stripes for me, or lost his arm for me, do you think I could do anything to hurt that Indian? And how could I commit sin, which you told us is the only thing which offends the good Jesus who died for me? I have no sins to confess, Father, and I hope I never shall have, and I will die rather than sin." The good missionary realized that he was in the presence of a saint.

The one thought, the one belief, that Christ had died for sin, was enough to make this savage a saint. Any one belief properly realized will guide a man securely to eternal life. The difference between us and the saints is that they realized the truths of faith. There is a vast difference between knowing and realizing. The purpose of religion is to enable us to have a realization of the saving truths which Christ taught, and to live by them.

St. Francis Xavier became the wonderful hero of God that he was by a realization of one truth. St. Ignatius often said to Francis in the midst of his triumphs at the University of Paris: "Francis, what does it profit to gain the whole world and lose your soul?" For a long time that saying was just so many words to Francis, but eventually it broke on him with all its meaning, with the result that he became the greatest Apostle of the Faith since the days of the Twelve.

In order to understand the effect of belief on conduct all we have to do is to look around us. Those who do not believe in hell seem to be going rapidly in the way that leads to it. The morals of to-day, except where religious belief prevails, are virtually pagan. Immodesty, impurity, dishonesty, dissipation, divorce, and despair meet us on all sides. Worldly people, who have discarded belief in revelation, are living as if they were a law to themselves. Their lives are the best argument against their false belief.

The Church of God teaches that we are creatures of God, and, as such, subjects of the Creator. It teaches that as subjects of God we are here to do His will, not our own. It teaches that Christ came to place us on the highway to everlasting life and blessedness, and that this highway is the way of the commandments. "If thou wilt enter into eternal life, keep My commandments."

Belief in the teaching of Christ, which is the teaching of His Church, is therefore a matter of vital importance. It makes a vast difference in life whether we believe that we are made for time or eternity. Christ proclaims that we are made for eternity. The world says our destiny is confined to this earth. Christ, Eternal Truth, is the Light of the world. Blessed are they who are guided by that Light.

CHAPTER IX

SALVATION OUTSIDE THE CHURCH

OUR divine Lord, in sending forth His Apostles to establish His religion among mankind, said to them: "All power is given to Me in heaven and in earth. Going, therefore, teach ye all nations; baptizing them in the name of the Father and of the Son and of the Holy Ghost. Teaching them to observe all things whatsoever I have commanded you: and behold I am with you all days even to the consummation of the world" (Matt. xxviii. 18-20). "Preach the Gospel to every creature. He that believeth and is baptized shall be saved: but he that believeth not shall be condemned" (Mark xvi. 15, 16).

This was Christ's commission to His Church. He said, moreover: "He who hears you hears Me." He thus constituted the Church His voice on earth, proclaiming the truth, pointing out the way to salvation, and leading mankind to eternal life. God is not only just—He is also merciful. Indeed, His mercy is over all His works. God requires the impossible of no one. It is impossible, humanly speaking, for those to be baptized who have never been within the reach or ministry of His Church. There are portions of the earth which have not been penetrated by the missionaries of the Gospel. Since the days of Christ there have been millions in pagan lands who have never heard of Christ. It is impossible to believe, if one has never heard what is to be believed.

That this was the mind of Christ is evident from the allocution of His representative on earth, the Vicar of Christ. The saintly Pontiff, Pius IX, in an official statement made to the whole world, August 10, 1863, declared as follows: "You know, my most dear children and venerable brothers, that those who, being individually ignorant of our holy religion, observe the natural law

57

and precepts that God has engraven on the heart of every man, and who are disposed to obey God and live virtuously and righteously, can, by the aid of divine light and grace, obtain eternal life; since God, who searches the heart, who sees clearly and knows the sentiments, the thoughts, and the dispositions of all, cannot, in His supreme mercy and goodness, by any means permit that even one soul should be eternally punished that has not separated itself from Him by voluntary mortal sin."

This papal pronouncement, which is the voice of Christ, clearly proclaims that no one incurs eternal damnation who has not separated himself from God by deliberate mortal sin.

Before a person can be guilty of unbelief he must have the opportunity of believing. Even in our own country there are persons in unfrequented places who have never heard the truths of revelation. Moreover, in our big cities there are many, very many, who have never heard the name of Christ except in profanity. And even among Christians there are many who have received the doctrine of Christ through false channels, and who have never heard His teaching from the true Church.

Doubtless many of those people are in good faith, and trying to live right. They are really Catholics in spirit because they have the desire to believe the truth and to live by it. Such as these belong to the soul of the Church, although they are not bodily united to it. God sees the heart and the intention. He knows those who are doing their best to know the truth and to live by it. In His own way He will conduct them to a blessed destiny. They, therefore, who are in perfectly good faith and who lead good lives are in God's hands, and need give us no concern.

But, if this is so, why make such ado about the Catholic Church being the only true Church, and about the necessity of belonging to it? Because it is the Church established by Jesus Christ to give the light to guide man aright and the means to help him attain eternal life, and because they who of their own fault fail to belong to her cannot be saved.

It must be distinctly noted that it is said that "they who of their own fault fail to belong to her cannot be saved." God is the sole judge of this matter. It may happen that persons born and educated in non-Catholic sects are in good faith in their belief. These, if they lead sinless lives, and have the will to belong to the true Church of Christ, are within the pale of the Church belonging to her in spirit, if not outwardly. God is the sole judge as to whether or not they are in good faith. The influence of environment and education may so affect people that they live on in ignorance that they are in error. This is termed invincible ignorance by theologians, and it saves from culpable error those who are in its grip.

But it is hard to see how some people among the non-Catholic sects can plead invincible ignorance. They are educated and well-informed on everything but the true Church of Christ. They doubt or discard their own religious doctrine, and fail to give the Catholic Church serious thought. Yet they see thousands from their ranks joining the Catholic Church every year. And those who leave their former sects are usually the most learned and the most virtuous. If they witnessed anything like that in any other affair of life it would move them to investigate their own position. But they merely shrug their shoulders or think of other things, as if religion were a minor matter, rather than man's supreme concern. Many of them admire the teaching and practises of the Catholic Church, but hesitate to inquire seriously into her claim, for fear of being convinced of the truth and obliged to live accordingly. Others find the non-Catholic sects so easy and congenial that they refuse to be concerned with the inconsistencies of their denomination, preferring to go on in the pleasant way their Church sanctions.

Yet these same people, if they were in a wordly concern which was as shaky as their Church would hasten to safety. God is the judge whether or not they are in good faith.

When, however, all has been said in extenuation of those outside the Church, the great fact remains that man is a sinner, that he is constantly tempted, that he frequently falls, and that unless he has a helping hand to enable him to rise and support him on his way he will fall again. A Catholic may fall, and fall lamentably, but he has the Sacrament of Penance to put him on his feet again and start him aright. The Catholic has a thousand reminders that there is a God above to whom he must give an account of his life. He has the holy Mass and the sacraments to keep him constantly in touch with the supernatural world. If a Catholic goes wrong it is because he deliberately refuses guidance and help from above. If Catholics, with the truth to guide them, and the grace of the sacraments to aid them, nevertheless find it hard at times to tread the path of virtue, what must it be for those who have not these wonderful helps?

I have often heard a man say that he started wrong and kept on wrong. Others have said that they lost their virtue and that they might as well continue on the broad road of vice. We Catholics know that if we fall and truly repent, the absolution of the Sacrament of Penance starts us off again with a clean score and on the right road. No matter how low we may fall we have at hand the means of rising. Not only that, but the means are pursuing us, so that to remain in sin is a constant rejection of the means of reconciliation.

It is not until we see God face to face in heaven that we shall realize what a blessed thing the Catholic faith is to those who live by it. It is the sure path to everlasting life with God. Outside the Catholic Church there is doubt, unrest, and a lack of nearly all the practical means of grace which the sacraments afford. It is hard to understand how a man of good life and of good logic can fail to see the truth of the Catholic Church. It can only be because he does not reason in matters of faith with the same honesty that he does in those of daily life. It is easy for a man to deceive himself into the idea that he is trying to be logical. One who is enjoying life wants nothing to disturb his ease and license. Hence, he either refuses to look for the truth, or if it is presented to him turns aside from it.

Suppose such a man commits serious sin, what is to bring about his reform and repentance? For if he does not repent and reform he will not be saved. There is within him a hazy or general notion that he must avoid sin to be saved, but a general notion is not enough to halt a man who is on the path of passion. He needs something definite and effective to make him turn aside from the broad road of sinful indulgence. It is possible for a man in any sphere of life to avoid evil and do good. But considering human nature as it is, its lust, its greed, its arrogance and its weakness, how few do what is barely possible.

That is why we Catholics have all but the assurance of salvation, since our religion gives those of good will every aid to walk in the way that leads to God. Let us, therefore, leave those outside the Church to God, and concern ourselves with our own selves. It is Catholic doctrine that those who of their own fault close their eyes to the truth cannot be saved. Only God knows those who thus reject the Catholic truth. And only those who are culpable in rejecting the Church are really outside her pale. We, thank God, are not looking for the truth, we have it. Its light may cause us to walk a narrow path, but what avails a broad and easy road if it lead away from final happiness?

Christ died for His Church, the Apostles gave their lives for her, the martyrs in millions shed their blood for her, countless millions have made untold sacrifices for her. She is the bride of Christ. By her He rears children for the kingdom of heaven. We should be grateful that we are her children. Our best gratitude is to live worthily of her. That will make us children of God.

CHAPTER X

ARE CATHOLICS CREDULOUS?

ONE sometimes hears the question, why are Catholics so credulous? In point of fact, Catholics are not credulous. Some Catholics are, just as some Americans or English or Chinese are. One is not credulous because one is a Catholic, but because one is ignorant or simple.

The Catholic Church embraces all classes of mankind, people of every condition, and of every race. There is a percentage of credulous people in every nation and among every class of people. In point of fact Catholics, as a body, are the most incredulous of people. Of course there is a good deal of credulity among the simpler element—that is so of every creed and nation and people. But Catholics as Catholics are the most intelligent inquirers in the world. There are no logicians anywhere comparable to Catholic theologians and philosophers. Recently Hilaire Belloc, himself a philosopher, wrote an article demonstrating that the keenest investigators of science and philosophy are Catholics. Any one who has opened a book of Catholic philosophy will find that it deals with the thought of all ages and all systems. Aquinas was probably the greatest intellectual genius of all time. This great Catholic theologian was conversant with Aristotle, Plato, Socrates, and all the philosophers who preceded him. He was so deep and broad that he touched upon almost every phase of thought that can occur to the human intellect. There is hardly a difficulty or doubt that can be proposed by modern sceptics that is not met with and solved in the works of Aquinas. It is safe to say that nowhere in the world will one find more logical people than among Catholic theologians and philosophers.

Ordinary persons would be amazed to know how keenly every subject of discussion is analyzed in our Catholic colleges, and particularly in our seminaries. If you think Catholics are credulous just try to dupe an ordinary Catholic priest. Among statesmen the Catholic clergy are noted for their common sense. No matter what wave of fanaticism or erroneous policy sweeps over the population it never carries with it the Catholic priests. Of course there may be an exception here or there, which only serves to prove the general statement.

It may be allowed that the clergy are not credulous, but how about the people?

First of all, a Catholic layman has right basic principles. Moreover, he has the best intellectual leadership in the world, and besides, Catholic philosophy is rigidly logical. The result of all, then, is that a Catholic has a mind trained to reason and to weigh evidence. It is true, of course, that in a body numbering several hundred millions, there are all classes of intellect and temperament. Any organization which numbers peasant as well as prince in its membership will reflect the attitude of mind of peasant as well as prince.

Religion does not necessarily change one's temperament nor give one brains. A man may be a saint and at the same time be very simple. Virtue does not necessarily imply culture, any more than vice necessarily implies vulgarity. Some of the most vicious people are externally cultured and respectable. On the other hand, some of the most virtuous have little or no refinement, according to society's standard. Vulgarity is not vice, nor are good manners virtue. Some of the most depraved and villainous men and women have the most exquisite manners, and conform most exactly to the external code of good-breeding.

The object of religion is not to make us society people, but children of God. Purity, honesty, reverence may exist along with crude manners and among the poor and ignorant. Wealth and culture usually go together. Some people judge religion by prosperity or respectability. The Apostles were neither wealthy nor cultured according to the world's standard of culture. Hence, a peasant as well as a prince may be of the true religion—credulity, poverty, and lack of culture notwithstanding. Moreover, it must be observed that the majority of mankind are influenced in their thinking and conduct by authority. How many citizens of the United States do their own thinking in matters of government?

It is safe to say not one in a hundred thousand. And there is a good reason for it; they have sense enough to know that others are better qualified to do it for them. Even among those who think they do their own thinking, there is but one in a thousand who really does so. Most people simply echo what they read or hear. An editorial or magazine article feeds the multitude with a set of ideas, which, after absorbing, many people consider their own.

Catholics if fed with any ideas have at least this comfort, that the ideas are correct. There is no body of people in the world so intelligently guided in matters of faith and morals as Catholics. No Catholic pronouncement is made without being submitted to the keenest scrutiny of philosophy, theology, and science. The result is that Catholics as a body are never misled. Take, for instance, Darwinism. Some forty years ago one was put down as unprogressive, ignorant, and opposed to science if one did not believe in Darwinism. To-day Darwinism is rejected by the greatest living scientists. So the poor, ignorant Catholics were, after all, in good company.

The Catholic Church realizes that the majority of mankind need leadership. She knows that the people at large must be guided and directed. And she gives her flock the wisest guidance that is to be found in this world. There is nowhere a body of intellectual men comparable to the various organizations of Cardinals, who at Rome, as the advisers of the Pope, examine every problem that concerns mankind with regard to faith and morals. It is safe to say that every Catholic seminary displays more real intellectual activity than can be found in any other institution of learning. Catholic men of intellect do not submit to the tenets and practises of faith without having a rational motive for their submission. A Catholic who lives up to his faith must make greater renunciations than are demanded by any other creed. The great body of intellectual Catholics the world over examine most critically the credentials of the faith. They use all the power of intellect to ascertain the credibility of the Church, but once they are convinced of her divine claims, they accept as from God her teaching. This is not credulity but faith.

Men put faith in chemists, in oculists, in statesmen if they are persuaded that they are trustworthy. Intelligent Catholics are convinced that the Church is a divine institution which cannot, consequently, mislead them. Hence they accept her doctrine without question. On matters not binding in conscience they may have their own views.

In Catholic colleges and seminaries and assemblages it is simply astonishing to witness the keen intellectual discussion that goes on. To say that a Catholic is limited intellectually by faith is the same as to say that a civil engineer is limited by mathematics. Truth is truth always, and to be limited by truth is merely to be safeguarded from error. History furnishes proof of this, for time and again Catholic truth has saved mankind from erroneous and extravagant courses.

Christ guaranteed His Church in matters of faith and morals. In other things she has no guidance or safeguard except human prudence and wise tradition. These may fail as at times they have failed, but that does not affect her position in her divinely guaranteed sphere.

But, it may be said, are not Catholics superstitious and credulous in some of their devotions? Do they not attach undue significance to minor practises of religion? Not any more than people of the same station do in other matters. Simple people readily attach undue significance to what is dear to their belief and practice. But why go to the simple and ignorant to estimate the Catholic Church? She herself is opposed to superstition. Often however, what is termed superstition by non-Catholics is something altogether different when understood aright.

Simple people have a way of speaking and acting which may give a wrong impression to those not acquainted with them. Often, too, these simple people, when questioned, cannot give an expression to their real sentiments and ideas. But, it may be objected, does not the Church encourage superstitious practices? By no means. The Church condemns superstition. Her devotions are of such a wide and varied nature that they appeal to all classes of people. What would help one class might be an obstacle to another. English piety is not French piety. Devotions which would appeal strongly to the Italian character might repel the American. What suits and helps the German might not make any appeal to the Spanish. It is so with various classes of the same nation. We see this illustrated in other fields of human experience. There are many people among us who would rather hear a brass band than a symphony orchestra. Governments recognized this human variance by their appeal to certain elements of the nation through parades and fireworks and other such things. Many imbibe patriotism from a parade who would not be affected by an eloquent address or a statesman's masterly proclamation.

Once we realize that human nature in all its phases has a place in the Catholic Church, we have gone a long way toward understanding that, together with the trust which characterizes her children, there is also among them the keenest intellectual inquiry. For a gentleman to judge the Catholic Church by the conduct or words of a servant girl is to be guilty of greater ignorance than that which he condemns in her. He would not judge of the merit of a symphony orchestra by his experience with the boy who carries the drum or passes out the music; yet too often men of supposed culture judge of the Catholic Church by their experience with a kitchen maid or a butler. What the Catholic Church teaches may be learned from any Catholic catechism or book of theology. The Church is not responsible for the errors of speech or conduct of her members. Christ guaranteed His Church against error. He did not guarantee her members against ignorance or sin. He made her to be like Himself, the Light of the world. The Light is one thing, to be guided by it another. Every member of the Church from the Pope down is peccable, that is, may sin. Infallibility is not impeccability. The Church is infallible because Christ, the Son of God, is her invisible Head, and is always with her and has given His guarantee that she will always teach truth, regardless of the virtue or vice of those who constitute her membership.

Catholics are not credulous for believing that Christ is true to His word. They are not credulous in trusting to His Church. Catholics may employ all their God-given intellect to ascertain if He speaks by His Church. If He does they are acting rationally and wisely in obeying her.

CHAPTER XI

WHAT USE IS FAITH?

WHEN the Christian missionaries first came to England they sought permission of the Saxon king, Ethelbert, to preach Christ to his people. While the king was hesitating what answer to give the missionaries a strange bird, having entered by an opening, flew across the council chamber and out into the open on the opposite side. As the king stood in deliberation a bard arose and said: "Sire, thou hast seen this bird of passage as it winged its way across the room. Whence it came we know not, nor do we know whither it has gone. We, like that bird of passage, are here for a brief space. Whence we came, or whither we go, we know not. If, therefore, these strangers can tell us, as they affirm, whence we have come and whither we are going, I say that we should welcome them and their message." On hearing this, Ethelbert permitted the missionaries from Rome to begin the preaching of the faith which eventually made Britain a Catholic land.

The importance of faith is that it gives us definite knowledge of our origin and our destiny, and of the way to our destiny. It tells us, moreover, much about God and heavenly things, of which we should otherwise be in ignorance. As we look up into the sky in daytime we see a canopy of blue. It is only with the coming of night that we may perceive the countless stars that fill the firmament. If it were perpetual day we should never know of the myriads of heavenly bodies which stud the sky, and which only the darkness of night reveals. Likewise faith reveals to us ever so many consoling and valuable truths which we should never be able certainly to know otherwise.

Faith is concerned with spiritual or heavenly things. It does not deal with agriculture or commerce or geography or with any earthly matters, except incidentally when it employs these things by way of parable or illustration in order to explain supernatural truths.

The late Cecil Chesterton said, in a public lecture, that concerning what was vital to man there was more knowledge in the first page of the penny catechism than in all the books of philosophy ever published. And he had read more widely than most men. As a young man he had renounced Protestantism, the religion in which he was brought up, because of its inconsistencies. As Protestantism was the only Christianity he was acquainted with he thought that in rejecting it he was rejecting Christianity. He became an agnostic, but a restless one, ever seeking a solution to the great problems which concern the origin, condition, and destiny of man. He ran the gamut of religious belief, taking up one system after another, only to reject each of them in turn. He finally came to the stage where he concluded that it was useless to try and get an answer to not a few paramount problems of life. He remained in this condition for some years, but never at rest. Meeting a Catholic priest while traveling in a railway coach, he casually touched upon one of the subjects which was uppermost in his mind, the existence of moral evil. The priest gave him the answer of faith. It was like a flash of light in a dark cave. It revealed what was hitherto a mystery. The priest told him that faith taught that God in creating man made him free. In order to be free man must have the power of choice between good and evil, otherwise he would be necessarily good. If there were no evil in the world there would be no choice between virtue and vice. God allows moral evil but does not approve of it. He permits the good and the bad to exist alongside each other, and to go on to the end, when He will reward the good and punish the wicked. This was the first time that Chesterton received a satisfactory solution of the problem of evil. It led him into further investigation of Catholic faith with the result that he became an ardent Catholic. It was after this and similar experiences that he declared that the penny catechism contained more philosophy than all the merely philosophic books of the world.

The existence of evil is, it is true, a mystery, even with the light of faith thrown on it. But it is a mystery of God's providence, not of the existence of evil as such. God could, if He wished, give us the full explanation of His dealings with mankind. But He has not seen fit to do so. Because He does not reveal everything about Himself is no reason why we should not be grateful for what He does reveal. He tells us, by faith, that He is the Creator of the world; that He made all things out of nothing; that He made man like unto Himself, immortal and free; that He gives man the period of this life in order to test his allegiance; that He does this by permitting good and evil, commanding him to do good and avoid evil; that man's destiny is to share the life of God Himself if he prove faithful to God; that He so loved the world that He gave His Only-Begotten Son as our Redeemer and example; that to as many as prove true to the precepts and example of His Son, Jesus Christ, He will give the power to become the children of God; that in order to help us if we fall through weakness, or even malice, He has instituted the sacraments to restore us to spiritual life and His friendship.

All these and other truths, not acquirable by human study, faith teaches us. Faith thus gives the solution to the problem of life. It tells us that we have not here a lasting city but that we seek one which is to come. It proclaims that this life is not solely enjoyment but probation, and that this world is not the goal but starting point of man. Not to mention other truths of faith, what we have enumerated show us the great value of faith. It explains life, which is otherwise a despairing problem. It gives a motive for patiently bearing the vicissitudes of life, which otherwise might crush us. It is a light guiding our steps unerringly to our home beyond, where our destiny is to become members of the divine family.

The most consoling and valuable thing about faith is its certainty. It is based on God's veracity. God can neither deceive nor be deceived. Heaven and earth may pass away, but His word will never fail. Consequently, people of faith never doubt about what faith teaches. They may not understand the mysteries of faith but they believe them on God's word. We do not understand how it is that the world rotates, and whirls through space with incalculable speed, but we believe it on the word of astronomers. Not one person in a million understands the processes of higher mathematics which convince astronomers of what they teach us. But though we do not understand these matters we have faith in men of science and on their word believe their teaching. We believe that the earth is round, yet most people do not understand how it is that those on the opposite side do not fall off, nor how it is that they stand toward us feet foremost. Scientists, of course, give the explanation, or what they call the explanation, namely gravity, but what gravity is neither they nor we understand. There are incomprehensible things in our own selves. We do not know how the bread we eat becomes our flesh and blood. All the chemists in the world cannot change bread into living flesh. But it is done by the marvelous chemistry of our own human laboratory, by a process all unknown to ourselves, and without our being aware of the transformation that is taking place.

If nature presents mysteries we should not be surprised that nature's God should also disclose mysteries. If we do not understand our own bodies, and what is going on in them, we should not be surprised that we do not understand Him who made us. Hence when God reveals to us something about Himself, the fact that we do not understand it should not concern us. If God only required of us to believe what we understood, He would be asking of us no more than what one man may expect of another. But He is God. He is the Author of truth. He is Truth itself. He is also our Creator, He gave us our love of truth, and our reason by which we discern the truth. He wants us, therefore, to show Him the respect and consideration and reverence and trust of believing Him, simply because He declares a thing to be so.

It may be asked why does God want our faith. He wants it because it is the highest homage we can pay Him. By faith we sacrifice on the altar of God's veracity our noblest faculty, our judgment. By sacrificing what is our most precious possession we show homage to God. Hence it is that God says, "I will espouse thee to Me in faith." Faith thus becomes the close bond of union and love between the Creator and the creature. It is the wonderful connection between God and man by which, as the Apostle Peter tells us, "we may become partakers of the divine nature." Of course the faith that thus lovingly unites us to divinity is not mere believing, but the living in accordance with the belief. Faith without works is dead. The truths of faith are so beautiful and consoling that every one would believe in them if it were not that belief implied conduct in accord with belief. People readily believe what Plato and Aristotle and other sages teach, because belief in these men entails no obligation to live as they prescribe. But if we believe in Christ, we acknowledge Him to be God, and that we must obey Him as God. That makes people apply a rule of belief with regard to Christ which they do not use with any other personage of history.

Everything about Christ and His claims is better attested than are the facts concerning any other historical person. But since faith in Christ means to acknowledge Him as Lord and Master, many reject the grounds of belief regarding Him which they accept for everything else. By faith the most comforting and sustaining truths are conveyed to man. What, for instance, could mean more to mortals than this truth, "To as many as receive Him He gives the power to become the sons of God." What a wonderful destiny that is! To reflect that in the warfare of life, and life is warfare, we may, by being true soldiers of Christ, win a divine inheritance, which will make us children of God! There are some people who enthuse over those truths of faith which tell of the goodness and love of God, but reject those which tell of His justice. They are willing to believe in a Christ who would let them live as they like, but not in Him who says, "If thou wilt enter into eternal life keep My commandments." In other words these people have a wrong idea of faith. They are willing to believe in themselves, not in God. They would believe in God if He would serve them, but they reject Him because they must serve Him if they believe in Him.

That is why Christ is judged by the world by a different standard from that applied to others. But to those who in sincerity seek the truth, Christ is indeed Truth itself. Hence when He says, "Amen, Amen, I say unto you, he that believeth in Me hath life everlasting," we of the faith know that by living as He directs we shall share in His blessed and eternal life.

It is a wonderful comfort for us to know from the very mouth of God that this life is not all of our existence, but only the first stage of it. Without revelation man might have attained a knowledge of immortality, but the fact is that it was a hazy and unsatisfactory notion of future life which prevailed outside the sphere of revelation. By faith we know that our destiny is to share in the glorious life of God. "That we may become partakers of the divine nature." By faith we also know that God is not merely a distant Creator, the First Cause of all that exists, omnipotent and omniscient, but that He is our Father, that He loves us, and that He manifested His love for us by giving His Only-Begotten Son, for our eternal welfare.

The Only-Begotten Son manifested His love for us by giving His life for us after enduring privation and suffering for us from the manger to the cross. Beholding how Christ suffered for us we are prepared, if need be, to suffer for Him. Hence, when for the sake of keeping His law we must put up with inconvenience, hardship, or downright suffering, we are strengthened by His example, and for love of Him to do manfully, and to bear with patience if not joy whatever the following of Christ entails. That is the life of faith. It is not academic belief in an abstract truth, nor an acceptance of some fact of history which does not personally affect us, but the firm conviction that what Christ, or His accredited Church, teaches, is a living truth which has a bearing on the conduct of life. It is thus that faith not only tells us that in God there are three Persons, but that the Second Person became man for our salvation. It shows us the infinite love of God the Father who gave His Son for us, and also the immeasurable love of God the Son, who died for us, and that of the Holy Ghost who sanctifies us by grace and enables us to attain a share in the blessed life of the Trinity. Faith manifests Christ to us as the Way, the Truth, and the Life. He is the way to eternal life, by His precepts and example; He declares the truth about ourselves and our destiny; and He is the life, the very life of God, which He desires us to share in. It will thus be seen that faith gives us that incentive to virtue which is so necessary in a sinful world, and that certainty about life which is so comforting in a doubting world. Catholics never doubt about the truths of revelation. They are as certain with regard to them as they are of their own existence. Difficulties they may have. But as Cardinal Newman has said, ten thousand difficulties do not make a doubt. We have difficulties about the nature of electricity and radio and other natural phenomena, but we have no doubts as to the reality of those things.

If there were no difficulties about faith, if everything that faith reveals were clear and agreeable to us what merit would there be in believing? If a soldier has faith in a general only when the general demonstrates the wisdom of his orders it is hardly faith at all. Soldiers show faith in a commanding officer when they follow him because of the confidence they have in him that he is worthy of their trust no matter how incomprehensible to them his orders may be.

God is the Commander-in-Chief of mankind. He can neither deceive nor be deceived. He wants us to trust Him and to obey Him because He is God. He does not explain Himself or His ways to us, because to do so would be to act not as Creator but as creature. Faith in Him, therefore, means the firm conviction that in being guided by Him we are being directed aright. It is not opinion, no matter how strong, or persuasion, or the highest probability that constitutes faith, but a conviction which is stronger than anything that reason can give, which constitutes faith. Hence it was that the martyrs laid down their lives in torments rather than prove false to the faith. It was the same firm conviction that inspired myriads of Christians in every generation to forego the most imperative cravings of nature, and to consecrate their lives to heroic service for God in the cloister or on missionary fields.

It is the same faith to-day which is the incentive for so many to live honestly and purely in a dishonest and impure world. If faith were not necessary, God would not have enjoined it. But the Apostle tells us that "without faith it is impossible to please God." Living faith of course is meant, according to the same Apostle,

"In Christ Jesus neither circumcision availeth anything nor uncircumcision: but faith that worketh by charity."

There are some persons who are known to profess the faith, but whose lives are a contradiction to all that faith teaches. These do real harm to religion. Their account is with God, who will hold them directly responsible for the great harm they do. Quite often this class of people make use of their faith as a means to attain some worldly object. In proportion as they proclaim their faith they live unworthy of it. The worst enemy of the true faith is that person who is known to profess it, but whose conduct belies it. Many a seeker after truth has been repelled from investigating the true faith because some of its adherents have given him a false notion of it by their lives.

Christ has said, "Not they who say Lord, Lord, shall enter the kingdom of heaven, but they who do the will of My Father." Faith, unless lived up to, will not avail unto salvation. Faith is all important, but an active faith which manifests itself in right living. For, after all, faith is not the end but only the means. St. Augustine said, "God who made us without our co-operation will not save us without our co-operation." We must do our part. If we do, we shall receive the reward of faith, which is so inexpressibly great that "eye hath not seen nor ear heard, nor hath it entered into the mind of man to conceive what God hath prepared for them that love Him." It is no less than companionship with God Himself, a share in His immortal blessedness. "But they that shall be accounted worthy shall die no more, for they shall be as the angels and are the children of God."

Sometimes one hears a person say that it is undesirable to have the faith because it imposes so many obligations. As well say that it is undesirable to have the expert prescription of a medical specialist in a serious malady because it imposes certain restrictions and remedies.

Christ is the Physician of the soul. By faith He has prescribed for eternal welfare. Blessed are they who trust Him and live by Him, for He conducts all who follow Him to the blessed end of life and joy everlasting.

CHAPTER XII

THE VIRGIN BIRTH

CHRISTIAN denominations, outside the Catholic Church, are now being rocked to their foundations by controversy over the Virgin Birth. The issue of the controversy will doubtless drive many into abandonment of religion altogether, while it will lead others into the Catholic Church. Some of the Protestant denominations are split in two on the subject. Ministers are opposed to ministers, and bishops find themselves at odds with their ministers. Recently, in New York, the controversy assumed such alarming proportions that some of the wise and influential heads got together and called a halt, fearing that the discussion, if continued, would discredit religion altogether.

Ministers whose sacred duty it was to preach the Gospel were using their pulpits to assail the Gospel. They were doing their best to strip revealed religion of revelation. The result was that gradually their churches were being emptied, except where a sensational preacher held forth. The truce which they entered upon was but a pouring of oil on the troubled waters. The storm is gathering again stronger than ever and will sweep all before it. Protestantism is reaching its logical conclusion. It began by private judgment, and that same private judgment is now rejecting the supernatural altogether. If the Christian religion is not supernatural it is a deception. It must stand as a religion revealed by God, established by God, and corroborated by divine deeds, or it has no legitimate claim on mankind. Christianity is entirely true or else it is false. A chain is no stronger than its weakest link. A religion from God cannot be partly true and partly false. If any one doctrine of Christianity is false the whole system collapses as a divine religion. And if it be not divine the sooner it is done away with the better, for it claims to be divine, and it is a fraud if its claims are false. No fraud should be tolerated.

But what has all this to do with the Virgin Birth? Everything. The Virgin Birth is rejected by a section of Protestants on the ground that it is supernatural. They maintain that the supernatural or miraculous cannot be admitted. They claim that the miraculous conflicts with science, and hence must be rejected. But, if the miraculous cannot be admitted, the logical thing to do is to reject Christianity altogether, for if Christianity is not miraculous it is nothing. If the opponents of the Virgin Birth were logical and consistent they would renounce Christianity. But this they will not do. They want to hold on to what appeals to them in Christianity and reject the rest. But Christianity is either divine or it is not. If it is divine it is supernatural, miraculous. If it is not divine it has no binding force on mankind, and has no reason for existence as a religion. Unless it can speak authoritatively to man it is only a school of ethics which we are free to accept or decline, and not a religion at all. For by religion we mean a bond between the creature and the Creator. A school of ethics or a system of philosophy is only a bond between man and man, an optional fellowship or association without any sanction.

Religion, to be effective, must be the authoritative voice of God. Systems of philosophy and ethics are very well in their way, but they will never reach the great body of mankind nor influence their conduct when human passion and selfishness are in the ascendant. Men do not give their lives for a system of ethics or philosophy. The martyrs were fools to die for the faith if it was not a divine religion. Until the Reformation, so-called, in the sixteenth century, all Christendom believed that the Christian religion was supernatural in its founder and its foundation. All that is worth while in the world to-day is the result of Christianity. A false creed could never endure so long in all parts of the world and produce such marvelous benefits for mankind.

So, to reject the Virgin Birth because it is supernatural, is to reject Christianity on the same ground. And it is coming to that. Modern Protestantism is fast drifting into a Christianized paganism. The Virgin Birth is only a test case. The opponents of the miraculous might just as well have fixed on any other Gospel event. In fact they have assailed another event with almost the same virulence with which they have attacked the Virgin Birth. The resurrection of Our Lord is flatly denied by this neo-Protestantism. But while denying the Virgin Birth and the resurrection they do not at the same time refrain from the celebrations of Christmas and Easter, the two great festivities of Christendom, one commemorating the birth of Christ from the Virgin Mary, and the other His resurrection from the dead. If Christ's Virgin Birth is a myth and His resurrection a legend, Christian scholars and people from the beginning have been deceived. For both Christmas and Easter have been more real as supernatural commemorations than the Fourth of July has been to Americans as a national celebration. Having premised this much let us now look into the matter of the Virgin Birth and see what the controversy is about.

First of all what does the Virgin Birth mean? Some think it refers to the Immaculate Conception. It has nothing to do with that dogma. Neither does it refer to the birth of the Blessed Virgin. It refers to the birth of Christ, and means that He was born of a virgin mother, that is, that Mary was a virgin before, during, and after the birth of her son Jesus. This signifies that Jesus had no human father, but that it was by the power of Almighty God that He was conceived in the womb of His Virgin Mother. Instead of being born as the rest of us were from a human father and mother, Jesus was conceived in the womb of the Virgin Mary by the overshadowing power of the Holy Ghost. God, by the same power by which in the beginning He created all things out of nothing, effected the birth of Jesus without a human father. If there is anything clear and certain in the Gospel it is the Virgin Birth. Reject it and you may as well treat Scripture as a fable. In the plainest words possible to human language the Virgin Birth is explicitly and repeatedly affirmed. So evident is it that to deny the Virgin Birth is to deny the truth of the most genuine and authentic document of history. Let me ask the reader to peruse carefully the narration of Christ's birth as given herewith from St. Luke, Chap. i, 26-38.

And in the sixth month, the angel Gabriel was sent from God into a city of Galilee, called Nazareth,

To a virgin espoused to a man whose name was Joseph, of the house of David; and the virgin's name was Mary.

And the angel being come in, said unto her: Hail, full of grace, the Lord is with thee: Blessed art thou among women.

Who having heard, was troubled at his saying, and thought with herself what manner of salutation this should be.

And the angel said to her: Fear not, Mary, for thou hast found grace with God.

Behold thou shalt conceive in thy womb, and shalt bring forth a Son; and thou shalt call His Name Jesus.

He shall be great, and shall be called the Son of the Most High: and the Lord God shall give unto Him the throne of David His father; and He shall reign in the house of Jacob forever.

And of His kingdom there shall be no end.

And Mary said to the angel: How shall this be done, because I know not man?

And the angel answering, said to her: The Holy Ghost shall come upon thee, and the power of the Most High shall overshadow thee. And therefore, also, the Holy which shall be born of thee shall be called the Son of God.

And behold thy cousin Elizabeth, she also hath conceived a son in her old age; and this is the sixth month with her that is called barren:

Because no word shall be impossible with God.

And Mary said: Behold the handmaid of the Lord; be it done to me according to thy word. And the angel departed from her.

If this narrative is not the account of a supernatural and miraculous event, it is the greatest fabrication in the annals of mankind. It was accepted as Gospel truth at the very time it was written. Men who lived at the time and afterwards, sacrificed their possessions, their liberty, and their lives for belief in it. It was intimately associated with faith in Christ as the Son of God. If it can be rejected the whole Gospel can be rejected and with it revealed religion altogether.

The verdict of the best scientific criticism in the world to-day is that the Gospels are the most genuine and authentic documents of history. In order to reject the miraculous, the opponents of the Virgin Birth are obliged either to reject the Gospels or to distort the plainest language that has ever characterized a historical record. In view of the verdict of the highest critics the Gospels cannot be rejected, hence recourse is had to distorting the words of the sacred text into a meaning which they cannot possibly bear. For instance, they assert that Joseph was the father of Jesus. But the sacred text explicitly states that he was not. When the angel told Mary that she was to be the mother of Jesus, she objected, "How shall this be done, because I know not man?" This expression was the Hebrew equivalent that she was a virgin. The angel removed her fears concerning her virginity by saying: "The Holy Ghost shall come upon thee and the power of the Most High shall overshadow thee. And therefore the Holy which shall be born of thee shall be called the Son of God."

Furthermore, St. Matthew narrates, "When as His mother Mary was espoused to Joseph, before they came together she was found with child, of the Holy Ghost. Whereupon Joseph, her husband, being a just man, and not being willing publicly to expose her, was minded to put her away privately." If Joseph were the father of the child he would not have been minded to put her away because of the child. Joseph was espoused to Mary for her protection and honor. If Jesus had been born outside wedlock, Mary would have been stoned to death as an adulteress, and Jesus would have been regarded as infamous. In God's plan Jesus was not to manifest His divine nature nor His mission until later. Meanwhile, before the world Joseph was His father. We find this confirmed by the incident in the Temple when Jesus was twelve years old. Mary said, on finding Him after three days' search, "Son, why hast Thou done so to us? Behold, Thy father and I have sought Thee sorrowing! And He said to them: Did you not know that I must be about My Father's business?" Here Joseph is referred to as father notwithstanding the fact that Jesus states that He was doing His Father's business. Furthermore, Isaias, in prophesying the birth of the Messias, says, "Behold a virgin shall conceive, and bear a son, and

His name shall be called Emmanuel." This prophecy was given by Isaias as a sign from heaven. If Jesus were born as the rest of us, His birth would not have been a divine sign. St. Matthew refers to this sign when describing Joseph's perturbation. "But while he (Joseph) thought on these things, behold the angel of the Lord appeared to him in his sleep, saying: Joseph, son of David, fear not to take Mary unto thee for wife, for that which is conceived in her is of the Holy Ghost. And she shall bring forth a Son, and thou shalt call His Name Jesus, for He shall save His people from their sins. Now all this was done that it might be fulfilled which the Lord spoke by the prophet, saying: Behold a virgin shall be with child and bring forth a son, and they shall call His Name Emmanuel, which being interpreted is, God with us."

In face of this distinct declaration, to maintain that Joseph was the father of Jesus is to deny language its meaning. St. Matthew certainly knew the meaning of the Scriptures as well, at least, as Modernists. He knew the meaning of virgin when he stated that Jesus was born of Mary, not by co-operation of man but by the power of the Holy Ghost. It would be stupid of him to apply the virgin prophecy of Isaias to Mary if she were not a virgin mother. To escape from this conclusive argument, Modernist critics affirm that the word virgin in Isaias does not necessarily mean virgin. St. Matthew should know, for he was a Hebrew, and he had, moreover, the tradition of his race. Besides, if the word does not mean virgin in the true sense, the prophecy would have no significance as a sign from heaven. Furthermore, the most learned Hebrew scholars assert that in the passage in question the word virgin means precisely what St. Matthew states.

In addition to this we have the confirmation of Mary's virginity and the true nature of Joseph's position toward her in the words of St. Luke: "Now it came to pass, when all the people were baptized, that Jesus also being baptized and praying, heaven was opened; and the Holy Ghost descended in a bodily shape, as a dove upon Him; and a voice came from heaven: Thou art My beloved Son; in Thee I am well pleased. And Jesus Himself was beginning about the age of thirty years; being (as it was supposed) the son of Joseph" (Luke iii. 21-23).

Unless we are prepared to discard the Gospels altogether, we must, in view of this plain statement, accept the Virgin Birth of Jesus. To reject this fact because it is a miracle means the rejection of Christianity altogether. Strip the Gospels of the miraculous and you have nothing left. Rather, you have a bigger problem on your hands than the miraculous. For in order to explain the establishment of the religion of Jesus Christ without miracles is a greater miracle than any recorded in the Gospels.

St. Augustine exclaims with regard to the resurrection, "The establishment of Christianity without the resurrection is a greater miracle than the resurrection." We may say, therefore, that it is impossible to deny the supernatural and to accept Christ's religion. Christ Himself was the greatest miracle. He was unique among mankind. It is impossible to understand Him if we reject the supernatural. His teaching never could have originated in a human mind. His character transcended all human standards. He proclaimed Himself the Light of the world, the Way, the Truth, and the Life, the Judge of the living and the dead, and He forgave sin, which God alone can do. It was fitting that being God He should come among us in the way He did. To deny the Virgin Birth is simply to cast Christianity overboard—and that is what the so-called Modernists are doing. Meanwhile the Catholic Church goes on undisturbed. This is but one of the many storms which have assailed her during the past twenty centuries. Christ Himself is with her and will be with her to the end of the world. Hence she fears not, no matter how violent the assaults on her may be. She has encountered worse storms and seen them break against the rock on which she is built. "Thou art Peter (a rock) and upon this rock I will build My Church and the gates of hell shall not prevail against it." That is God's guarantee, and our firm assurance.

CHAPTER XIII

THE POPE

WE often hear it said by non-Catholics that there is too much pomp and circumstance about the Pope. Christ, they say, was simple and poor—why should His representative be clothed with majesty and surrounded by royal splendor? Again, it is asked, why should the Supreme Head of a spiritual kingdom be burdened or decorated with the glory and dignity of temporal power? In the course of this chapter both these questions will be considered, and some others also, which frequently are asked or broached by non-Catholics. The best way to reply to queries concerning the Pope is to give a clear idea of who and what the Pope is. Once we know the duties and station of the Vicar of Christ most questions concerning him will answer themselves.

The word Pope comes from the Latin *Papa*, which was derived from the Greek *Papas*, meaning father. Greek was the most universal language at the time of the establishment of Christianity, which accounts for the fact that the New Testament was written in Greek, not in Hebrew. In the beginning the word Pope was applied to priests, bishops, and patriarchs, who were considered to be spiritual fathers of those in their charge. Gradually the term became restricted to the Chief Pastor of all the faithful, the Roman Pontiff. Whenever the Pope is referred to now it is always understood to mean the Holy Father of all Christendom. Christ Himself constituted the Pope, in the person of Peter, Head of His Church. "And I say to thee: That thou art Peter (a rock); and upon this rock I will build My Church, and the gates of hell shall not prevail against it. And I will give to thee the keys of the kingdom of heaven. And whatsoever thou shalt bind on earth, it shall be bound also in heaven; and whatsoever thou shalt loose on earth, it shall be loosed also in heaven" (Matt. xvi. 18, 19).

By these words Christ made Peter the foundation on which His Church was to rest. In all nations the key is the symbol of authority. By giving the power of the keys of His kingdom to Peter, Christ clothed him with authority to rule over His Church. Furthermore, Christ promised to be with Peter as Head of the Church to the end of the world. Hence He was speaking to the Apostle in his official capacity as Supreme Head. The office was to last to the end of time. Peter and the other Apostles lived only a few years, more or less. But the Church and its official Head were to go on until the consummation of the. world. The Church without a Head would be like a headless body, and not the living organization instituted by Christ for perpetual life. Hence the successor of Peter, the Head of the Church, is called the Vicar of Christ. Vicar means one who acts in the person of another. After the Ascension Peter represented Christ as Head of the Church, and after Peter's martyrdom and triumphant entrance into heaven, his successor became the visible Head of the Church, the representative on earth of Christ, the invisible Head. Christ's words to Peter, therefore, constituted a permanent office in His perpetual Church. That office was to be filled by whoever succeeded Peter as Bishop of Rome, which was the official bishopric of Peter up to the time that he sealed his service to his Master by dying on a cross for Him. As proof that Peter's office passed to his successor, and not to other Apostles, after his death, we have the facts of history. In the year 96, St. Clement, who was the third successor of Peter as Bishop of Rome, exercised authority over the Church of Corinth during the lifetime of St. John, one of the Apostles. And in exercising this authority he proclaims that his words were spoken by God through him. Only a few years later (about 107) St. Ignatius of Antioch in his letters to the Roman Church, refers to it as presiding over all other churches. From the very beginning all disputed matters of importance were referred to the Roman Pontiff for final adjudication. Unless this primacy of authority were conferred on the Pope by Christ Himself we may be sure that the bishops and other prelates of early Christianity never would have submitted themselves to it, for they were tenacious of their prerogatives. If the primacy was not instituted by God, no man could have asserted and exercised it, because it made every prelate, even the highest, dependent on it. The primacy of the Pope is really one of the strongest proofs of the divinity of the Church.

The supreme headship of the Church of Christ is attached to the bishopric of Rome. The Pope becomes supreme pastor because he is the Bishop of Rome. The Cardinals, who are the chief of the Roman clergy, constitute the electorate. The Pope is elected for life; he cannot appoint his successor. Christ compared His Church in its beginning to a mustard seed, which, although so small, develops into a herb so large that the birds of the air may repose on its branches, and its foliage gives shade and comfort to the wayfarer. The mustard seed was the crucified Christ and the insignificant band of Apostles. From this tiny origin developed that Church which is now spread over the entire world. Catholic means universal, and our Church is Catholic because it is everywhere in the world. It is the only corporate organization that is universal. By this is meant that the Catholic Church is the only organization in the world which, like the human body, is a unified society, having all its members joined together in one faith and under one Supreme Head, and at the same time existing throughout the entire world. Other societies or organizations or religions are local or national or regional in one way or another. The Catholic Church, on the contrary, is one compact organization, spread over the whole world, with hundreds of millions of members, hundreds of thousands of clergy: priests, bishops, archbishops and cardinals, yet all absolutely and vitally united under one Head, the Pope, who is the Bishop of Rome, Peter's successor. The word corporate comes from the Latin word which means body. It is because this union of Head and members is so real that the Church is called a corporate society, her unity resembling that of a living body.

In consequence of the world-wide existence of the Church and of her marvelous unity there is need of vast and intricate organization. Christ's Church in His own day consisted of Himself and His few disciples. Simplicity was, accordingly, not only possible but necessary. To-day His Church is the largest corporate society in the world. The United States Government at Washington is now vastly different from what it was when our first President was in office. No one would expect the great machinery of our government to be as simple now as it was in the early days of the Republic. The Catholic Church is more extensive and has more subjects than the United States Government. In the Church we have first of all the parish, comprising the faithful people and their pastor. The pastor receives his commission from his bishop, just as a captain does from army headquarters. The bishop, in turn, receives his commission from the Pope, just as a general receives his from the Commander-in-Chief. A priest is ordained by the bishop, the bishop is consecrated by the designation of the Supreme Pontiff. By means of bishop and priest, therefore, the Pope is in close association with the hundreds of millions who constitute the flock of which he is Chief Shepherd. In order to carry on the spiritual work of Christ's kingdom on earth there is need, therefore, of a vast and intricate machinery of administration. This administration of the Church is centered in what is called the Vatican, the Pope's governmental headquarters. Here is transacted a variety and bulk of business that is staggering in its proportions. Every quarter of the globe is in close communication with this central bureau of affairs. The work is so vast and so delicate that it is assigned to various commissions presided over by high dignitaries of the Church, usually Cardinals. The Cardinals may be called the Pope's cabinet. Every important question that arises is submitted to them for deliberation and advice. As the Catholic Church is active in every nation of the world, and as various questions arise between Church and State and between bishop and priest, and even between priest and people, and sometimes among the faithful themselves, it is evident that the Vatican is one of the vastest administrations in the world. With vast and intricate administration there is associated necessarily a great deal of formality. This results in what some are pleased to call the pomp of the papal court. As well expect the Church to go back to the Catacombs as to return to the primitive simplicity of apostolic times.

Why, it may be asked of non-Catholics, should they build cathedrals like that of St. John the Divine since the Apostles had only the Catacombs as a place of worship? The Catholic answer is that nothing is too good for the Lord. In the early ages, when Christians were obliged to worship as best they could, they realized that any place of worship was better than none at all. Hence a private house or an underground passage of the Catacombs frequently served as a Christian temple. But when persecution ceased and the Church could worship God openly, she felt that God should have a dwelling in some way worthy of Him. At least she considered that God's dwelling should not be inferior to man's. And so under the Christian emperors there arose those wonderful basilicas which were the admiration of Christendom. Besides having regard for God's dwelling, it was felt that there should be regard for God's Vicar. Hence, when the Roman empire became Christian, the Pope, the Head of Christendom, was regarded with the respect and reverence which became the Representative of Christ. Christian emperors and Christian people desired to have their Supreme Pastor in a position of dignity and honor. It was the office that was honored, not the individual. Christ's Vicar was, by his official position, the most sacred and exalted personage in the world. Christ, though born in a stable, did not live there all His life. His Vicar, in the lifetime of St. Peter, dwelt, as it were, in a stable. Christ is content with a hut as a dwelling for His Eucharistic presence, if a hut is the best that man can give Him. But when His followers are in a position to build Him a temple more worthy of Him, He certainly is not pleased to see them more solicitous for a dwelling for man than for Himself. Christians, knowing this, have always striven that their best in architecture and art should be dedicated to the Lord. Hence we behold the wonderful cathedrals of Christendom, the expression of Catholic faith and devotion to their sacramental Lord.

So likewise in honoring Christ's Vicar Christians felt they were honoring Christ Himself. As soon, therefore, as the Church rose from the Catacombs the faithful began to surround the person of the Pope with tokens of respect, reverence, and loyalty. Gradually the Pope became the most revered personage in Christendom, as was right, seeing that he was Christ's Vicegerent. Emperors, in order to honor him and to facilitate his work, conferred on him donations of temporal domains. This necessitated civil administration, which, by degrees, eventuated in what is termed the temporal power of the Pope. We see something similar to this in the Trinity corporation of the Episcopal Church of New York City. Non-Catholics who question the temporal power of the Pope make no question of the temporal power of the rector of Trinity church of New York, and hundreds of similar instances. Non-Catholics who speak of the simplicity of Christ in contrast with the pomp of the Pope, might well turn their attention to the pomp and possessions of the Episcopalian hierarchy in England and elsewhere, and of the gorgeous temples erected to divine worship. If non-Catholic Churches have no Vatican it is because they have no corporate unity. If the non-Catholic Churches were a unified organization like the Catholic Church there would soon be evident the need of an institution similar to that of the Vatican. But as they have no corporate unity in the true sense, they have no need of head-quarters and all the administrative offices and formality such an establishment implies.

It may be said that the need of a central bureau for the administration of spiritual matters is understandable, but that Rome is immersed in material affairs. The best reply to this is that if an ordinary rector of a non-Catholic Church finds himself taken up considerably with the material affairs of his parish, what must be the needs of a world-wide Church administration?

The Church of Christ is spiritual in the sense that it serves the spirit of man and employs spiritual means of grace, but the agencies are material. Men, not angels, are the ministers of God's sacraments. A Church which has to deal with literally hundreds of thousands of clergymen the world over must necessarily have a stupendous administration of a material nature. All this seems clear and reasonable, it may be said, but why does the Pope assume royal state and pomp? The Pope, as the head of the largest corporate society in the world, is a most important personage. An Episcopalian bishop, who is head of a single diocese only, and whose office is spiritual not temporal, is clothed, nevertheless, with considerable dignity. It is most reasonable that the Pope, who is Bishop of bishops, should also be clothed with corresponding dignity. We must remember that for many centuries the Pope was the Father of Christendom, and as such the most consequential personage in the world. Besides being the Head of the Universal Church he was also a temporal ruler. The Pope became ruler mainly because when the Roman emperors neglected Italy, the people turned to him for guidance and protection. Later on, the emperor presented to the Pope certain dominions which became known as the Papal States. This donation was given to the Pope in order that he might have revenues for his vast and beneficent undertakings throughout Christendom. The Pope having been presented with the Papal States it was only right that he should govern them and have the dignity attached to a temporal sovereign. In every part of the world the clergy of various denominations are clothed with dignity befitting their spiritual and temporal station. The bishops of the English Church are also lords of the realm and maintain a dignity becoming their state. The Pope as temporal sovereign was not only a Lord of the realm but also the reigning monarch. He would be lacking in self-respect and in the respect due his position and people if he did not conduct himself as a sovereign. With very few exceptions, the Popes, with all their high titles and dignities, have been men of very simple lives. No body of men in the history of the world can begin to compare with them for simplicity of life, holiness and justice.

There remains a final matter of importance for our consideration, namely the present position of the Pope with relation to the Italian Government and to what is termed the temporal power. The Pope, as the Head of the Universal Church, should be in a position to act impartially toward the people of every nation of the world. As father and teacher and guide of all Christians he should not be subject to the interference or domination of any one nation. If he be subject to any particular power, that power may pass laws interfering with his freedom of action, or may endeavor to use his influence to its own advantage and the consequent disadvantage of other nations. This is no mere fancy. France, during the time when the Papacy was at Avignon, is an historical instance. The Church was so much hampered by the French Government during that period that the sojourn of the Popes at Avignon is called the Babylonian captivity. It resulted in such a state of affairs that the other nations of Christendom demanded the return of the Papacy to Rome to escape the predominant influence of France at the papal court. In our own day the Italian Government has forbidden a representative of the Pope to represent him at the Hague Conference. Besides, at any moment, the present Italian Government may enact laws which would seriously interfere with the office and duties of the Sovereign Pontiff. In fact it used its power recently to keep the Pope or his ambassador from the World War peace conference. There is no question that had the Pope's influence been exerted at that conference it would not have resulted in the sad condition of affairs we now behold.

The Vicar of the Prince of peace was banned from participation in the treaty of peace which concerned the welfare of the whole world. By temporal power it is not meant that the Pope should be monarch of a great state, but that he should, at least, be independent of any temporal ruler. For centuries the Popes held and exercised temporal sovereignty by a clearer title than any sovereign of Europe. That was due to the exigencies of times and conditions now past. But although that particular temporal power may never be restored, a temporal power greater or less is nevertheless necessary for the best administrations of the Papacy. That temporal sovereignty, even if it embraced only a few square miles, would make the Holy Father equally accessible to the people of all nations and enable him to act impartially or without suspicion of partiality to those of every nation of the world. As it is now, whatever liberty of action he enjoys is by tolerance only. We of the United States can readily understand the need of the Pope's being independent of any power, for we have before our very eyes an example of a similar case. The framers of the Constitution, in order to have our federal government free from the influence of any particular State, created the District of Columbia. This small territory is not part of any State of the Union. Its citizens do not vote on national or State issues. Congress is the sole ruler of this territory, and in consequence our federal government has that liberty and independence requisite for just legislation and executive action.

The Pope, who rules over hundreds of millions of people, not of one nation but of all nations, should have independent sovereignty if he is to exercise his authority in the most beneficial manner. It is thus seen that the temporal power, rightly understood, is in every way just and desirable.

A word with regard to the present Italian Government and the Papacy. Every reader of history knows that the Papal States were for centuries the dominions of the Papacy. Every reader of history also knows that the papal rule was the mildest and most just in the world. Every reader of history knows, too, that it was because the Papal States were so peacefully governed that they became the victim of conspirators, who by trickery, intimidation, and force wrested the dominions from their rightful sovereign. Every reader of history knows that the title to the papal states was a just title—as just as any on earth. Having unjustly taken away the defenceless states of the Church, the newly created Italian Government tried to appease the outraged sovereignty of the Pope by bribery. They offered him money and many immunities, all of which he declined and continues to decline. It was like a man depriving you of your house, and then, to settle matters, offering you the use of a room in the house. The Pope did all in his power to defend his dominions, but as he had only a handful of soldiers, principally for maintenance of order, he was forced to witness agitators and revolutionists stirring up strife and discontent until they eventually succeeded in overturning and dominating a loyal state. The Pope protested against this national crime, in the only way that an unarmed victim can protest against an armed aggressor, by appeal to public conscience. But as the nations of Europe from whom he expected aid were at the same period engaged in similar schemes of aggrandizement, his appeal and protest were of no avail. The Pope then did the only thing left him to do. Before the world he proclaimed that he was the rightful sovereign of the Papal States and that in principle, if not in fact, he would act accordingly. Hence he regards himself as a sovereign ruler, independent in his own right and title, as every sovereign ruler and sovereign state is. In Rome he does not acknowledge, in principle, another sovereign. If a diplomat or embassy or royal personage wishes to pay him an official visit it must be done as to a sovereign. This is why that even royalty must pay its respects to him in his own dominions by calling on him direct from the embassy of that nation, and not from the palace of the King of Italy. It is not done out of pride or pomp, but out of fidelity to the office entrusted to him.

It may be said that this silent protest has had no appreciable effect, and that in consequence it should end. That would perhaps be an argument for one whose policy is expediency, but not for him whose policy is principle. Christ Himself protested His innocence, although it apparently availed not. But it did avail and availed mightily as the ages rolled on. So the Pope's protest, although seemingly vain, is not without its effect on a world, which, no matter how much ruled by force, cannot be dead to principle. Whatever may come of the Pope's protest, this at least is certain that the Papacy stands for justice among nations as well as among individuals. To-day the Papacy is the most benign and most respected authority in the world. Considered merely as a personage, leaving out the matter of religion altogether, there is no more highly esteemed ruler in the world than the present Sovereign Pontiff. The Catholic Church may well be proud of her Head, and Catholics the world over may be grateful that their Holy Father is such an exalted personage in Christendom.

CHAPTER XIV

PAPAL INFALLIBILITY

PAPAL infallibility is one of the doctrines of the Catholic Church, which, if not rightly understood, repels people, but which, rightly understood, attracts them to the faith.

Almost every day this subject comes up among those who discuss religion. A short time ago a priest was invited by a body of professors of one of our great non-Catholic universities to discuss with them the doctrine of papal infallibility. They were intensely interested in this subject, and realized that it was a matter of great importance to religion. Hence I shall endeavor in simple style to present to my readers just what the doctrine of papal infallibility is. A right view of this doctrine will enable us to understand better the nature of our religion and to impart to others correct notions on the subject.

Infallibility means immunity from liability to error. We say, for instance, that the needle of the mariner's compass points infallibly to the north. No matter what its position nor how much it may be upset, it invariably returns to its position pointing northward. Its value consists in its practical infallibility. This quality which it possesses is due to certain laws of nature. By virtue of the true direction of the needle, the mariner can always guide his ship aright, no matter how storm-driven his vessel may be. The compass in so directing the mariner does not hamper his progress but instead helps it. It does not interfere with the mariner's safe liberty, but only protects him from the danger of losing his course.

So with the papal infallibility. It does not put a check on right reason, but saves fallible reason from going astray. If one is on a wrong path it matters not how fast or far one goes, one makes no progress. Papal infallibility serves to keep reason in the right path in matters of religion. Of course all this implies that there is such a thing as papal infallibility. Every one realizes that if there is on earth a certain norm of truth it must be a boon to man since it would keep him from the pitfalls of erroneous reasoning. Having said this much by way of introduction, let us take up the subject of papal infallibility and inquire into its nature and claims.

Infallibility means immunity from liability to error. In reference to the Pope it signifies that he is by special, divine assistance, preserved from liability to error in definitive dogmatic teaching regarding matters of faith and morals. Infallibility is sometimes confused with impeccability. Impeccability means immunity from sin. A man may be a sinner and yet have correct ideas. The infallibility of the Pope does not mean that he is impeccable. It does not mean that he may not sin. But it does mean that as the official Head on earth of the Church of Christ he may not officially teach false doctrine; and this not because he is wiser or more learned than other men, but because Jesus Christ, the Son of God, has pledged His divine word that His Vicar on earth will always be safeguarded against erroneous teaching in his office of visible Head of the Church.

There are many non-Catholics who are ready to concede infallibility to the Church of Christ. But they maintain that it resides in the Church at large, that is, in the assembled episcopate. They grant that a universal Church council may be infallible in its teaching, but deny that the Pope himself is infallible. We shall first show that infallibility resides in the Church at large, and afterwards that it is a prerogative of the Pope himself, a personal endowment which attaches to his official position as the Head of the Church.

Before we proceed it is well to recall who Christ was and what was the nature of His mission.

Christ was God. In saying this we mean that He was divine in the true sense, namely that He was Jehovah. Unless He was truly God His religion has no binding force on mankind. His mission was to redeem mankind and to be the Light of the world. His mission extended not merely to the people of His own day but to all mankind to the end of the world. By His passion and death He redeemed mankind once for all. By His example and teaching He was the Light of the world. That Light did not go out when

He returned to His heavenly Father. It did not come to shine in a distant corner of the world only, nor for the few people who lived at the time. Before He returned to His heavenly abode He established on earth a Church to carry on the work which He had begun. This Church was so truly to be a continuation of His own ministry that He said of it, "He who hears you hears Me." From the very nature of His Church, therefore, we should expect from it truth not error. A Church divinely established by God Himself to teach mankind in His Name must necessarily be qualified to fulfil its purpose. Unless it were safeguarded against error it could teach falsehood in His Name, and thus lead men astray in His Name. Since Christ commanded us to listen to the Church as to Himself He was bound to see to it that the Church should be the voice of truth. We should, therefore, infer the infallibility of His Church from the very fact that Christ is God and that the Church is the perpetuation of His ministry to mankind. But, apart from what the nature of the case demands, we have the explicit declaration and guarantee of Christ that His Church is to be immune from liability to err.

Christ in His solemn commission to the Apostles to carry on the work which He inaugurated, said: "All power is given to Me in heaven and in earth. Going, therefore, teach ye all nations; baptizing them in the Name of the Father and of the Son and of the Holy Ghost; teaching them to observe all things whatsoever I have commanded you: and behold I am with you all days, even to the consummation of the world" (Matt. xxviii. 18-20).

By this solemn commission Christ enjoined on His Church the duty of preaching to mankind the doctrines which He imparted to her, and gave mankind the assurance that He was to be with her always, thus guaranteeing that her teaching was His. It was because of this guarantee that He added: "He that believeth and is baptized shall be saved; but he that believeth not shall be condemned" (Mark xvi. 16).

If His Church was to teach error He would not have commanded mankind to receive her message, otherwise He would be responsible for false doctrine. Moreover, Christ, who is Truth, cannot be with error, and since He is always to be with His Church it is guaranteed that she is truth. Again, Christ declared that "the gates of hell shall not prevail" against His Church (Matt. xvi. 18).

If the Church should teach what was false she would be doing Satan's work, not Christ's, and the gates of hell should prevail. Hence, since Christ is God, it is evident that His assurance will stand and that His Church will never teach error.

Finally, at the close of His life, on the night before He laid down His life for the life of the world, He clearly announced the infallibility of His Church. "I will ask the Father and He shall give you another Paraclete, that He may abide with you forever. The spirit of truth . . . He shall abide with you, and shall be in you . . . the Paraclete, the Holy Ghost, whom the Father will send in My Name, He will teach you all things" (John xiv. 16, 17, 26).

It was because of this presence of the Holy Ghost in the Church that St. Paul speaks of her as "The house of God, which is the Church of the living God, the pillar and ground of the truth." Such a description could never be applied to a fallible Church. The same Apostle, writing to the Thessalonians, says: "When you had received of us the word of the hearing of God, you received it not as the word of men but (as it is indeed) the word of God." It was because of the abiding presence of the spirit of truth in the Church that the Apostles, in proclaiming the decree of the Council of Jerusalem, began with the words, "It hath seemed good to the Holy Ghost and to us." If words have any meaning we must conclude that the Church established by Christ to carry on His ministry, and to represent Him on earth, is here to represent Him, not to misrepresent Him. Christ owed it to Himself to see to it that His Church should not be subject to error. Twenty centuries of experience has confirmed His guarantee, and gives, if that were necessary, added assurance that He is with His Church as He foretold, and that in consequence she is His infallible organ on earth. So much for infallibility of the Church at large, and to which many Christians outside the Catholic Church willingly subscribe.

Papal infallibility, however, finds no adherents outside the Catholic Church. Nevertheless, the infallibility of the Pope has all the justification and guarantee which substantiate the infallibility of the Church at large. The Pope is the visible Head of Christ's

Church. The Pope is the successor of Peter, the rock on which Christ built His Church. In the language spoken by Christ, Peter means rock. In establishing His Church, Christ said, addressing Peter personally: "Thou art Peter (a rock) and upon this rock I will build My Church." The Church built on this rock-foundation was to last forever, and "the gates of hell shall not prevail against it." The Pope, Peter's successor, is the rock-foundation of Christ's Church. A building is no stronger than its foundation. An infallible Church cannot rest on a fallible foundation. This personal infallibility is due to no merit of the Pope's but to the concern which Christ had for the Church. Our divine Lord, having appointed Peter head of the Church, said to him: "I have prayed for thee that thy faith fail not, and thou being once converted, confirm thy brethren." We cannot doubt the efficacy of Christ's prayer, nor that it was made in behalf of Peter in his office as head of the Church.

It was evidently intended for the Head of the Church for all time, since the Church was to last forever. It was so understood by the Christian world in the early ages of Christianity. The early Christians were certainly in the best position to know the nature of the Church and its Head. Augustine voices the universal sentiment regarding the Pope's infallibility, when in relation to the Pelagian affair he declares in a sermon: "Rome's reply has come; the case is closed." The Fathers of Ephesus give as their reason for the condemnation of the heresy of Nestorius, "the letter of our Holy Father, the Bishop of Rome." The Fathers of Chalcedon having received an epistle from the Pope on a doctrinal matter declared: "So do we all believe . . . Peter has spoken through Leo." Instances might be multiplied, but these are sufficient to show that the early Church regarded the Pope as the infallible voice of God on earth in matters of religion. The Pope, like the rest of us, is human. He may sin, as Peter sinned. But, in spite of Peter's sin, Christ made him the head of the Church. Men, not angels, are the ministers of God's religion.

God can make use of weak instruments to do His mighty work. And He does. Christ was the Light of the world. Christ was very God. By His divine power He can see to it that His representative will not lead men into error. How He does it is His affair. It is enough for us to know that He, the Lord and Ruler of the universe, has established on earth a personal representative, and that He owes it to Himself to see to it that He is rightly represented. The very meaning of Vicar is "one who stands in the place of another." The Pope, who is the Vicar of Christ, stands in Christ's place, and Christ will see to it that His Vicar falls not into error when, as Head of the Church, he defines the creed of the Church.

The Pope is infallible only when he speaks *"ex cathedra."* What does that mean? *Cathedra* means chair or throne. We get the word cathedral from it. A cathedral is the church where the bishop presides or has his episcopal seat or throne. An *"ex cathedra"* statement therefore means, as it were, a speech from the throne. It is a proclamation by the Pope, in the exercise of his office as pastor and teacher of all Christians, wherein he defines, by virtue of his supreme apostolic authority, a doctrine of faith or morals to be held by the whole Church.

By such proclamations the Pope does not add a new doctrine to the deposit of faith given by Christ to His Church, but only clarifies some point which circumstances require to be more explicitly stated. The Supreme Court of the United States does not add to the Constitution by its decisions, but simply states the meaning of a certain clause with reference to certain conditions. Virtually a Supreme Court decision is infallible, because there is no appeal from it. The Supreme Court has no guarantee of infallibility, but the Pope has.

An illustration may make clear the meaning of the Pope's action when, in defining faith or morals, he speaks *"ex cathedra."* Suppose a gentleman who has a collection of art objects entrusts them to a curator to place them in a gallery and to care for them. The curator duly places and safeguards these art treasures. People come in and admire the collection. After some time a controversy arises as to the genuineness of a certain painting. As there is much interest in this special object, the curator takes it from its usual place and puts it in prominence and under better light. In so doing he does not add to the collection, but simply brings out his particular object more prominently, and shows more clearly and explicitly its genuineness. So with papal dogmatic decisions. They do not teach new truths, but only state more clearly and explicitly some truth which was, from the beginning, a part of the deposit of faith entrusted to the Church by Christ Himself.

Papal infallibility, for instance, was a doctrine of the Church from the beginning. This is evident from the fact that whenever there was a doctrinal dispute, both sides sought the approval of the Pope. Once he decided the matter the case was ended, or if either party held out against the Pope that party was adjudged heretic. Practical infallibility resided in the papacy always. Circumstances in recent times made it advisable to state papal infallibility explicitly, which was done by Pius IX.

The Pope, outside an *"ex cathedra"* statement (there have been only a few such during the past three hundred years) may claim that credence only to which his scholarship, character, and ability entitle him. The Pope may fall into personal sin and error, but as the official representative of Christ, speaking *"ex cathedra,"* he cannot teach false doctrine; and this in virtue of Christ's guarantee. Either Christ was God or He was not. If He was not God His religion has no claim on us. If He was God His guarantee is divine, and we can rely on it absolutely. A physician may prescribe correct remedies for others although he himself may not be in sound health. So the Pope, by God's guarantee, proclaims correct doctrine when speaking *"ex cathedra,"* regardless of his personal views or virtue. As our government clothes its ambassadors abroad with special prerogatives not for themselves but for the country they represent, so Christ has endowed His representative on earth, the Pope, with infallibility in his official capacity of Pastor of the universal Church. Christ commissioned Peter to feed the Christian flock, both lambs and sheep. As Chief Shepherd of the fold the Pope has the assurance of God Himself that divine assistance will safeguard him from leading the flock into fields of poisonous pasture. If the Catholic Church is not a divine institution it has no valid claim on mankind. But if it is divine its founder is God, and we should expect that God would see to it that His own Church should not lead men astray. Papal infallibility is not only a historical fact, but it is also a necessary prerogative of a Church which is of God.

The sad state of confusion into which non-Catholic churches have fallen is the best argument for papal infallibility. There is but one Church in the world which speaks with the authority of Christ. That Church is the one whose Chief Pastor is listened to as the voice of God. God cannot mislead. Neither can His Vicar. Objectors to papal infallibility point to certain facts of history which tend to show that the Pope has erred. In all such cases careful study will show that the Pope did not speak *"ex cathedra."* The Pope is infallible only when he enjoys full liberty of action, and states a doctrine which he intends to be binding in conscience on the whole Church. He cannot delegate his infallibility to any person nor to any congregation. Moreover, it does not extend to anything outside matters of faith and morals or to what is necessarily associated with faith and morals. In this sense the history of twenty centuries proves that in very truth papal infallibility has been a prerogative of the Vicar of Christ's Church. Christ is the Light of the world. His infallible Church with its infallible Head is the torch of truth which He Himself has lighted and cared for, as a beacon to guide mankind unerringly over the sea of life to the haven of eternal bliss.

CHAPTER XV

ANTI-CATHOLIC PREJUDICE

THE word prejudice comes from two Latin words—*pre*, which means before, and *judicium*, which means judgment. Prejudice, therefore, means judgment passed on something before sufficient data has been obtained on it. Most people who have prejudices lose them when they inform themselves better on the objects of their prejudices.

It is well known among scholars that men who have had strong prejudice against the Catholic Church have become her admirers and frequently her adherents and champions after examining into her history and teachings.

The Catholic Church is the oldest corporate organization in the world. She is the only universal Church. She is the Light of the world. In the course of centuries she has had to do battle against evil measures and evil men. She has never compromised on Christ's teaching and morality. Consequently she has frequently had evil men and evil forces arrayed against her.

We know from the World War what enemy propaganda can do. It was debated recently which branch of the military won the World War, the army or the navy. After long discussion the conclusion was reached that neither army nor navy had won the victory, but that propaganda had won it.

War propaganda means trying to influence opinion against the enemy. Directly after the World War was over, people on both sides were astonished to learn that nearly all the reports they had accepted and believed concerning the enemy were so many fabrications or exaggerations.

The Catholic Church is at war with the world. The World War had an end. The war between the Church and the world will never end. Consequently, propaganda in one form or another will always be active against the Catholic Church. The Church and the world can never come to terms. They are as opposed as day and night. Light and darkness cannot exist together. Christ preached a kingdom not of this world; the world declares that there is no kingdom except her own here. Christ stands for eternal life; the world lives for the present only. Between the two, therefore, there is bound to be antagonism. This explains the hatred of the world for the Church of Christ. And it explains its propaganda and misrepresentation with regard to the Church.

The world is prejudiced against the Church because it sees her in a false light, will not try to see her right, does not want to see her right. In our day the prejudice of the world takes the form of either hatred or indifference. Of the two, indifference is the worse. You can combat hatred, but indifference refuses parley.

To-day the prejudice of the world is shown by hatred in Russia, France, and Mexico, and other places, where those in power are doing everything possible to destroy belief in Christianity. It is shown by indifference in our own country, where many people are so little concerned about religion that they are not interested enough in it to care, one way or another, what people believe or how they worship.

So much for the prejudice of the world at large with regard to the Catholic Church.

There is another prejudice harder to understand, namely that of non-Catholic Christians, or, as they are sometimes called, the Evangelical Churches. It is sad to say, but true, that at times the prejudice of Protestants or Evangelicals is greater and more intense than that of the world at large. This is due to the fact that they are contenders for what the Catholic Church holds that she alone possesses, namely, the true religion of Jesus Christ. A rival is the bitterest of opponents. Protestantism challenges the claim of the Catholic Church to be the sole true Church of Jesus Christ.

There would be little or no antagonism between Catholics and Protestants if the Catholic Church would drop her claim to being the sole true religion of Christianity. There is virtually no antagonism between the various Evangelical Churches. There may be differences of creed and various forms of worship, but since they all proclaim that one religion is as good as another, they are mutually tolerant of one another, and whatever rivalry may exist among them is of a friendly kind. Episcopalians, Presbyterians, Methodists, Baptists, Congregationalists and the hundreds of other Evangelical bodies extend to one another the hand of fellowship.

No matter what their differences they form a solid front against the Catholic Church. This is due mainly to two reasons. First, if the Catholic Church is right, they are wrong. And secondly, in order to make the Catholic Church wrong they are prepared to credit whatever discredits her.

Let us take up these two points. Nobody wants to admit he is wrong. But if a Protestant admits that the Catholic religion is right, he condemns himself. An Episcopalian may admit that a Presbyterian is right without surrendering his own position. That is why all the Protestant sects harmonize and fraternize, more or less. But an Episcopalian cannot admit that the Catholic is right, and yet remain an Episcopalian. One excludes the other.

The basis of the Protestant position is that one religion is as good as another. This is the outcome of the doctrine of private judgment. If the judgment of one person impels him to be a Baptist, that of another may cause him to be a Methodist. Of course such procedure is illogical, for it comes to the same thing as saying that truth and falsehood are equally right.

For example, if the Episcopalian creed is true, the Presbyterian cannot be true, for the simple reason that one affirms what the other denies. The Episcopalians hold that the Episcopate is essential to the Church of Christ. The Presbyterians deny this. Both cannot be right, since what one affirms the other denies. Truth may be with one but not with both at the same time. One or the other must, therefore, be false. To say, therefore, that one religion is as good as another is to maintain that falsehood is as good as truth.

Incidentally this demonstrates the false basis on which the Evangelical Churches rest. We see to-day the logical outcome of this principle by the trend of Protestantism toward Modernism, which is only another name for Rationalism or the rejection of revealed religion.

Modernists are logical and consistent at all events. Following their doctrine of private judgment it has led them to reject virtually everything that Protestantism proclaimed in the beginning. The Bible was to take the place of God's living Church. The Bible, the whole Bible, and nothing but the Bible was the constitution of the Reformers. It did not matter that the Bible proclaimed one thing to one person, and its contradiction to another. In their exaltation over discovering what they supposed to be a new religion, wherein every one was to be Pope, they overlooked what their Modernist descendants are forced to look at face to face, and in consequence of which they discard the religion of their forefathers.

One religion cannot be as good as another, for the simple reason that falsehood cannot be as good as truth. That is as evident as that water is wet. But because the various Evangelical Churches close their eyes to a contradiction in religion which they would not tolerate in other matters, they live on together in harmony. They call this broad-mindedness. It is broad. Very broad. As broad as saying that two and two make five. But such a broad-minded person would not find a bank equally broad. A bank happens to be a practical concern.

Protestants, therefore, are mutually liberal and considerate because their position is weak. One cannot afford to declare the other wrong because to do so would be to pronounce condemnation on self. Hence their envy, their antagonism to that Church built upon a rock which proclaims that every creed different from hers is wrong. And this brings us to the second point of our consideration.

It was necessary for the Reformers to discredit the Catholic Church. Unless they could show that she was false they themselves could not be true. Unless they could show that she had erred there was no justification for their establishing a new religion. Now Christ had said that His Church would never err. He did not say that members of His Church would not sin or err. In fact He foretold sin and scandal even in high places. He established the Sacrament of Penance for sinners in His Church. Christ guaranteed His Church against error, but not its members against sin or error.

The first little Church of Christ with Jesus as Pastor and the twelve as members had its sin and scandal. Judas was a thief and traitor, Peter was weak and denied his Lord. The first council of the Church, a few years after the resurrection, was held, among other things, to remedy abuses. There will always be abuses in the Church of Christ. Men, not angels, are its ministers. The proof of the divinity of the Catholic Church is that in spite of the weakness of some of its members and rulers it is in the world to-day. Unless it were divinely guided and sustained it had perished long ago from storms without and weakness within.

Protestantism, with all the support of state and all its concessions to human nature, and all its esthetic appeal, or lack of it, is now, after a few centuries, crumbling. But the Church built on the rock is, after twenty centuries, firmer than ever. It is the one Church in the world that is universal, the only one that speaks with the authority of Christ and the only one that even claims to be unerring.

Consequently, to return to our argument, the Reformers had to discredit the Catholic Church to gain credit for their own. This is not the place to go into details. I content myself with saying that those who in the beginning broke away from the Church which alone was founded by Christ, employed every means possible to blacken the Bride of Christ. As proof of this let it suffice to say that scholars who have gone back to original sources declare that, since the Reformation, history was poisoned at its source, with the result that after-generations have been nourished on falsehoods. This accounts for the dreadful prejudice of Protestants against the Catholic Church.

I have met many non-Catholics who have told me of their firm belief in charges so damnable against Catholic teaching and practice, that if I were in their place I should hate the Church worse than they. Some of the best scholars and the highest type of manhood among Protestants have become Catholics as a result of searching for accusations against the Catholic Church. Their investigations led them to enter the very Church which they set out to assail. That ought to be a convincing argument.

Protestant prejudice is due mainly to the falsehoods which have deluged the Protestant mind.

Let me conclude with a statement of a man who for forty years fought the Catholic Church and sought in every way to discredit and destroy her, but who, eventually, seeing the Church as she is, not as she is caricatured, embraced her and is now her defender. This statement is from the celebrated John L. Stoddard, who for twenty-five years was the foremost lecturer in the English-speaking world.

"When I am asked what I have found within the Catholic Church superior to all that Protestantism gave me, I find that language is inadequate to express it. One thinks of the familiar metaphor of a stained-glass window in a vast cathedral. Seen from without by day, this seems to be an unintelligible mass of dusky glass. Viewed from within, however, it reveals a beautiful design, where sacred story glows resplendently in form and color. So it is with the Church of Rome. One must enter it to understand its sanctity and charm.

"When I reflect upon that Church's long, unbroken continuity, extending back to the very days of the Apostles; when I recall her grand, inspiring traditions, her blessed sacraments, her immemorial language, her changeless creed, her noble ritual, her stately ceremonies, her priceless works of art, her wondrous unity of doctrine, her apostolic authority, her splendid roll of saints and martyrs reaching up like Jacob's ladder, and uniting earth and heaven; when I reflect upon the intercession for us of those saints and martyrs, enhanced by the petitions of the blessed Mother of our Lord; and, last not least, when I consider the abiding presence of the Saviour on her altars;—I feel that this One, Holy, Apostolic Church has given me certainty for doubt, order for confusion, sunlight for darkness, and substance for shadow. It is the Bread of life, and the Wine of the soul, instead of the unsatisfying husks; the father's welcome, with the ring and the robe, instead of the weary exile in the wilderness of doubt. It is true the prodigal must retrace the homeward road, and even enter the doorway of the mansion on his knees; but, within, what a recompense!

"Favored are those who from their childhood up are nurtured in the Catholic Church, and to whom all her comforts, aids, and sacraments come no less freely than the air and sunshine.

"Yet I have sometimes wondered whether such favored Catholics ever know the rapture of the homeless waif, to whom the splendors of his Father's house are suddenly revealed; the consolation of the mariner whose storm-tossed vessel finally attains the sheltered port; the gratitude of the lonely wanderer, long lost in cold and darkness, who shares at last, however undeservedly, the warmth and light of God's great spiritual home!"

Catholics are so accustomed to the wonderful benefits of their faith that they fail to realize its value and glory. Like children brought up in the palace of a king they take everything as a matter of course. What some go through fire and water to attain is ours from infancy. We should set a high value on our religion, and for its sake endure generously and cheerfully the prejudice and hatred with which our inheritance is confronted.

CHAPTER XVI

INTOLERANCE

WE not infrequently hear the Church accused of intolerance. The Catholic Church stands for truth, as Jesus Christ did. The Catholic Church is no more intolerant than was her divine Founder. Intolerance is a much misunderstood and much abused word. A mathematician must be intolerant with regard to the multiplication table. A civil engineer cannot tolerate any trifling with or abuse of mechanical laws. Our government must be intolerant of anarchy. Truth is necessarily intolerant of falsehood. Christ, who was the most patient and gentle person that this world has known, was also the most intolerant of everything opposed to His teaching. His Church would be untrue to Him if she were not intolerant where He was intolerant. He established His Church as a depositary of His truth. Consequently she can make no compromise with what He has committed to her charge. If a commander-in-chief entrusted an officer with a message to the army, that officer would be guilty of disloyalty, or perhaps treason, if he allowed the message to be altered.

Intolerance under certain circumstances is the highest virtue. A good woman will tolerate no trifling with her chastity. An upright man will tolerate no charge against his honesty. Our government will tolerate no trifling with the Constitution. The deposit of faith, entrusted to the Church by her divine Founder, is more sacred than the Constitution. If the Church did not uphold the faith she would be guilty of the betrayal of the most sacred trust ever committed to mankind. Christ, who died for sinners, was intolerant of sin. He who flayed the hypocrisy and vice of the Scribes and Pharisees opened his merciful heart to the woman taken in adultery, to Magdalen, and to the thief on the cross, when they showed repentance. He castigated the Scribes and Pharisees because they upheld falsehood, and defended their evil course. We see therefore that intolerance is not necessarily reprehensible. A father does not tolerate impertinence from his children. A mother does not tolerate immodest conduct in her daughters. An officer of the law does not tolerate violation of the law. But, it may be said, is not intolerance an evil thing, is it not narrow, inconsiderate, an enemy of liberty? To this it may be said that intolerance may be considered under two aspects, theoretic and practical. Theoretically, error, vice, anarchy, etc., must never be tolerated, since that were to approve or at least silently encourage these vicious monsters.

Practically, the victims of error, vice, and anarchy are to be dealt with patiently, with a view to rescuing them from their unfortunate condition. Oppose error, but extend a helping hand to the erring. When, however, the upholders of error, vice, or anarchy become a menace to the public weal, they must be repressed. And so with regard to the Church established by Jesus Christ; to error she is absolutely opposed, toward the erring she is tolerant to the point of indulgence. It is only when those in error become a menace to faith or morals that she protects herself against them by every legitimate procedure. The Church will expend all her resources for the conversion and true welfare of those who are in error. So long as the erring ones are in personal error only, she leaves them to God. A man's conscience is sacred. God alone is judge of the individual soul. But if one in error endeavors to spread error, and openly proclaims error, advocates error, defends error, the Church has the right and duty to protect herself against error, and in so doing to repress and chastise the upholder of error. In our country, which is most liberty-loving, a citizen may have privately what opinions he chooses about the Constitution and laws. But if he becomes a public opponent of law and order and constitutional rights, he will be proceeded against by the government. There are men now serving prison sentences for upholding and advocating doctrines subversive of our Constitution. The Church has a constitution and she must protect it against attack.

She first warns those of her subjects who may be the victims of error. She does all in her power to cure their spiritual malady. But if they refuse her kindly efforts, and by their aggressiveness threaten to spread contagion she excommunicates them. Our government has established quarantine to protect her citizens from physical contagion. The Church has her spiritual quarantine to protect the faithful from the blight of error. It is only when everything of a kindly nature has failed that she has recourse to extreme measures. It should be well understood that she employs her measures only against her own subjects. Her weapons are spiritual, mainly. In the days when entire nations were Catholic, and when Church and State ruled hand in hand, an open offense against faith was regarded as an assault on the nation, and as such was punished by the State. The Church simply judged the case, deciding if the faith had been openly assailed. That ended her participation in the matter. She meted out, of course, her spiritual penalties on the obstinate champion of error, but left him to the State to deal with regarding corporal penalties.

The Church's part was, therefore, only to pass judgment on the person accused, declaring him innocent or guilty. The State then took the matter in hand and acted according to the statute law. At times, as in everything concerning human nature, there may have been excesses and mistakes. But we should have to know intimately the customs, circumstances, and temperament of the times before passing judgment. It must be remembered that in the ages when heresy was punished corporally and cruelly, heresy was regarded as one of the greatest offenses against the common peace and welfare. In our own country witches were burned at the stake in Massachusetts, and citizens were exiled for their religious views. And all this was done by people who championed liberty and who themselves had suffered for the practise of religious liberty. One fact will show the wonderful tolerance of the Catholic Church. When the Jews, who for various reasons were persecuted in the different countries of Europe, sought a secure place for the unmolested practise of their religion they found their best place Rome itself. It was the Pope, moreover, who most efficaciously mitigated the rigors of the Inquisition when the Spanish Government was using it as a weapon of State. The English Government, under Elizabeth, perpetrated, in the name of religion, greater injustice and cruelty on her subjects than is recorded elsewhere in the annals of Christendom.

When, therefore, we speak of intolerance, we must reflect that religion has been made to bear many a load which should be placed on civil government. In the ages when religion was dominant in the State, government frequently sought to use it as a means and justification for unjust acquisition or unlawful and ambitious procedure. It may be said, in general, that whatever the intolerance existing at any time in Christendom it would have been worse but for the influence and action of the Church. Always the Church stood out as the champion of the people and their rights. One, and perhaps the main, reason why she was opposed by certain monarchs, was because she opposed their tyrannical and unjust measures toward the people. It is so to-day. Look out over the entire world and you will find no greater protector of the common people than the Church of Christ. Every Catholic knows that in time of need the priest is a friend indeed.

Having said this much about tolerance in general, it may not be out of place or uninteresting to consider some aspects of tolerance. We may consider tolerance with regard to its personal, civic and governmental aspects. Personal tolerance refers mainly to our private association with others. It means that we bear patiently with what we disapprove of or even condemn as evil. We may be tolerant with people whom we dislike and of whom we disapprove, by making allowance for their shortcomings and habits. This tolerance may degenerate into a vice, if by our silence we encourage others in wrong-doing. But if, all things considered, we realize that tolerance is the advisable thing, and not another form of cowardice, it is best to show ourselves patient and silent toward persons and things that are apparently beyond our influencing or changing. But if we have a duty toward others, such as that of parents in regard to children, tolerance may be participation in wrong-doing.

Another aspect of this subject is civic tolerance. This is very important, particularly in a country like ours, where there is such a mixture of nationalities, religions, and temperaments. Civic tolerance is concerned with our attitude toward our fellow citizens who differ from us in religion, or politics, or race, or social standing. We confine the present consideration to religious tolerance. Briefly, religious tolerance means respect for the religious convictions of others. It is based on the Christian teaching that we should love our neighbor. Our neighbor is not only the man who agrees with us in our convictions, but every man. Christian kindness and love extend not merely to those who please us or agree with us, but toward our fellowman as man. We are to presume that other people are sincere in their convictions just as we are ourselves, and we should esteem and love those who differ with us, just as we expect the good-will of those with whom we differ. It is certainly right to credit others with good faith unless we know they are in bad faith. For the most part God alone is judge of that. Hence we read in Scripture, "Judgment is Mine, saith the Lord." Pope Gregory IX. in the year 1233 exemplified this doctrine of religious tolerance, when he proclaimed that "Christians must show towards Jews the same good-will which we desire to be shown to Christians in pagan lands." Tolerance thus practiced for the love of God becomes a charming Christian virtue. It is not the easiest virtue to practice, by any means, as we see from its frequent violation. Dean Swift remarked that "many have just enough religion to make them hate one another, not enough to make them love one another." It is the characteristic of really pious people to be very kind toward those of other religious convictions. St. Francis de Sales won more converts from heresy by his benevolence toward heretics than by his arguments.

It was so with all the saints, and especially with the great missionary and apostolic saints. Without compromising on error they esteemed and loved the erring persons. The more sincere a man's religious convictions, the greater is his virtue of tolerance toward those who differ with him. Tolerance must not be taken for indifference. Religious indifference makes one care little or nothing for what others believe. But that is not the virtue of tolerance. Religious tolerance means that although a person may be absolutely convinced that he has the truth, and is willing to die in its defense, he nevertheless, for the love of God, shows esteem and love for those whom he holds to be in error. God Himself gives us an example of this tolerance, since He allows the wheat and tares to grow side by side, and permits the sun to shine on just and sinners alike. Yet God so hates sin that He gave His life on the cross to atone for it and to prevent it. Even while nailed to the cross He prayed for sinners as His blood poured out for sin. It may be said that the practise of religious tolerance will be mistaken for approbation of error. Christ was known to love sinners, yet no one thought that He condoned sin. The more religious one is the more resplendent is his religious toleration. The saints were the most tolerant of men. A saint will give his life to bring the truth into the life of others, but, like Christ, his Master and Model, he will be all goodness and kindness to those who err. It is only a small mind that is intolerant. Indeed intolerance brands one as narrow. Intolerant people are hated. They stand in their own way. Their power for doing good is shackled. Tolerant people are loved, and in the end accomplish most good. Tolerance, when practiced by those who have no religion, is a natural virtue, very beautiful and very admirable. When practiced as a supernatural virtue, that is for the love of God, who so loved us, it becomes a very meritorious act of religion. Very often intolerant people think they are virtuous when they are simply stubborn or narrow. It is easy to be intolerant, difficult to be tolerant. Tolerance implies patience, unselfishness, and due regard for the feelings and traditions of others.

Tolerance is necessary for friendly intercourse and for right living. In proportion as one is a true Christian one will be tolerant. Catholic missionaries, who sacrifice the delights of home, friends, and country, in order to spread the Gospel of Christ in foreign lands are recognized as the most tolerant body of men in history. It may be objected that tolerance opens the door to religious indifference. The best reply to this objection is that the most tolerant Catholics are the most devout Catholics. The present Supreme Pontiff is proof of this. Although condemning the anarchy and irreligion of the Russian Bolshevik regime, he was nevertheless one of the first and most magnanimous in sending relief to the distressed Russians, regardless of creed. Cardinal Mercier was another example of magnanimous tolerance. The Pope would readily sacrifice his very life for the faith, but at the same time he leaves individual private conscience to God. God has not asked His followers to pass judgment on others, but He has commanded them to love their neighbor. In our country, where there are so many various creeds and races, anybody or anything that is prejudicial to religious tolerance is a menace to true citizenship.

This brings us to our final consideration of the subject, namely, governmental tolerance. Government has for its object to safeguard the rights and liberties of its subjects. Provided that the practise of religion does not unjustly conflict with the public weal the State is obliged to protect her citizens in their right to worship God as their conscience dictates. Government as such has to do with external order and welfare. No government as such has been divinely commissioned to safeguard and proclaim the deposit of faith. This commission was given to the Church founded by Christ. Hence the Church cannot be tolerant of erroneous doctrine in her fold. It would make her false to her trust. She must, accordingly, do all in her power in her own sphere to guard and proclaim the faith. It is not so with the State, however. The State is pledged to protect the liberty, property, and life of her citizens. This is the conception of the modern State. Since the right to one's religious convictions is conceded by modern government, it follows that the State must allow her citizens to worship God as they wish, provided that that worship does not conflict with the just laws of the country. Hence the State must tolerate the various religions which her subjects adhere to. And since worship usually implies external service, the State is bound to protect her citizens in their public worship.

Religious toleration by the State therefore means freedom of faith, of profession, and of worship. Hence the principle of Roman Law *"De internis non judicat praetor."* (The judge is not concerned with matters of conscience.) The modern State, therefore, is neutral with regard to religious worship, neither advocating one religion nor proscribing another. Certain States, England for instance, and Spain, establish a State religion, allowing, however, freedom of worship to all others which do not interfere with public order and welfare. In the United States, where religious freedom is guaranteed by the Constitution, every cult has equal rights before the law. Our government has always respected the religious convictions of her variegated population, and it is safe to say that the principle of religious toleration finds its best expression in the United States of America. For any citizen or group of citizens to attempt to infringe on this constitutional freedom of worship is paramount to treason. The glory of our country has been respect for law and order. To stir up religious strife, directly or indirectly, is to undermine the very basis of peace and welfare. People of all religions make sacrifices for the common welfare, and are entitled to serve and worship God as their consciences dictate, without hindrance from those who worship differently or who do not worship at all. In these days of widespread education intolerance is fast vanishing. Sometimes, however, it shows its sinister head, but mainly where bigotry is rampant. If a man does not respect his conscience he is not going to respect government. Intolerance assails a man for respecting his conscience. Intolerance thus attacks the firmest basis and support of the State.

By all means let us uphold truth and oppose error. But let us also leave the individual conscience to the judgment of God. That is what Christ did. That is what we must do if we would be His true followers.

CHAPTER XVII

THE BIBLE

ONE of the accusations made by the Reformers against the Catholic Church was that she kept the Bible from the people. In proof of this they affirmed that the Church chained the Bible in the Middle Ages. The Church did chain the Bible, and for a very good reason—to keep it from being stolen. Before the invention of printing a Bible was worth as much, if not more, than an automobile. It took several years to make a Bible before printing was invented. It was all done by handwriting. If you wish to know what that means, take a pen in hand and copy word for word, in careful penmanship, the four or five thousand pages of Scripture.

Moreover, paper was not in common use as it is now. Books were mostly made on thin sheets of parchment or skin. A man who possessed a few books in those days was rich. On account of the value of a book there was a temptation to steal it. Most of the books were in the libraries of monasteries under careful guardianship. The Church, however, wishing to have the Bible at the service of all, put it in a public place, and chained it to a reading desk in order to keep it there for the people. Before doing that the Bible had frequently been carried off and the people deprived of its use. The solicitude of the Church for the Bible was construed into the false charge that she chained the Bible to keep it from the people, whereas in reality she chained it to keep it for the people. I have mentioned this matter in some detail, since it throws light on the unprincipled manner in which the Reformers acted toward the Church in many other things. Another false accusation made against the Church with regard to the Bible was that she was opposed to its publication in the language of the people. The Reformers asserted that they were the first to open the Bible to the general public. How false this charge is, may be seen from the fact that previous to the Reformation the Bible was printed in every language of Europe.

Before Luther's German version of the Bible appeared, there were one hundred ninety-eight versions of the Bible printed in the languages of the various peoples of England, Italy, France, Spain, Germany, etc. In face of these documentary proofs of the Church's desire to bring the Bible to the people, it is hard to understand how she was ever accused of preventing the people from reading the Scriptures. It is another instance of how she was misrepresented by her opponents. It must be remembered, in connection with this subject, that printing was invented only shortly before the Reformation. Consequently, books were few, and those who could read were few. Outside the clerical and governmental classes there were very few who could read. Indeed some of the greatest monarchs of the Middle Ages were unable to read or write. It was because of the fewness of books of any kind that the Church spoke to her children by the various arts of sculpture, painting, and architecture. Stained-glass windows in churches presented to the constant view of the people scriptural events, especially those associated with Our Lord. The Stations of the Cross told graphically the story of Christ's passion and death. Statues and images brought to the mind the blessed Mother of God, and the saints. The church itself, with its sky-piercing steeple, pointed a finger heavenward to remind man of his true home beyond. Critics of history say that no man can be rightly estimated except by those who know his epoch and circumstances. It is easy for those of one generation to misjudge those of another with which they are not acquainted. Hence good historians always study the period into which their investigations lead them. The Church has a right to equally just treatment. Until recently so-called historians have not accorded her this just treatment. Now, however, there is beginning to be shown a fairer attitude toward her, with the result that many of the accusations formerly made against her are being converted into praise for her wise and benevolent measures. The Catholic Church welcomes investigation. The more light thrown on her the more she stands out divine. Her greatest foes have always been ignorance and bigotry.

To return to the subject in hand, the Bible. The word Bible comes from the Greek *Biblia,* which means books. The Bible is a collection of books known altogether as the Scriptures. In Latin the word *Biblia* became the expression for this collection. Gradually *Biblia* referred to the Scriptures only, becoming a new word in the Latin language, and designating the Scriptures as *The Book,* by way of eminence. Sometimes we hear it referred to as the Good Book, God's Word, the Holy Scriptures, the Inspired Volume, etc., but generally, among English-speaking people, it is called the Bible. The Bible is made up of two separate collections of writings: the Old Testament, containing the Scriptures of the inspired writers previous to Christ, and the New Testament, containing the writings of the Apostles and Evangelists. Scripture literally means writing. In early days all books were in script, or handwriting, as we term it. The Jews regarded the Old Testament Scripture as sacred writing. They believed that they were entirely different from the writings of man, being in fact the work of those who were inspired by God. They regarded them as of divine authority. Christ confirmed them in this belief. He frequently appealed to the Scriptures in proof of His divine mission. He declared that the Scriptures must be fulfilled, etc. If they were not of divine authority there was no reason why they should necessarily be fulfilled. The New Testament, containing the writings of the Apostles and Evangelists, records Christ's life and teaching, and the truths revealed by Christ Himself or the Holy Ghost. It contains in part the deposit of faith, to which nothing has been added since the apostolic era.

The Old Testament was written, originally mostly in Hebrew. But when the Jews were dispersed, and gradually lost their language, the Hebrew Scriptures became a sealed book to many of them. The scholars among them translated the sacred writings into the language of the place where they resided. The result was that the Old Testament existed in various versions, principal of which were the Syriac, the Aramaic, and the Greek Septuagint. At the time of the Apostles Greek was the most universal language. The early

Church thus used, mainly, the Greek Old Testament, instead of the Hebrew, which was little understood even by the Jews themselves. The New Testament, for the same reason, was originally written in Greek. It is this Greek text of the Bible, Old and New Testaments, that was in general use in the early ages of Christianity. Some people think that the Bible made the Church. In point of fact the Church gave us the Bible. The Church was firmly and permanently established before a line of the New Testament was written. The Old Testament existed, but not as the solemnly recognized Bible. The Bible, as we now have it, owes its origin to the divinely established Church of Jesus Christ, which assembled its contents, and by the guidance and authority guaranteed her by Jesus Christ proclaimed that it was the word of God. Now what does the Church mean by saying that the Bible is the inspired word of God? She does not mean that God spoke the words of Scripture or wrote them. She does not even mean that God directly dictated Scripture. What she means is that the writers wrote under the inspiration or guidance of God. Each writer, employing his own individual style, wrote, consciously or otherwise, what God wanted him to write. The Bible is thus the message of God to man. The primary author is the Holy Ghost, or, as it is commonly expressed, the human authors wrote under the influence of divine inspiration.

Cardinal Manning gives the following idea of inspiration: "Inspiration, in the special and technical sense, includes the three following operations of the Holy Ghost: (1) the impulse to put in writing the matter which God wills they should record; (2) the suggestion of the matter to be written, whether by revelation of truths not previously known, or only by the prompting of those things which were within the writers' knowledge; (3) the assistance which excludes the liability to error in writing all things, whatever may be suggested to them by the Spirit of God, to be written." The dictation, therefore, of each word, is by no means essential to a true notion of inspiration. Hence it is that the Evangelists, each in his own manner, recorded what they were inspired to record. The prophets of the Old Law did the same. God could have given a message direct to mankind if He had wished, and as He did in fact to Moses, but it pleased Him to use men as instruments of His communication, just as He uses men as the ministers of grace in the sacraments, instead of directly imparting grace as He could easily do.

Having considered the inspiration of the Bible, we may now take up the subject of its interpretation. No book interprets itself. The most carefully drawn legal paper is open to various constructions. Even the Constitution of the United States, a document most studiously prepared, has need of an official interpreter, the Supreme Court of the United States. That the Bible, though a divinely inspired book, does not interpret itself, is evident from the fact that it has had almost as many different interpretations as it has had readers. Nor can it be said that being a divinely inspired book, its prime Author, the Holy Ghost, will guide the reader to the right meaning. The Holy Ghost cannot guide readers to contradictory meanings, and we know that many passages of Scripture have been interpreted by various people in an absolutely contrary sense. The Bible, besides being a divinely inspired volume, is also a literary composition, with the style, figures of speech, and various characteristics of literature. Every work of literature has its literal and figurative passages, its allusions to conditions of its own time and place, and various other peculiarities which constitute its distinctive feature. Shakespeare and Dante have had hosts of interpreters, learned men, scholars of highest repute, yet reaching different and often contradictory conclusions. It was because of this inherent quality of literature that the framers of our Constitution designated the Supreme Court of the United States as the official interpreter of its meaning.

Christ, in instituting His Church, clothed her with infallibility. She was to speak in His Name and with His authority to the end of time. "He who hears you hears Me." "As the Father hath sent Me I also send you." "I am with you all days, to the consummation of the world." It was this Church of Christ's that solemnly proclaimed the Scriptures of the Old Testament as God's inspired word, and moreover specified just what books constituted Scripture. Scripture itself does not state what writings make Scripture. And so with the New Testament. It was the Church which decided which were inspired writings, and formed them into the New Testament. The Jews themselves were not united on what books constituted the Old Testament. And among the early Christians there was much controversy over the inspired writings. It was the Church, acting as God's official representative, that solemnly proclaimed just what writings constituted the Bible. It is all very well to say that Scripture is inspired, but we must also know what is and what is not Scripture. It was the Church that made this decision and thus made the Bible. Now just as Scripture does not state what constitutes Scripture, so it does not state what is the interpretation of Scripture. The Church which made the Bible, likewise interprets the Bible. The Reformers began by making each reader his own interpreter, with the result that there were as many meanings of Scripture as there were readers.

They began by saying that the Bible and nothing but the Bible was the rule of faith. Now, many of them have come to the point where they discard the Bible altogether as a divinely inspired book. They who accused the Catholic Church of being the enemy of the Bible, now find that she is its sole defender in the only sense in which it can be defended as a divinely inspired volume. Outside the Catholic Church there are two extreme parties with regard to Bible interpretation. One party holds to literal interpretation, the other entirely rejects every supernatural feature. The Catholic Church, while upholding the divine inspiration of Scripture does not maintain its literal interpretation, exclusively. She holds that the various writers wrote what God wanted them to write, each one employing his own peculiarities of style and environment. In consequence they at times used words in their literal meaning, again in their figurative, and at other times in their obvious, or commonly accepted meaning. We say, for instance, that there is a full moon, or half moon, or quarter. The moon is always the same. It shows itself differently, that is all. We say the sun rises in the east and sets in the west. It does nothing of the sort. Yet it conveys a meaning, just as does the expression full moon or quarter moon. So with Scripture; some parts are to be literally interpreted, while others are to be taken figuratively or typically. The description of the heavenly Jerusalem (Tobias xiii. 21) (Apoc. xxi. 18) is obviously figurative. If there be question of the interpretation of any particular passage of Scripture, it is not left to conjecture, or to individual penetration, but to the living voice of the Church, constituted by Christ as the official interpreter of revelation.

Pope Leo XIII. in his great encyclical, *"Providentissimus Deus,"* declares that the biblical authors "did not seek to penetrate the secrets of nature, but rather described and dealt with things in more or less figurative language or in terms which were commonly used at the time, and which, in many instances, are in daily use at this day, even by the most eminent men of science. Ordinary speech primarily and properly describes what comes under the senses; and somewhat in the same way the sacred writers—as the Angelic Doctor also reminds us—'went by what sensibly appeared,' or put down what God, speaking to men, signified, in the way they could understand and were accustomed to." St. Augustine, fifteen hundred years ago, wrote a long and learned treatise on the Six Days of Creation. He interpreted the Six Days to mean six epochs or cycles. He also interpreted creation to mean creation of the universe from certain primitive forms made in the beginning, by the Creator, and endowed by Him with the power of developing into present forms. Centuries ago, therefore, the Church recognized that literal interpretation of Scripture was not necessarily required. As previously stated it is for the Church to declare in what sense a specified passage of Scripture is to be taken, and to determine the precise meaning of the part in question. She very rarely does this; never, in fact, unless the text becomes a matter of dispute, and cannot be otherwise settled, and is, moreover, concerned with religion directly or indirectly. The Creed of Pope Pius IV, 1564, states the matter briefly: "I admit the Sacred Scriptures according to that sense which holy Mother Church has held and does hold, to whom it pertains to judge of the true sense and interpretation of the Holy Scriptures."

Although the Church is the divinely appointed custodian and interpreter of the Bible, we must not think that she acts arbitrarily in her interpretation of it. On the contrary, before she hands down a decision on a disputed text she gives it more time and attention than does our Supreme Court to a matter under judgment. There is no tribunal on earth more learned or judicious than that which examines and decides scriptural matters. But no matter how learned a commission may be its decision is not final, or of faith, unless it be ratified by the highest Church authority and promulgated as Catholic doctrine. It will be seen, therefore, that the Bible, although under the guardianship of the Church, is not in any way restricted by her solicitude and interpretation, but rather made more serviceable. The Constitution of the United States does not lose but rather gains by the action of the Supreme Court. Every Supreme Court decision tends to clarify the Constitution. And so with the Church's interpretation of the Bible, instead of interfering with its message she brings out even more clearly God's communication to man. When we realize that the inspiration of Scripture extends only to the original text, as written by the one who was inspired, we may understand better the need of an authoritative and infallible interpreter. To make this clear we must recall that the Old Testament was written originally mostly in Hebrew and the New mostly in Greek. Not a single line of these original Scriptures exists in the world to-day. What we have are copies of the original, or copies of copies. Even the oldest of these copies or versions do not go back to the Apostles, or to the time when the Bible was made. Only the original Hebrew and Greek texts were inspired. The translations or copies were declared to be faithful renditions of the original. It is only the versions so accepted as true translations by the Church that she regards as the Word of God. She has declared authentic the version known as the Latin Vulgate and has proclaimed it to be the official Bible of the Church.

Luther's version of the Bible had over three thousand faulty translations. The King James version of the English Bible had even more mistakes than Luther's German version. It is for this and similar reasons that the Catholic Church wants only those English, German, or French versions of the Bible to be used by her children, which she approves of as being faithful translations of the original, or of the Latin Vulgate which is her official version. When it is said that the Church is opposed to the reading of the Bible in certain schools and assemblages, it is not to the Bible she is opposed, but to a version of the Bible which she knows is not a faithful translation, and which, consequently, tends to inculcate erroneous doctrine. Far from being opposed to Bible reading the Church is the greatest encourager of it. She even grants an indulgence to those who spend fifteen minutes a day reading the Gospels. But while so encouraging Bible reading the Church does not forget that she is the custodian of the Bible. In an Encyclical in the year 1893 Pope Leo XIII. wrote: "The solicitude of the apostolic office naturally urges and even compels us, not only to desire that this great source of Catholic revelation should be made safely and abundantly accessible to the flock of Jesus Christ, but also not to suffer any attempt to defile or corrupt it." Previously Pope Pius VII. wrote to pastors "to encourage their people to read the Holy Scriptures; for nothing can be more useful, more consoling and more animating, because they serve to confirm the faith, to support the hope, and to influence the charity of the true Christian."

It will be seen, therefore, that the Bible's friend and protector is the Catholic Church. But it is the true Bible that she guards and which she exhorts her children to read. She obliges her priests to read portions of the Bible every day. Indeed in the course of a year every priest reads almost the entire Bible. He spends about an hour a day reading the Breviary, which is mostly composed of Scripture. But for priest as well as people the Bible must be the Bible. It must not be mutilated, altered, or have any omissions. If you take up a Protestant Bible you will find that it lacks seven books of the Old Testament and not a few Epistles of the New. This shows the necessity of guardianship. The Bible did not drop from the sky. It was not originally a single book. Even when its parts were assembled and made into the Bible it was not a permanent book, but subject to decay as others. It could only continue by being copied and translated. It could not do this of itself, nor of itself guarantee its true copying or version. The Church, God's guaranteed representative on earth, saw to it that inspired writings, and inspired writings only constituted the Bible, and that copies and versions were truly made therefrom. The Jews themselves had two sets of Scriptures, one in Hebrew, which was that of the Jerusalem Jews, and one in Greek, which was that of the Alexandrian Jews. They differed as to their contents. It was the Church which pronounced which was the right one. She proclaimed the Greek

Septuagint version the true and complete Old Testament. It was the same with the New Testament. There were many writings which claimed to be inspired in the early ages of Christianity. It was the Church that decided which were apostolic and incorporated them into what is now known as the New Testament. In this way the Church made the Bible. She existed prior to the Bible and in no way depends on it for her establishment. But once having set her seal on the Bible, as God's word, she now appeals to it, and abides by it in matters of faith.

The Bible, therefore, is God's communication to mankind through the inspired prophets of the Old Law, and through the Apostles and Evangelists of the New. God might have written His communication in the sky or on imperishable granite, but He has seen fit to speak to us by men like ourselves. We should not be surprised that He manifested His will to us by men, when we reflect that He manifested His love for us by man, giving His Only-Begotten Son to us, Jesus Christ, born of the Virgin Mary, who in all things except sin was like unto us. Having given His communication to us by the Bible He did not leave it to itself to perish or become distorted by the action of time and human caprice but committed it to the keeping of His divinely guided Church. In her hands it has been kept intact from the beginning, and has been accessible to all. The Church is above the Bible. The Church received her divine charter from Jesus Christ, the Son of God. She taught the truths of Scripture before the Bible was made, and will continue to teach them if the Bible should perish. Christ guaranteed perpetuity to His Church, not to a book. Christ constituted as His teacher, not a book, but His Church. The Church is Christ in the world. "He who hears you hears Me."

CHAPTER XVIII

THE MASS

ONE of the first things the Reformation assailed was the Mass. The so-called Reformers proclaimed that the Mass was idolatry. They destroyed altars, abolished the priesthood, and forbade the celebration of the Mass. The Mass is the distinctive act of worship of the Catholic Church. It is the central service of the religion established by Jesus Christ. The altar is erected for the sacrifice of the Mass, the Church is built as a sacred dwelling for the altar and for the celebration of Mass, the priest is consecrated for the service of the Mass, and Jesus Christ, the Son of God, dwells in person in the tabernacle of the altar, as a consequence of the Mass. If the Mass is not the most sacred act of worship on earth it is the most idolatrous and abominable. For the Mass claims to bring down on our altars the Son of God, and to offer Him in sacrifice to the Godhead. Unless the Mass is just that, it is mockery. Being that, it is the holiest act of worship that can be rendered to Almighty God. Having said this much by way of introduction, let us now consider the nature of the Mass, and some of its important aspects.

The Mass is the *unbloody* sacrifice of the Body and Blood of Christ. Calvary was the *bloody* sacrifice of Christ. The Mass is essentially the same sacrifice as that of the cross. This is no figure of speech, no metaphor, or exaggeration. The sacrifice of the altar and the Crucifixion are the very same sacrifice in all the essentials. They differ merely with regard to the manner of the offering. The Crucifixion was the offering of Himself by Jesus Christ in a bloody manner, His Body being delivered to suffering, and His Blood poured out unto death. In the Mass Jesus Christ sacrifices Himself in an unbloody manner, offering His Body under the form of the host, and His Blood under the form of the sacred species of the chalice. Christ instituted the Mass at the Last Supper. It was then that He Himself said the first Mass, gave the first holy communion, and ordained the first priests.

It was the eve of Calvary. He was taking leave of the Apostles who had been His companions during the years of His public ministry. Before His departure He made His last will and testament, leaving to them not gold nor possessions nor fame, but Himself. In what follows we must bear in mind that Jesus Christ was God. He knew all things, He could do all things. He read the secrets of hearts, foretold the future, healed the incurable, gave sight to the blind, multiplied the loaves and fishes, changed water into wine, walked on the sea, raised the dead. At the Last Supper He worked His greatest miracle. First He took bread into His sacred and venerable hands, and by the power of which, in the beginning, He made all things out of nothing, He changed the bread into His own Body. How He did this we do not know, any more than we know how He changed water into wine at the wedding-feast of Cana. But this was a greater miracle, because the change actually took place without anything outward to indicate it. The Apostles had only the word of Christ for it. But that is more than sufficient. He declared that the bread which He held in His hands was His Body. There was no outward change whatever. The shape, form, and color were the same, yet on Christ's word there was a substantial change. What He held in His hands was now His Body. It may seem strange that there was nothing exterior to indicate the interior change. But that is why it is called the mystery of faith. If we saw the bread transformed into actual flesh before our eyes there would be no mystery of faith. It would be evidence. There is no credit in yielding belief to evidence. Evidence compels belief. But Christ instituted the Mass as a mystery of faith. He wanted us to believe on His word, even though there was no evidence to support it. That is why faith is meritorious. It sacrifices our noblest faculty, our intellect, on the altar of God's word. We believe because God speaks, who can neither deceive nor be deceived. It may help us somewhat to understand that this change was effected internally, although there was no outward indication of change, by considering an electric rail before and after the current is turned on. The third rail is said to be dead when the current is off, but live when it is on. To outward appearances there is no change perceptible when the rail is dead or live. Yet when live the rail has the power of a thousand giants, when dead it has not the power of a fly. People can see no difference in the live and dead rail, but when they see a sign reading "Live rail, danger, keep off," they believe in the sign and act accordingly. This does not explain the change which Christ effected at the institution of the Eucharist, since there was a substantial change in the bread, while in the rail there is no substantial but merely an accidental change. However, this illustration helps us to realize that when Christ said that the bread was His Body, it was really so, even though there was no evidence of change. We have only God's word for it, therefore, that this change was effected. But God's word is enough. Heaven and earth may pass away, but God's word will never fail.

Therefore, Jesus having changed the bread into His Body, offered it in sacrifice to the Father, saying, "This is My Body, which is given for you." By these words Christ there and then offered His Body in sacrifice for us. He was not referring to the sacrifice of His Body on the cross, which was to be offered in a bloody manner the next day. His Body was indeed given for us on Calvary, but here He is speaking of an actual, present offering; "This is My Body, which is given for you." It was given there and then, in an unbloody manner, under the outward form of bread. Our Lord, therefore, offered His Body in sacrifice for us at the Last Supper. Immediately afterwards, in like manner, "Taking the chalice He gave thanks and gave to them saying: Drink ye all of this. For this is My Blood of the New Testament, which shall be shed for many unto remission of sins."

He says distinctly, "This is My Blood," not that it will be, but that it is His Blood. It is the very Blood which on the morrow will be shed on Calvary for remission of sins. Here and now it is offered in an unbloody manner, to-morrow it will be flowing from His bruised Body on the cross.

This was the first Mass, of which Christ was the first priest and He Himself was also the victim, in unbloody form, the same victim as He was to be in bloody form on the cross a few hours later. Having instituted the Eucharist, by changing bread and wine into His Body and Blood, and having said the first Mass by offering Himself in this unbloody form as a sacrificial victim to the Father, He proceeded to give holy communion to the Apostles: "Take ye and eat, this is My Body; drink ye all of this, for this is My Blood." That was the first holy communion. But this was not all. Having said Mass, He commissioned His Apostles to say Mass also. "Do this in commemoration of Me." By these words He ordained them priests to offer the sacrifice of the Mass. Equivalently He said: "Do what I have just done. I have offered My Flesh and Blood under the form of bread and wine to My heavenly Father. I ordain you to do the same." Hence it is that at Mass the priest does precisely what Christ did at the first Mass in the Cenacle of Jerusalem. The priest at the Consecration of the Mass does not say "This is the Body of Christ," but "This is My Body," using the very words of Christ, and speaking them as the representative of Christ. At Mass it is Christ Himself who offers the sacrifice, the priest acting in His stead.

Christ is a priest forever, as Scripture declares, and it is at Mass day after day that He offers the victim of the altar. That is why the Mass is so sacred. It does not depend on the holiness of the priest, since Christ Himself it is that offers the victim, which is none other than Himself.

The Mass, although a real and true sacrifice, is not the actual slaying of the victim, as was the slaying of Christ on the cross. Christ is now in glory. He can die no more. In what way, therefore, is the Mass a sacrifice just as real as the Crucifixion? The sacrifice of the Mass is the continual renewal, the unbloody representation of the sacrifice of the cross. Consequently the Mass must put before us in some way what took place on the cross. On the cross Christ offered Himself by dying, His death being the result of the separation of His Blood from His Body. To represent the death of Christ this separation of Body and Blood must be reproduced. Since the resurrection the humanity of Christ has been glorified, so that His Body and Blood are no longer capable of being separated. In the Mass, in order to represent the separation of Christ's Blood from His Body, which took place on Calvary, the two forms of bread and wine, one solid, the other liquid, are necessary, and by the separate consecration of the host and the chalice there is typified the separation of Christ's Body and Blood. If the host alone were consecrated Christ would indeed be on the altar. This would be the Blessed Eucharist. But in order to be the Mass there must be represented the slaying of the victim, Christ. By the separate consecration of the chalice the separation of Christ's Blood from His Body is represented, thus constituting the sacrifice of the altar, which, as regards the victim and the one who offers it, is the same as the sacrifice of the cross, differing only in the manner, the Crucifixion being a bloody sacrifice, the Mass an unbloody sacrifice.

Consecration of the bread alone would be the Eucharist, the Blessed Sacrament. But the Eucharist is not the Mass. The Mass requires a mystical slaying of the victim, and this is done only by the separate consecration of the chalice, following the presence of the victim, Jesus Christ, on the altar, as a consequence of the consecration of the host. The separate consecration of the chalice is the mystical separation of Body and Blood which represents the death of the victim. If a priest should, for any reason, be interrupted after the consecration of the host, and before the consecration of the chalice, there would be, indeed, the Blessed Eucharist on the altar, but no Mass. It requires, I repeat, the separate consecration of the chalice after the consecration of the host, in order to constitute the sacrifice of the Mass, which is none other than that of Calvary, but in an unbloody manner.

To put briefly what has been stated, let it be said that the Mass is essentially the same sacrifice as the cross. On the cross Christ offered His Body and Blood as a sacrifice to the heavenly Father. This was a bloody sacrifice. At Mass Christ becomes really present on the altar by the consecration of the host. "This is My Body." Where Christ's Body is there He is. He offers Himself to the heavenly Father as a sacrifice, not by shedding His Blood, since He is now in glory, but by the separate consecration of the chalice, which represents the separation of Blood from the Body, constituting a real sacrifice, but in an unbloody manner.

At the Mass, therefore, the altar is the cross, the priest is Christ, the victim of sacrifice is Christ, and the slaying of the victim is represented by the separate consecration of the chalice, which shows the separation of Blood from the Body, the cause of Christ's death on the cross. Hence St. Paul, writing to the Corinthians, speaks as follows: "The Lord Jesus, the same night in which He was betrayed, took bread, and giving thanks, broke, and said: Take ye, and eat: this is My Body, which shall be delivered for you: this do for the commemoration of Me. In like manner also the chalice, after He had supped, saying: This chalice is the New Testament in My Blood: this do ye, as often as you shall drink, for the commemoration of Me. For as often as you shall eat this bread, and drink the chalice, you shall show the death of the Lord, until He come." The Mass therefore shows the death of the Lord. It represents in an unbloody manner the bloody death of Christ on the cross. The Mass was instituted before the Crucifixion. It was a sacrifice by itself. In the first Mass the living Christ offered Himself to the heavenly Father. In every Mass it is the glorious, living Christ, who, by the priest, offers Himself to the heavenly Father. In every Mass the death of Christ on the cross is commemorated, as He ordained, by the consecration separately of His Body and His Blood. This is the mystical slaying of the victim which constitutes the Mass the holy sacrifice of the altar, and makes it to be essentially the same sacrifice as that of the cross. St. Paul brings this graphically before us when he says: "Whosoever shall eat this bread or drink the chalice of the Lord unworthily, shall be guilty of the Body and the Blood of the Lord." On the altar, after the consecration, Christ is truly present. He is there to be our spiritual food in holy communion, to be worshiped by us in the Blessed Sacrament of the altar, to be our friend and consoler in the tabernacle, and to be offered up in Holy Mass as a sacrifice to His heavenly Father for the remission of sins. It is by the Mass that we have the Blessed Eucharist for holy communion, for viaticum, for adoration. And it is by the Mass that Christ is offered up, in an unbloody manner, for the salvation of sinners, and in thanksgiving, praise, and petition for mankind.

By the Mass Christ has put in our possession a gift of infinite value, which we may offer to God as worthy of God. By attendance at Mass we, with the priest, offer to God this supreme gift, the most acceptable thing that can ascend from earth to heaven. When we attend Mass with the right spirit we are standing with Mary at the foot of the cross. This is the meaning of that Scripture which says: "You shall show the death of the Lord until He come." The Mass shows the death of Christ. The Mass offers to God what Christ offered on Calvary. It is a privilege to assist at holy Mass. It is the holiest act of worship in which a Christian can participate. If the Mass were offered in one place only, and but once a year, Christians doubtless would flock to its celebration from all over the world. But because God has made it so easy, for us to assist at Mass we are apt to value it lightly or hold it cheaply, whereas in God's estimation it is the most precious thing in the world.

If the sun should rise but once a year what a wonderment would its rising cause among men. But because it rises every day we take it as a matter of course and pay little or no attention to it. Yet if the sun failed to rise even for a week what a dismal and dreadful place the earth would be! The Mass is that sacrifice which the prophet Malachias foresaw when he uttered the divine words: "I have no pleasure in you (the Israelites) saith the Lord of hosts, and I will not receive a gift of your hand. For from the rising of the sun even to the going down My Name is great among the Gentiles, and in every place there is sacrifice, and there is offered to My Name a clean oblation." This prophecy did not refer to the sacrifice of the cross, which was offered in one place only, once for all, and in a bloody manner, but to the Mass, the clean oblation, offered everywhere from the rising of the sun to its going down. For there is not an hour of the day in which the Mass is not celebrated somewhere in the world. Moreover, the prophet states that this sacrifice is to be offered, not among the Jews, but among the Gentiles, which means the nations other than the Jews. And it is among the Gentiles of the world over that this clean sacrifice is offered to God from the rising of the sun to its going down.

A Catholic church is not a mere meeting-house nor a platform or pulpit—it is a temple in which there is the altar of sacrifice. Every Catholic church is a Calvary and every altar a cross. On this altar is shown the death of the Lord. On this altar, in the tabernacle, is Christ Himself, and from this altar He comes to us in holy communion, to be our strength and joy. It is the Mass that brings Christ among us and offers Him in our behalf to the heavenly Father. Christ is both Gift and Giver, the victim and the priest of the unbloody sacrifice of the altar. No greater boon has God bestowed on man than the Mass. No greater offering can man make to God than worthy participation in the holy sacrifice of the Mass. For in the Mass Jesus Christ, the great High Priest, offers Himself to the heavenly Father for mankind. The offering He made of Himself on Calvary is thus perpetuated in an unbloody manner. On the cross His sacred Blood flowed from His wounds. He was the victim slain for sins. On the altar the same Christ offers Himself for mankind, offering the same Body and Blood. But as He is now glorious in heaven and can die no more, He offers Himself in an unbloody manner, yet representing the sacrifice of the cross by the separate consecration of the chalice, which indicates the separation of the Blood from the Body, the slaying of the victim.

It is thus that the Mass brings constantly before us the passion and death of the Lord. It is a constant memorial of Calvary, and at the same time the sacrifice of the same victim as hung on the cross. The Mass differs in manner only from the Crucifixion. In both cases it is to God that the offering is made, it is Jesus Christ that is offered, and it is Jesus Christ who makes the offering. The nature of a sacrifice requires that it be offered to God alone, that there be a victim or gift offered entirely, and that there be a sacrificing priest. On Calvary, Christ as priest offered Himself as victim to the heavenly Father, shedding His own Blood, because He suffered of His own will. On the altar Christ, the great High Priest forever, offers Himself as He is now, to the heavenly Father, commemorating the sacrifice of the cross by a mystical shedding of Blood, by means of the separate consecration of the chalice. Christ, in ascending to His heavenly Father, did not leave us orphans. By instituting the Mass He devised a way of always being with us. He was called by the prophet, Emmanuel, which means: "God with us." He is with us as our perpetual High Priest, daily offering the sacrifice of the Mass. He is with us in the Blessed Sacrament of the altar. He is with us in holy communion. There is no surer means of our being with Him forever in heaven, than by worthy participation in the holy sacrifice of the Mass. The Mass not only brings Christ down to us, it also raises us up to Him. The Mass glorifies God, by offering Him what is of infinite worth, and sanctifies man by putting before him the price of redemption. The Mass commemorates God's love for us, a love that proved itself by the supreme sacrifice. The Mass thus becomes a powerful incentive to serve and love God, no matter what sacrifice His service may entail.

CHAPTER XIX

PURGATORY

THE doctrine of Purgatory, rightly understood, is one of the most reasonable and consoling truths of revealed religion. Luther saw so much to admire and approve in it that for a long time he hesitated about rejecting it. Finally he rejected it because it was distinctly Catholic. Many modern Protestants, while avoiding the word Purgatory, teach the real doctrine of Purgatory. They call it the Middle State. Martensen, for instance, writes: "As no soul leaves this present existence in a fully complete and prepared state, we must suppose that there is an intermediate state, a realm of progressive development, in which souls are prepared for the final judgment" (Christian Dogmatics, Edinburgh, 1890, p. 457). See also Farrar, "Mercy and Judgment," and Campbell, "The Doctrines of the Middle State." Another non-Catholic, Mallock, speaks as follows: "It is becoming fast recognized on all sides that Purgatory is the only doctrine that can bring a belief in future rewards and punishments into anything like accordance with our notion of what is just and reasonable. So far from its being a superfluous superstition, it is seen to be just what is demanded at once by reason and morality; and a belief in it to be not an intellectual assent only, but a partial harmonizing of the whole moral ideal" (Is Life Worth Living? xi. p. 290).

It stands to reason that God is just. It is also evident that many of us depart from this life not altogether saints and yet not altogether sinners. Moreover some, who have been notoriously wicked repent at the last moment, and God has declared that He will not reject the penitent sinner. Such a penitent, although assured of God's forgiveness, must nevertheless atone for his lifelong transgressions. Unless there is a place beyond where atonement can be made, the death-bed penitent would entirely escape chastisement for sin. It is true that Christ forgave the sins of the thief on the cross, and also remitted the chastisement of them. He may do that with every sinner if He so wills. But that is not His ordinary way, as we know from Scripture. God forgave David his sin but chastised him dreadfully nevertheless. So, too, He punished Moses and others after He had pronounced forgiveness of their sins. We have, therefore, the fact that God is just and merciful, and also the fact that not all of us depart this life holy enough for companionship with God, and yet not wicked enough for perpetual banishment from His presence. Scripture declares that nothing defiled can enter heaven. They, therefore, who have lesser sins on their souls, or who have repented but not received chastisement in this life for their wickedness, must be made worthy of entrance into the all-holy presence of God in some place beyond this life. That is what is meant by Purgatory.

Purgatory may be defined as a place or condition of temporal punishment for those who, departing this life in God's grace, are not entirely free from lesser sins, or have not fully paid the satisfaction due to their transgressions. Christ Himself proclaimed that the sinner must pay the penalty of wrong doing. He said of sinners, "Unless you shall do penance you shall all likewise perish" (Luke xiii. 3).

How many sinners have done adequate penance for their offences? Christ, who redeemed all mankind, did not thereby relieve us of doing our part for sin's atonement. By redemption He made it possible for the greatest sinner to obtain pardon, but on condition that the sinner make reparation as far as he is able. Some either neglect or have not the opportunity of making due satisfaction for their sins in this life, hence unless there is a place beyond where this can be done they can have no companionship with the all-holy God in the kingdom of the blessed. Let us take, for example, the case of a man who has been dishonest all his life, even to the extent of depriving the widow and the orphan of their substance. Let us add to all this the crime of deliberate murder, in order to obtain possession of another's goods. Now such a man is despicable in the sight of angels and men. Yet God's mercy is not closed against even such a malefactor. While there is life God's forgiveness may be had. Suppose such a one turns to God at the very last. God will forgive him if he truly repents. God, who knows the heart, is the sole judge in these matters. But if the guilt of sin is remitted by a merciful God, it does not follow that chastisement is not required by a just God. Such a sinner might indeed be forgiven, the guilt of his wickedness might be blotted out by the merits of Christ's redemption, but chastisement might be exacted by a long, a very long suffering in the life beyond the grave. Some non-Catholics object to Purgatory because there is no specific mention of it in Scripture. There is no specific mention of the word Sunday in Scripture. The Sabbath is mentioned, but Sabbath means Saturday. Yet the Christians of almost all denominations worship on Sunday not on Saturday. The Jews observe Saturday. Nowhere in the Bible is it stated that worship should be changed from Saturday to Sunday. The fact is that the Church was in existence for several centuries before the Bible was given to the world. The Church made the Bible, the Bible did not make the Church.

Now the Church which gave us the Bible, instituted, by God's authority, Sunday as the day of worship. This same Church, by the same divine authority, taught the doctrine of Purgatory long before the Bible was made. We have, therefore, the same authority for Purgatory as we have for Sunday. But although there is no specific mention of the word Purgatory in Scripture, there is specifically mentioned the very thing that Purgatory means. Purgatory means a place or condition of purification after this life. The Jews offered sacrifice for their deceased brethren. The high priest in person performed the sacrificial rites for the dead. Now, unless there was a place such as Purgatory, sacrifice for the dead would be meaningless. For if there was only heaven or hell hereafter those in heaven would not need help, and those in hell could not profit by it. Consequently there must be a middle state which is temporary and purificatory. This we call Purgatory.

We read in Scripture that Judas Machabeus sent an offering to Jerusalem for the dead, because "It is, therefore, a holy and wholesome thought to pray for the dead, that they may be loosed from sins" (2 Mach. 12, 46).

Even if this text were history only, and not Scripture, it would prove the reality of Purgatory—since it shows that the Jewish people believed in prayer for the dead, and Christ did not correct that belief, as He was bound to do if it were erroneous. But He himself taught the doctrine of Purgatory; He declared that certain sins were not forgiven either here or hereafter (Luke xiii. 27). This means that at least some sins are forgiven in the life beyond. That is the meaning of Purgatory. St. Paul also states that some will be saved yet so as by fire (1 Cor. iii. 15). Hence from the very time of the Apostles sacrifice was offered for the souls of the departed. In the great central act of worship of the Apostolic Church prayers for the dead were an integral part of the service. Even to-day we can obtain visible evidence of prayers for the dead by inspecting the tombs in the Catacombs. The Church of Christ from her very origin taught the doctrine of Purgatory, and, what is more, exemplified the doctrine by her ritual and devotions. Christ guaranteed His Church against error. Consequently what His Church taught was true. If the Church of Christ taught what was false, Christ was not God, for God's promise cannot fail, and if Christ be not God all Christianity is false. Christ also promised that His Church should last forever. It was, therefore, in the world from His day, down to our own, and is in the world now.

The only Church recognized as His from the beginning taught the doctrine of Purgatory. If, therefore, Purgatory is not true, His Church was not true, and Christianity is a deception or worse. The Reformers denied the doctrine of Purgatory. They therefore admitted that the only Church in the world which up to their time was Christ's was abandoned by Him. That was making Him false to His guarantee and virtually declaring Him to be either impotent or untrue, either of which would be a denial of His divinity. In order to avoid this undesirable conclusion the Reformers maintained that Purgatory was not taught in the early centuries of the Church but was an abuse introduced later. But it can be shown that Purgatory was a received doctrine in that era of the Church which even the Reformers admit was the period of truth in the Church. Before we give proof of this let it be said again that the Reformers, by asserting that Purgatory was not taught in the early and pure ages of Christianity but only in a later period, condemn Christ Himself, and with Him His Church altogether. For Christ did not guarantee His Church for a few centuries only, but forever.

Now for our evidence. Tertullian states that prayers for the dead were an apostolic ordinance (*De Corona Militis*). Moreover he charges the faithful that they have a sacred duty of praying for their departed brethren (*De Monogamia*). Tertullian lived in the second century, only a few years after the Apostle St. John had gone to his everlasting reward, hence his testimony shows what the Apostolic Church believed and taught. Prayers for the dead imply that the faithful departed need prayers and may benefit by them. This is the very meaning of the doctrine of Purgatory, for unless there was a middle state between heaven and hell, prayers for the dead would be useless, since the dead would be either in heaven where they need not prayers, or in hell where they could not profit by them. After this life there are only two permanent states, heaven and hell. Purgatory is a temporary state where the not altogether good and the not altogether bad may be purified for the kingdom of eternal bliss. This is a most consoling doctrine, for very few of us are altogether what we ought to be. Some of us are purified in this life by prayer, penance, and affliction of one kind or another, but others depart this life so stained with the dross of earth that before they can become the pure gold of God's kingdom they must be purified in the crucible of Purgatory.

St. Cyril of Jerusalem, describing the liturgy of the Mass, writes: "Then we pray for all those who have departed this life in our communion; believing that the souls of those for whom prayers are offered receive very great relief, while this holy and tremendous victim is sacrificed upon the altar." In accordance with this doctrine, lists of the dead were placed prominently in every place of Christian worship as a perpetual reminder to pray for them. Now all this was done in the very beginning of Christianity. The Reformers claimed that although the early Church was pure in doctrine it had become corrupted in the course of centuries. But at the very period to which they pointed as the purest in the

Church's history, the doctrine of Purgatory was an integral part of the Christian faith. The Reformers therefore not only contradicted themselves by denying the doctrine of Purgatory, but they also made Christ untrue to His word, which guaranteed that His Church should never fail. When Christ guaranteed His Church against error and against decay He was not referring to individuals, but to His Church as an institution established by Himself to last forever and to be the light of the world. One of the Apostles fell lamentably under Christ's very eyes. Another denied Him with an oath within His hearing. Man is free and may fail under the holiest environment. But Christ's Church is His own special creation and is guaranteed by Him to teach the truth and to last until the end of time. The mistake of the Reformers was to identify individuals as the Church. As well identify Benedict Arnold with the patriotic army which he sought to betray. There have been and doubtless will be bad priests and prelates to the very end of time. Christ foretold scandals, at the same time warning us that it would be woe to them that should be guilty of scandal. In this matter of Purgatory, as well as in every doctrine of the Catholic Church, we must bear in mind that a chain is no stronger than its weakest link. If the Catholic Church has taught but one false doctrine it is not the Church of Christ. And if the Catholic Church is not Christ's no other is, because for centuries after Christ the Catholic was the only Church which all true Christendom recognized as the Church established by Jesus Christ.

In assailing the Catholic Church, therefore, one is assailing, unconsciously perhaps, Christ Himself. For if the Catholic Church has failed Christ's promise has failed, and that ends His claims to divinity. Away, then, with all revealed religion, and with Christ Himself if the Catholic Church is not altogether true in her doctrine. And we see that it is rapidly coming to a denial of Christ and revealed religion among non-Catholics. Modernists, one great branch of Protestantism, are now engaged in stripping supernatural religion of the supernatural. They seek to reduce Christ to their own level, and His teaching to the same class as that of human sages. But unless Christ is God, as He said He was, and unless His Church speaks to us with divine certainty and authority, as

He declared it would, why should we accept Him or His Church? Why not be a follower of Plato or Aristotle? Why not be a pagan? There is no obligation to follow Christ unless He be divine. But if He be divine we must hearken to Him or bear the consequence. To put it briefly, a religion, unless it be authoritative, does not oblige man to live by it. And unless it be divine it is not authoritative. Moreover if it is divine it is all true. The Catholic is the only consistent Christian. A non-Catholic Christian may indeed be sincere, but it is because he is inconsistent or illogical, or perhaps so influenced by education and environment that he never seriously reflects on his religious tenets. When Christ established His Church He endowed it with truth and perpetuity. His doctrine would have perished with His voice unless He had devised some means of transmitting it down the ages. Christ never wrote a line. He left nothing in a book. What He did leave was a living book, His Church, which was to be His voice in the world to the end of time. He spent years in instructing His Apostles, and moreover sent upon them the Holy Ghost, who recalled to them all His teaching and inspired them with all that they should do in their apostolic ministry. Hence it was that in the first apostolic decree we find these opening words: "It hath seemed good to the Holy Ghost and us." The early Church spoke in the name and with the authority of God. It was this early Church which established prayers for the dead, and made a commemoration of the dead an integral part of its solemn service, the holy sacrifice of the Mass.

Unless we have faith in the living Church, we have no grounds at all for faith. The Catholic Church is the only living Church which goes directly back to Christ without interruption. Hence if we do not accept her doctrine we have no source of belief. In the Apostles' Creed we say: "I believe in the Holy Ghost, the Holy Catholic Church, the communion of saints, the forgiveness of sins, the resurrection of the body, and life everlasting." The communion of saints signifies that union which exists among the faithful on earth, and between them and the faithful departed, both those in Purgatory and in heaven.

By this holy union we can pray to the saints in heaven for help, and we can pray for those who are in Purgatory that they may the sooner join the blessed host in heaven. Scripture exhorts us to pray for one another, and also to pray for the faithful departed: "It is a holy and wholesome thought to pray for the dead." It is certainly consoling for us to know that our dear ones departed are not beyond our help. Christian piety has always followed the faithful departed by prayer and alms, and especially by the holy sacrifice of the altar. God's mercy is over all His works. Surely His mercy is manifest in the comforting doctrine of Purgatory, by which we know that in spite of minor transgressions, and sins forgiven but unsatisfied for, we may nevertheless hope to be made worthy to associate with God in that blessed kingdom which He has prepared for them that love Him. Purgatory, although a place of suffering, is also an abode of peace. All who are in Purgatory have the comforting knowledge that they are friends of God and on their way to everlasting blessedness. This makes them happy in the midst of pain, because they realize that their suffering is preparing them for entrance into their eternal Father's home and to a share of His unbounded love.

Suffering is relative. A person who suffers without hope of relief is indeed in sad case. But one who knows that suffering will end in perfect freedom from pain or disease gladly endures the severest pain. A patient of an incurable disease finds no solace in suffering, nothing but the dead weight of pain. But a patient who has the assurance of recovery willingly endures the surgeon's knife or the unpleasant remedies of the physician. Purgatory is the vestibule of heaven. It is the certainty of eternal salvation. All its sufferings are inflicted in love and endured in love. It is because the souls in Purgatory love God so much that they suffer so much. In Purgatory they realize what God is, are drawn to Him most powerfully, and yet repelled from Him by the state of their souls. They cannot themselves hasten their union with God, since the time of meriting ends with life. But they can be helped by the charity of their friends on earth. By the communion of saints we on earth can offer to God our prayers, good works, alms-deeds and sacrifices of one kind and another, in their behalf. Above all, we may assist at the holy sacrifice of the Mass for them, and best of all we may have the holy sacrifice offered up especially for them. When St. Monica the mother of St. Augustine felt that she was about to die she said to her son: "Lay this body of mine where thou wilt; one thing only I ask of thee, remember me, when I am gone, at the holy sacrifice of the altar." Thus spoke one saint to another, in the first ages of Christianity. By praying for the souls in Purgatory the Christian practices his religion in a most salutary manner both for himself and for those for whom he prays.

In aiding the faithful departed we are practicing first of all an act of charity. We are doing something for those who are beyond self-help. This act of charity is also an act of the love of God, for it is done for love of God, and to unite to Him the sooner those who are dear to Him. Of course God could, if He wished, terminate the period of suffering in Purgatory at any time, but we must remember that God is just, as well as merciful. He shows His justice by requiring chastisement for wrong-doing, and His mercy by permitting us to go to the aid of those being chastised. By our faith and charity we can offer to God satisfaction for the souls in Purgatory, and trust to the goodness of God to accept our satisfaction for them in the most generous measure compatible with justice. For, after all, when we pray for the faithful departed, it rests with God to accept our prayers and good works in their behalf. God is wise and just as well as merciful. A lifelong sinner of the most heinous character, but who repented at the last, might have offered for his soul thousands of Masses by his friends' generosity or by a stipulation in his will, yet Almighty God might see fit not to accept them in his behalf. Such a soul, forgiven by God's pursuing mercy, might have to suffer chastisement for his sins to the day of judgment. One cannot purchase one's way to heaven. In praying for the faithful departed we do so by way of suffrage, that is, we offer our good works to God in their behalf, leaving it to Him to accept them for those for whom they are offered. Of this, however, we may be certain, that since He bids us pray for them no prayer of ours in their behalf goes without rendering them some assistance. It will thus be seen that the doctrine of Purgatory is a great help to the living, since it enables them to practice charity in a high degree, and a consolation to the faithful departed since it gives them hope that their period of probation may be shortened. It also helps the practise of faith, by causing us to make sacrifices in daily life in accordance with the teaching of faith; and finally it aids in the practise of Christian hope, because we trust that the good God will not only be merciful to those for whom we pray, but to ourselves also, who for love of Him pray for those who love Him, and whom He loves, and whom He desires to welcome home as soon as they are made ready for His loving embrace. "It is a holy and wholesome thought to pray for the dead that they may be loosed from their sins."

CHAPTER XX

INDULGENCES

ONE of the things most misunderstood by non-Catholics is indulgences. Frequently Catholics are asked most surprising questions about this subject. Some will ask if an indulgence is permission to commit sin. Others want to know how it is that the Catholic Church can usurp God's place in dealing with the sinner. An indulgence is not permission to sin, nor does the Church usurp God's place by granting indulgences. Like everything connected with the Catholic Church, the doctrine of indulgences, rightly understood, becomes an argument for the divinity of the Church, and leads many to embrace the Catholic faith.

A Catholic can do his Church no better service than to be well informed on this and other subjects which are the occasions of misunderstanding between us and non-Catholics. Cardinal Newman, in his Preface to "Lectures on the Present Position of Catholics in England," says: "his object has not been to prove the divine origin of Catholicism, but to remove some of the moral and intellectual impediments which prevent Protestants from seeing it." In the concluding lecture, he said: "What I desiderate in Catholics is the gift of bringing out what their religion is . . . You must not hide your talent in a napkin, or your light under a bushel. I want a laity, not arrogant, not rash in speech, not disputatious, but men who know their religion, who enter into it, who know just where they stand, who know what they hold and what they do not, who know their creed so well that they can give an account of it, who know so much of history that they can defend it . . . I wish you to enlarge your knowledge, to cultivate your reason, to get an insight into the relation of truth to truth, to learn to view things as they are, to understand how faith and reason stand to each other, what are the bases and principles of Catholicism. . . ."

One of the intellectual impediments which prevent Protestants from seeing the divinity of the Catholic Church is their false ideas on indulgences. Let us begin our explanation of this doctrine by giving the meaning of the word itself. Indulgence means consideration of kindness or pity or mercy.

A judge shows indulgence to a convicted criminal by taking into consideration the mitigating circumstances of the crime, the grief of relatives, the shame and sorrow of the criminal, and other such things. A defiant criminal, one who shows no regret for his deed nor gives evidence of reform, ordinarily receives strict justice from the judge. But a criminal who shows regret for the past, and evidences a determination to reform, finds justice tempered with mercy. Such a one would receive indulgent treatment from the court, perhaps being allowed freedom on suspended sentence, or paroled, or at least have the term of imprisonment shortened. The indulgence of the court does not obliterate the guilt of the criminal but only lessens or remits the penalty ordinarily affixed to the crime. Such indulgence by the court does not encourage crime but rather aids reform. We see, therefore, that in a certain sense the State grants indulgences. Government attaches certain penalties to certain violations of the law. Government cannot remove the guilt of crime, but it can and does mitigate or remit the penalty affixed to the crime.

Sin is an offense against God. Sin has two consequences. First, it defies God by violating His law, and secondly, it incurs a penalty for this violation. The forgiveness of sin is the remission of its guilt, which means the restoration of the sinner to God's friendship, and in consequence the remission of the eternal chastisement due to sin.

After the guilt and eternal punishment have been remitted there remains the temporal chastisement due to an offense against God, which must be suffered either here or hereafter. It is satisfied for here by penance, good works done voluntarily, alms-deeds, and by patience and resignation in the trials of life. It is satisfied for hereafter by the suffering of Purgatory.

Now an indulgence has to do solely with the temporal chastisement due to sin after the guilt has been remitted. It means that the Church, by the power conferred upon her by Christ, mitigates the temporal chastisement due to sin. We speak of the Church as our holy Mother the Church. This is not an empty title. She is our Mother, indeed. It was she who made us children of God by the Sacrament of Baptism. She has the heart of a mother toward us, her children. A mother will gladly remit or lessen the punishment of a child's offense if she finds that the child is truly sorry and determined to avoid offending again. So our holy Mother the Church, on seeing the proper dispositions in a repentant sinner, rejoices to lessen or remit altogether the temporal chastisement of sin. This power was given the Church when Christ said, "Whatsoever you shall loose on earth shall be loosed also in heaven." In the early ages of the Church it was not unusual to assign public penances for sins. These established penances were called canonical because they were in accordance with the canon or rule of the Church. These penances were for various periods of duration, thirty days, a year, or several years. In some rare cases they were lifelong.

When the Church first granted indulgences it was with reference to these canonical penances. Afterwards, when public canonical penance ceased, she still retained the terms of these earlier days in granting indulgences. Hence we hear of an indulgence of thirty days or of a year or of a plenary indulgence. When, in the earlier days, the Church gave a penance for a sin it did not mean that that penance necessarily satisfied for the chastisement—much depended on the sinner's dispositions. God alone knows just what chastisement satisfies for sin. It depends on many things known only to Him, such as the degree of guilt in the commission of sin and the degree of sorrow for the sin committed. The same outward sin committed by a hundred different persons may have a hundred different degrees of guilt in God's sight. Also an act of true and intense sorrow for sin, or of sincere love of God, of which God alone can be judge, may atone for sin more than a multitude of penances performed in the ordinary way.

Here it is advisable to explain a term in connection with indulgences, which if not rightly apprehended may give rise to mis-understanding, especially to non-Catholics. When it is said that the Church grants an indulgence, the word *grant* has a technical meaning. If there is question of an indulgence applicable to the souls in Purgatory, it means that the Church offers to God, by way of suffrage and appeal, the superabundant merits of Christ and the saints; the good works enjoined on the penitent for gaining the indulgence being a condition only. The superabundant suffer-ings of Christ and the martyrs form, as it were, a treasury from which the Church draws in behalf of the penitent sinner, on con-dition that he comply with everything that is necessary for the gaining of the indulgence.

That is the meaning of an indulgence applicable to the faithful departed. It rests with God. He may see fit to have the in-dulgence benefit entirely or only partly those for whom it is offered. That is why the Church offers Masses for years and years, sometimes perpetually for the souls departed. If the bene-fit of one Mass were applied totally to a soul in Purgatory, that soul would straightway enter paradise. But God knows what jus-tice and charity require. A lifelong sinner might repent and be saved at the very last. Such a soul would be saved, but it might have to remain a long, long while in Purgatory. Such a one might have acquired wealth by dishonest and oppressive meas-ures. His family might have hundreds of Masses offered up for his soul, but the application of the Masses to his soul rests with God. God, who showed the sinner unlimited mercy while he lived, and accepted his conversion at the very end, may see fit to have him pay the full temporal chastisement for his sins in Purgatory. Nothing defiled can enter heaven. However, since God Himself bids us to pray for our dead, "it is a holy and wholesome thought to pray for the dead," we may feel assured that no indulgence we gain for our dear ones departed fails to aid them in some measure.

The technical meaning, therefore, of the word *grant,* when there is question of an indulgence applicable to the faithful departed, is that the indulgence is offered to God by way of suffrage and appeal. When there is question of an indulgence for the living the meaning of the term *grant* is that the Church absolves the penitent from the temporal chastisement due to sin, and in its place offers to God a part of the superabundant sufferings of Christ and His saints. When an indulgence is gained by a sinner for himself it means that if his dispositions are perfect he is absolved from the chastisement which he should otherwise have to undergo either here or hereafter for his sin. An indulgence cannot be gained by one person for another living person. A sinner has it in his own power to merit forgiveness and mercy while he lives. We may pray and offer good works for a sinner's conversion, but we cannot free him from his evil ways without his own will. Our prayers and good works may win for him grace to help dispose his will, but conversion is, with God's grace, his own doing. While living, the sinner has it in his power to merit. The faithful departed cannot merit for themselves. Merit for oneself terminates with life. But God enables us through the communion of saints to aid the souls departed who are beyond self-aid. We aid them, however, not as we do ourselves, but by way of suffrage, leaving it to the goodness and mercy of God to accept in their behalf what we offer for them. Christ loves them and died for them and desires them to be happy with Him. Therefore we may trust Him to do what is merciful and charitable. Nothing defiled can enter heaven. God is the benign Judge of the living and the dead. Mercy is over all His works.

We may presume, therefore, that since God authorizes His Church to grant indulgences for the dead, He hears her appeal in the most benign and generous manner.

Having explained in detail the nature and significance of an indulgence, we are prepared to understand the formal definition of an indulgence, which may be stated briefly as follows: An indulgence is a remission in whole or in part, outside confession, of the temporal chastisement due to sin, after the guilt and eternal punishment have been remitted. We say temporal chastisement to distinguish it from the eternal, which is remitted when the guilt of sin is absolved. As said previously, sin disinherits one from the family of God. This disinheritance means not only losing heaven but incurring the punishment of hell. There is no place in heaven for those who are not friends of God. A sinner is an enemy of

God, one who deliberately violates God's solemn orders. Here-after there are only two permanent abodes, either with God or away from God. Away from God forever means hell. Purgatory is a temporary abode for the purification of those friends of God who are not ready for admission into His presence. A sinner whose sins have been forgiven by absolution in the Sacrament of Penance is restored to God's friendship, but unless the chastisement due to his sin is satisfied for by penance here it must be done by suffering hereafter in Purgatory. The reason we are eager to gain an indulgence is, therefore, in order to obtain the remission of the chastisement due to sin. By gaining an indulgence we know that we are receiving from God, through His Church, a remission of the temporal chastisement of our transgressions.

Let me add here an explanation of some aspects of indulgences. An indulgence, say of a year, does not mean a year less in Purgatory, but the remission of a chastisement equivalent to that which was remitted in earlier times when a public penance of a year was remitted by an indulgence.

Indulgences are classified, therefore, in terms of former canonical penances. Furthermore, to gain a specified indulgence one must be perfectly disposed. That is why Christians practice penance voluntarily. They seek by self-imposed acts of denial or of charity to atone for their transgressions, realizing it is better to suffer here than hereafter in Purgatory.

Presently I shall sum up briefly the doctrine of indulgences in a way which I trust, after the foregoing explanations, will make it clear to everybody.

We must bear in mind that God, who forgives the repentant sinner and restores to him his inheritance, nevertheless chastises him for his sins. An indulgence is the substitution of a milder for a severer penance, enjoining instead of chastisement, some good works which advance piety, charity, and religion. An indulgence is thus seen to be an aid to sanctification.

Having given at length, and with no little repetition, the origin and nature of indulgences, we may conclude by a final statement.

An indulgence is a remission, outside confession, in part or in full, of the temporal chastisement due to sin, after the guilt has been remitted. An indulgence is an impossibility except a sinner has repented and has the will to reform his ways.

Far from encouraging a sinner in evil, an indulgence is a most powerful help to reformation and sanctification. It is, moreover, an incentive to charity, since it enables us to do a service for our dear ones departed who can no longer merit for themselves, and who in consequence turn to us for help. We often wish that our dead were with us again in order that we might have the opportunity of showing them our love. The doctrine of the communion of saints and of indulgences enables us to do for them what our loving hearts long to do.

Moreover, every indulgence we gain for the faithful departed or ourselves is associated with some act of piety which helps to make us dearer to God and more worthy of being with Him hereafter. God, who made us, knows best our nature and our needs. In conferring upon His Church the power of granting indulgences He gave her what was helpful to our own sanctification and consoling in our tender concern for the dear ones departed.

CHAPTER XXI

HELL

HELL is a subject not supposed to be mentioned among up-to-date people except with a shrug of the shoulders or a tilt of the nose. If one takes hell seriously one is regarded with pity or scorn by those supposedly advanced thinkers.

What about hell? Denying smallpox does not do away with it. If there is a hell, our indifference to it or denial of it will not affect its existence. Hell is the most dreadful doctrine of Christianity. Christianity is a religion of love. Hell seems to be the very enthronement of fear. The Old Testament made its appeal mainly through fear. Christ came to inaugurate the new law of love. Yet He proclaimed the dreadful dogma of hell. How are love and hell reconciled?

Christ, the most gentle being that ever lived, proclaimed the most dreadful doctrine that ever fell on human ears. It seems to be a contradiction, this God of love and this dogma of eternal punishment. God is love. God loves us. God so loved the world as to send His only Son among us in order to make us members of the divine family. Christ, the Son of God, when He came among us, showed His love by a life of gentleness, mercy and kindly deeds, surpassing everything in the annals of mankind. Finally, for love of us, He made the supreme sacrifice, laying down His life in pain and shame for our sakes. The love of God for us is therefore beyond question.

But how reconcile this love with the awful doctrine of hell? Hell is the punishment of those who spurn God's love. God exhausts every device of love, appealing to the heart of man to the very last moment of life, but if man reject the divine Lover in life the rejection is forever, and that is hell. Eternity without the love of God is eternity of banishment from God, for none may be His companions hereafter who ignore Him here. Nothing defiled can enter heaven. The man who departs this life stained with grievous sin is branded so repulsively that heaven, the home of God's friends, could not harbor him.

In heaven all is love, because God is love. Only those who love God in life can be His lovers in eternity. Now this love of God required of us here is not a sentimental or emotional love, but a love shown by service. Christ says: "If you love Me keep My commandments." Words or sentiments avail nothing if deeds do not attest love.

Christ was not content with declaring His love for us. He lived it. And if we love Him we must show it by our lives. "Not he who says Lord, Lord, shall enter the kingdom of heaven, but he who doth the will of My Father."

Service, therefore, becomes the test and measure of our love of God. Unless we manifest our love of God by keeping His commandments, the rest does not count. Sentiment and emotion are the outcome of fervid natures. The love of God must be shown by our will to do His will. No one can say he loves another if he opposes the will of that other.

A sinner is one who opposes God's will. A sinner is one who defies God's authority. A sinner is one who refuses to be subject to God. Hell means that one terminating one's life as a rebel to God cannot be friends with God in His eternal kingdom. After this life there are but two permanent abodes, either heaven with God, or hell away from God. Man must choose his eternal abode while he lives. God does everything to induce man to choose the path of the commandments which leads to eternal blessedness. But if man prefer to be a law to himself, and take the broad road that leads to destruction, God will let him have his way, for God made man free.

It will thus be seen that God sends no man to hell. On the contrary He warns the sinner against hell, He shows him whither the path of sin leads, and by appeals to conscience and by His grace poured out in the sacraments, endeavors to change the sinner from his evil and dreadful course.

But if God's warnings and love are spurned, the sinner goes inevitably to his eternal ruin. Instead, therefore, of questioning God's goodness with regard to hell, we should rather be astonished at man's temerity in taking the path that leads to hell. God distinctly proclaims that if His love be rejected the one who rejects it will be in turn rejected. What rashness in man to presume that God can be trifled with! Do we fancy that because God is love that He is a weakling? That He will submit to have His authority and dignity set at naught? Because a sinner is not physically forced to do God's will, does it mean that he can mock God?

For a sinner is a mocker of God. A sinner snaps his fingers in God's face, defying Him. That is the meaning of mortal sin. It is a deliberate transgression of God's law in a serious matter. A man who dies in the state of deliberate transgression against God's law is not qualified to receive welcome into God's kingdom.

But some may say God is too good to punish everlastingly. Is God too good to be true? If He distinctly declares that the sinner goes to everlasting punishment do we honor God by refusing to believe Him? Why be so solicitous for God's goodness and not solicitous for His truthfulness?

It all comes to a question of fact, did or did not Christ proclaim the doctrine of hell? If He did He is to be believed. If the doctrine is dreadful, it is for us to dread sin, which leads to hell. Now Christ proclaimed over and over again, in the clearest and most emphatic manner, that the punishment of him who dies an unrepentant sinner is hell.

If we do not believe Christ let us put Him down as an impostor and reject Him. But no one can logically believe in Christ and hesitate to believe in hell. Both fall or stand together. If hell is a false doctrine Christ is a false teacher. And if Christ be false Christianity is a fraud. Let us be done with this matter of sitting in judgment on God, saying what we shall believe and what we shall not believe.

Revelation must be accepted whole and entire as God's truth, or rejected whole and entire as a fabrication. If one single truth of revelation be false all the Christian religion is false. A religion from God cannot be partly true and partly false. Our sentiments are not to be the standard of judging God. If we went by sentiment, we should deny the compatibility of the Crucifixion with God's love for His Son. If we went by sentiment we should judge that world calamities are inconsistent with a good God.

We know God is good—He gave us our mothers—He gives us the power to become His children for all eternity in heaven. We know He is good—and yet how explain wars and pestilences and earthquakes and widows and orphans? We simply cannot sit in judgment on God. God does not ask us to understand Him, but to obey Him. We shall understand God hereafter if we do His will here. God wants our love here and wants it shown by service, not by sentiment. It is all nonsense to enthuse over God's goodness and then turn around and presume on His goodness to insult Him. Every deliberate grievous sin is an insult to God. It is equivalently saying to God, "I defy You." We are not brave enough to say that in words, but sin says it in action.

Some may say that sin is not so serious as all that. Well, God is the Judge, and He says it is. After all, it is God's judgment in the matter that counts. Our Lord said, "What does it profit a man to gain the whole world and suffer the loss of his soul?" The world is quite a considerable thing, yet put in one arm of the balance and the soul in the other, the soul outweighs the world, in Christ's judgment. Sin destroys the soul. The martyrs were not mistaken. They lost their lives in torture rather than sin. The Apostles were not mistaken. All of them suffered direst torments in the fulfilment of their mission.

When we recall what sin is it should alarm us. If a soldier should deliberately violate the orders of his commander-in-chief in a serious matter, he would know what to expect if detected. God is the Ruler of mankind. His orders are the commandments. No one who violates the commands is undetected. Every sin is committed in God's presence. Because God is so good as not to punish on the spot does not mean that He is the less offended, but that His patience and mercy are almost without limit to mankind. It is because God is so good that frequently the sinner is so bad. But just because God is so good He is also so dreadful when His patience and goodness are abused.

However, when all is said, hell remains, more or less, a mystery. It is an awful thing, eternal punishment. To understand hell we should have to understand the infinite majesty of God. Eternal punishment is an awful thing. It is also an awful thing to despise the majesty of the Infinite God. And that is what sin does. It is only those who die unrepentant who go to hell. Let me make this clear, for a right understanding of this point is important in this consideration.

First of all a sin must be mortal to deserve hell. A mortal sin is a deliberate violation of God's law in a serious matter. Minor or venial sins do not consign a sinner to hell. Purgatory is a temporary cleansing place for minor transgressions, for nothing defiled can enter heaven. A mortal sin is a serious matter. It means a deliberate doing of something which is known to be seriously forbidden by God. Two things enter necessarily into a mortal sin, knowledge that the thing is grievously wrong, and deliberation in doing the wrong thing. If either of these factors be missing there is no mortal sin.

It will thus be seen that hell is not a trap for the unwary, but a terminal whose path is labelled, a path by which no one can travel without knowing its awful destination. Besides this a sinner is free to turn aside from this path whenever he wills to. If, therefore, a man wills to go along this path to destruction in spite of God's clear warning it is not because God is not good but because the sinner is bad.

Up to the last moment of life the sinner is free to turn from the evil path. But God, who has promised forgiveness to the repentant sinner, has not promised him his own time for repentance. The road of sin may terminate any moment without warning. A sinner may mock or defy God, and God may put up with him for long or short but if, when the angel of death summons him to judgment, he is in mortal sin he is in hell.

No sin is too great for God's mercy, nor are any number of sins too many for His forgiveness. But if the sinner go along counting on his own time for conversion or presuming on God's goodness to defy Him, he may find that God's justice will overtake him when he least expects it. This, therefore, must be borne in mind in the consideration of hell, that the sinner has it in his power to turn aside from his doom whenever he wills. Hell is for those who, with open eyes, rebel against the Creator and persist in their rebellion to the end.

Even so, hell is, in a way, a mystery. We believe it not because we understand it, but because God proclaims it. We do not understand the doctrine of the Trinity, yet it is the basis of our faith. We have the same authority for hell that we have for the Trinity. Deny either, and you part company with Christ.

For us it is enough to know that God so detests sin that He banishes forever from His presence the unrepentant sinner. Leprosy is a dreadful thing. We do not understand why a good God permits such an awful scourge to afflict man. But because we do not understand we do not therefore trifle with this dread disease. We avoid it and its proximity. That is what God wants us to do with regard to hell. He wants us to avoid it. He tells us that but one key opens the door to hell, and that no one can turn the key but ourselves. If, therefore, we think that eternal punishment is something terrible, let us keep away from it. We have it in our power to avoid it. Instead of complaining against God's chastisements, let us keep His commandments.

We take precautions against smallpox and cholera. It would do no good to deplore or deny those diseases. That would not prevent our contracting them. If instead of decrying hell we would try to lead good lives we would not be disturbed by the thought of it. Most people who deny hell are doing things which lead to hell. Worldly people scoff at the idea of hell. But look at the morals of these people. Some of our theatres and magazines and amusements are just what should be expected from people who close their eyes to hell. A man might shut out the light at noonday and say it was night. But that would not make it night. A traveler might close his eyes and walk along gaily in spite of warnings that a precipice was ahead, but that would not keep him from falling into it.

There are times when temptation so strongly assails us that the fear of hell is the only thing that can save us from falling. The fear of hell has saved many souls. We should try to serve God from love, but if ever our love grows cold the dread of hell should keep us from offending Him.

If there is no hell what is the significance of the Incarnation and Atonement? If there is no hell the Christian religion is false. But there is a hell. God has said it. Christ died on the cross to keep us out of it. If we are wise we will take measures ourselves to keep out of it. Hell is for those only who turn their backs on God.

"Then He shall say to them also that shall be on His left hand: Depart from Me, you cursed, into everlasting fire which was prepared for the devil and his angels. For I was hungry, and you gave Me not to eat: I was thirsty, and you gave Me not to drink." (Matt. xxv. 41-42.) "If thy hand or thy foot scandalize thee, cut it off, and cast it from thee. It is better for thee to go into life maimed or lame, than having two hands or two feet, to be cast into everlasting fire." (Matt. xviii. 8.)

CHAPTER XXII

THE IMMACULATE CONCEPTION

OUTSIDE the Catholic Church the Immaculate Conception is in great measure misunderstood and consequently assailed. Frequently Catholics themselves, when asked about this dogma by non-Catholics, find that they are not sufficiently informed on it to explain it satisfactorily. Every Catholic knows in a general way what is meant by the Immaculate Conception of the Blessed Virgin, but not every Catholic may know how to make it clear to those without the faith. The Immaculate Conception means that the Virgin Mother of God was an exception to the rest of the human race with regard to original sin. By this is meant that "in the first instant of her conception, by a singular privilege and grace, granted by God, in view of the merits of Jesus Christ, the Saviour of the human race, the Blessed Virgin Mary was preserved exempt from all stain of original sin."

This doctrine has nothing to do with what is termed the Virgin Birth. The Virgin Birth refers to Christ's birth from a Virgin, that is, His birth without a human father. Mary was born of human parents, like the rest of us, but she was not conceived or born in the same condition as we were. We were born in the state of original sin. Mary was not only born without original sin, as was St. John the Baptist, but she was conceived without original sin. John the Baptist was sanctified in his mother's womb. The Blessed Virgin was sanctified always, from the very instant that her soul was created and infused into the body. Original sin was not removed from her soul, as it is removed from others, by baptism; it was excluded, it was never in her soul. This privilege was granted to Mary by a singular exemption from a universal law, through the merits of Christ, by which the others are cleansed from sin by baptism. Mary being the new Eve who was to be the Mother of the new Adam, Christ, was by the eternal wisdom of God and by the merits of Christ exempted from the original law of original sin. Her redemption was the very crown of Christ's redeeming sacrifice. He is a greater redeemer who pays the debt that it may not be incurred than he who pays after it has fallen on the debtor.

The Immaculate Conception, therefore, means that Mary's soul, from the instant of its creation, was sanctified. This means that she was never under the ban of original sin. Now just what do we mean by original sin? Unless we understand what original sin is we shall not have a right understanding of the Immaculate Conception. Adam, the first man, was the beginning or origin of the human race. Every human being is descended from Adam. Original sin derives its name from the fact that it was a sin committed by the origin of the human race. The human race may be compared to a chain which is united link by link to the first link. If the first link becomes weakened or defective the whole chain becomes weakened or defective.

Adam, as the head of the human race, besides being a perfect man, was over and above endowed with special gifts or favors to which human nature of itself was not entitled. Chief of these supernatural endowments was sanctifying grace, by which man was so beautified and elevated that he found favor in the sight of the Trinity, and was raised up to the dignity of child of God, and heir to heaven. Adam by his sin lost sanctifying grace and with it the supernatural favors accompanying it. By losing sanctifying grace he lost God's friendship, and moreover, incurred God's displeasure. Since sanctifying grace made him a child of God and an heir to heaven, he lost both of these supernatural endowments when he lost sanctifying grace. If a monarch should richly endow one of his subjects, and raise him to the dignity of prince and then find him plotting against the throne, and guilty of treason, and should punish him by depriving him of princely dignity and royal favor and the possessions bestowed on him, all the family and descendants of this traitor would suffer the loss he incurred. It was so with Adam and his descendants. Having lost sanctifying grace, and with it God's favor, and adoption into the heavenly family, Adam, like a disinherited subject, incurred wrath and punishment for his offense.

and by his fall brought on his descendants that consequence which we call original sin. Original sin is, therefore, that state in which we are born disinherited from God's favor and the title to children of God and heirs of heaven. This sin of Adam was actual. In us it is not actual, but an inherited condition. Unless this condition or state of sin is removed from us we cannot regain our lost inheritance. It was to enable us to regain our inheritance as children of God that Christ became man.

By redemption Christ puts it into the power of Adam's descendants to say with St. John, "Behold what manner of charity the Father hath bestowed upon us, that we should be called and should be the sons of God." To this St. Paul adds: "And if sons, heirs also; heirs indeed of God, and joint heirs with Christ." If, therefore, original sin is our inheritance by descent from Adam, Christ, the second Adam, puts it into our power to regain the supernatural endowments which Adam as head of the human family lost. Original sin should always be viewed in association with the redemption. By the redemption the descendants of Adam may rehabilitate themselves with the grace of God and the title of children of the heavenly Father.

The meaning, therefore, of the Immaculate Conception is that by the special design of God, and by the merits of Christ, the human being who was to be the Mother of the Redeemer was exempt from the state of sin which was the lot of the children of a sinful parent. Sin was not in the original plan of God. Man was made after the image and likeness of the Creator, and was pleasing in His sight. If man had not sinned he would, in God's own time, have shared the life of God in heaven forever. In God's plan every human being was to be conceived and born as was Mary, immaculate. Sin changed that benevolent design of God. However, not with regard to Mary, who was to be the Mother of the Redeemer, Jesus Christ the Son of God. Our Lord was the only being who could choose His own Mother and have her to be what He wished her to be. If we had the choosing and fashioning of our mother we should certainly see to it that she was all that love could make her.

God, infinite wisdom and power, and loving His Mother more than we love ours, saw to it that she was at least as favored as

Eve, who was immaculate before the fall. It was because God had so wonderfully honored her that Mary exclaimed in the inspired *Magnificat*, "He that is mighty hath done great things to me." The Immaculate Conception was one of the great things which He that was mighty had done to her. Of course the greatest thing was His selecting her from among all womankind to be His Mother. After conferring on her that honor we should not be surprised at any less favor bestowed upon her. Indeed we should be surprised if His Mother were not immaculate always. Once we understand that Mary is the Mother of God it should amaze us if she were not immaculate in her conception rather than that she was immaculate.

How it is that any one who reverences Christ should expect Him to be born of one who was ever under the ban of sin is indeed hard to understand. He who came to redeem mankind deigned to be born of woman rather than to come among us as a mature man like Adam. He could have assumed human nature in the same creative way that He made all things out of nothing. But He chose to be born of woman and to come among us as one of us. He took His human nature from a human being. He derived His Body and Blood from His Mother Mary. The Body in which He suffered for us, and the Blood which He shed for us came from her. Strange indeed would it have been if the origin of His Humanity, His blessed Mother, had ever been branded with what He came to atone for. The more we realize who her Son was, the more we perceive the necessity of her immaculate conception, if not for her own sake, at least for the sake of Him to whom she gave birth. Mary, it is true, was a creature and her Son the Creator. She was only human, He was divine. No matter how holy she was or how exalted, she was infinitely inferior to Him. But because He was God, all powerful and omniscient, He made His Mother the masterpiece of creation. It was possible for Him to have Mary conceived, as Eve was created, immaculate. Can we believe that He wished His own Mother to be inferior to the mother of man? Can we believe that He permitted her, from whom He derived His human nature, to be tainted by even the slightest stain? Even if the Immaculate Conception were not a dogma of faith, we should nevertheless expect it to be a truth of our divine religion. For in the very beginning, when God promised a Redeemer to our first parents He said to Satan, "I will put enmity between thee and the woman and her seed; she shall crush thy head and thou shalt lie in wait for her heel." The conqueror from the seed of the woman who should crush the serpent's head is Christ, the woman at enmity with the serpent is Mary.

God puts enmity between her and Satan in the same manner and measure as there is enmity between Christ and the serpent. Mary was ever to be in that exalted state of soul which the serpent had destroyed in man, that is in sanctifying grace. Hence it was that the angel of the Incarnation saluted her as "full of grace." The Church of God employs this same expression in that wonderful prayer the "Hail Mary." This prayer begins with the Angel Gabriel's message from the Blessed Trinity to the Holy Virgin of Nazareth: "Hail (Mary) full of grace, the Lord is with thee; blessed art thou among women." To these words from heaven are added the inspired words of St. Elizabeth, the mother of St. John the Baptist: "blessed is the fruit of thy womb (Jesus)." The whole first part of the Hail Mary is therefore from heaven: "Hail, Mary, full of grace, the Lord is with thee; blessed art thou among women, and blessed is the fruit of thy womb, Jesus!"

In his salutation the angel declares Mary "blessed among women," singling her out, as it were, from all others. When thus addressed she was not yet the Mother of God, nevertheless she was proclaimed "blessed among women." She was blessed because she, of all women, was never out of favor with God. But although Mary was blessed among women she was, notwithstanding, only a woman. She was one of God's creatures. She owes her life and all her blessedness to God. She was born, as we are, from a human father and mother. She was not divine in any sense. She owes her salvation to Jesus just as much as we do. It was in virtue of His redemption that she was conceived immaculate. But although she owes her salvation and immaculate conception to our Saviour she is withal His Mother, and, with the exception of her divine Son, the most exalted being of all creation, and the closest to divinity that it is possible for a created being to be. In honoring Mary we are honoring her whom God honored. He sets us the example. He chose her for His Mother. In honoring her we are honoring Him, because all her glory and prerogatives are from Him. In honoring a masterpiece of an artist we honor the artist. Mary is God's masterpiece. We worship God alone. We honor His saints, Mary is first among the saints. Next to God we love and honor her.

We adore God, we venerate His Mother, we pray to Mary, not as we do to God, but as we do to the saints. Her power is only that of interceding with her Son. But can we doubt her power when we know His love for her? And because He desires us to honor her He grants through her what He might not otherwise bestow. Hence it is that we go to her. Saints pray to her that they may become holier. Sinners pray to her that they may break from sin. She is the Mother of God. She is also our Mother, given us to replace Eve. With reverence and love, therefore, we go to her and pray: "Hail Mary, full of grace, the Lord is with thee; blessed art thou among women, and blessed is the fruit of thy womb, Jesus. Holy Mary, Mother of God, pray for us sinners, now, and at the hour of our death. Amen."

CHAPTER XXIII

MARRIAGE

PERHAPS there is nothing about the Catholic Church which causes more inquiry than her position with regard to marriage and divorce. It is a subject which comes up constantly wherever people discuss social questions. Moreover, in a country like ours, where people of every religion and of no religion live side by side and frequently form intimate friendships, which may result in marriage, it is a matter which concerns us intimately.

Sometimes we hear of a so-called Catholic divorce and wonder how it can be, since the Catholic Church never grants a divorce to her children where there has been a consummated valid marriage. Again we may read of a divorced non-Catholic marrying a Catholic, and we are at a loss to understand how this squares with the Catholic doctrine that divorce with right to re-marry is not allowed among Christians. And so of other things pertaining to marriage and divorce.

Let me preface my treatment of the subject by stating first, that the position of the Catholic Church with regard to marriage is precisely what God has ordained, as we shall see. In the second place, the Church never has, and, moreover, never can, grant a divorce among Christians in case of a consummated valid marriage. Divorce with right to re-marry is altogether different from divorce which grants separation only. When we say that the Church cannot grant a divorce in case of a consummated valid marriage, we mean divorce with right to re-marry.

There are three things to keep in mind in this matter: first, that marriage among Christians is a divine institution, the nature of which has been expressly declared by Christ Himself; secondly, that marriage means a valid and consummated marriage; and thirdly, that divorce means not separation only, but separation with right to marry again. Keeping these points in mind, and also understanding that Christ, after instituting the Sacrament of Matrimony and declaring marriage to be indissoluble, left to His Church the regulation and formalities of the marriage ceremony, we are in a position to have a correct idea on this important matter, and to be able to inform others when occasion requires.

Catholic means universal. The Church of Christ is the only universal Church. That is why it is called Catholic. It is the only Church in the world which has corporate existence in every nation and every part of the world. Catholics everywhere are under one Supreme Head, the representative of Christ on earth, the Sovereign Pontiff, known as the Pope. The Church, being universal, legislates for all mankind. National churches and those of local or temporary character have to consider only a certain class of people. The universal Church has to consider human nature universally.

Legislation regards the welfare of the many. Every law entails hardship on some individual, but makes for the peace and security of the multitude. This must be kept in mind in considering the Church's legislation on matrimony. Take, for instance, the law about automobile speeding in our cities. It protects the great body of the people, but at times causes inconvenience and serious loss to the individual. Every law looks to the general welfare, and puts society as a body above the individual.

Marriage is the most vital factor of social existence. A nation or people will not be better than its marriage status. Christ, who knew human nature best of all, for He was its author, considered marriage so important that He raised it to the dignity of a sacrament. He made it an especially holy thing, realizing that Christian marriage called for virtue in order to fulfil its duties and abide by its consequences. Marriage is easily the most important contract into which a man may enter. If you buy a piece of property or an interest in a business, you are careful to comply with all the legal requirements. But property or business may be disposed of at will. A family cannot be bartered or abandoned. A family is the ordinary outcome of marriage, and the universal Church in legislating for marriage has in view its ordinary, not its exceptional, nature.

We have then, the universal Church legislating for mankind as a whole on the most vital contract that affects the individual and society. All this must be kept in mind in the consideration of this subject. Also we must bear in mind that the Catholic Church is the official mouthpiece of God. God, in dealing with us, has in view not merely our welfare here, but especially hereafter. Moreover, life is not the end of man, but the way to the end. Furthermore, and this needs to be particularly kept in mind, God's commandments, all of them, oblige us to their observance regardless of inconvenience or loss to ourselves.

For instance, the commandment not to steal obliges the poor man as well as the rich. A man by stealing might procure comfort for himself and his family, or be spared great hardship, but he is not allowed to steal. By stealing, he might be able to educate his children, but they must go without education rather than get it as the result of dishonesty. And so on. Therefore to plead hardship as a reason against a law is to do away with all law. All our civil laws cause hardship to individuals at times. No one brought before a judge for theft would think of pleading the hardships of poverty as a defense for violating the law.

They, therefore, who oppose God's laws on marriage on the ground of hardship, or other such reasons, are acting in a way which would not be tolerated by any court of law. I am saying this because there is so much flippant talk nowadays on the most sacred contract that may bind mankind. A proof that the Catholic Church is divine is that it is the only Church which upholds marriage as instituted by Jesus Christ. All the others have made concessions more or less to the pressure of passion or advantage.

For sixteen centuries there was no such thing as divorce among Christians. The first divorce granted was by Martin Luther. And that tiny trickle has resulted in a flood which now threatens society. The Catholic Church could have retained England in her fold had she been willing to grant Henry VIII. a divorce. But she could no more do it than she could grant him permission to murder.

Unless the Catholic Church were divine, she could not maintain her position with regard to marriage in face of the demands of a clamoring world. But because she is God's representative on earth, she will always teach what He taught, and do what He commanded her to do. I have said this much in order to make plain and reasonable what I am to state on marriage as a sacrament instituted by Jesus Christ and entrusted to His Church for its administration.

A consummated valid marriage among Christians is indissoluble. No power on earth can dissolve such a marriage. No Catholic may marry a divorced person whose partner of a valid Christian marriage is living. This is the legislation of Jesus Christ, not of any man nor of any human institution. The Catholic Church does no more than carry out Christ's commission. One may defy the Church and her laws, but in doing so one is defying Christ. People have said to me that if the Church would open her doors a little wider with regard to marriage, many more would enter. But God does not want any one to enter except in His way, and that was fixed long ago, and the Church could not change it if the whole world would enter. The nature of marriage was stated by Christ Himself. Find fault with Him, but not with His Church for being faithful to Him.

No legislation was ever more explicit than Christ's on marriage. Let us hear Him: "What, therefore, God hath joined together let not man put asunder" (Mark x. 9). Again, "His disciples asked Him concerning the same thing, and He saith to them: Whosoever shall put away his wife and marry another, committeth adultery against her. And if the wife shall put away her husband, and be married to another, she committeth adultery" (Mark x. 9-12). That is about as plain as it can be put. Again Christ said: "Everyone that putteth away his wife and marrieth another committeth adultery; and he that marrieth her that is put away from her husband committeth adultery" (Luke xvi. 18). It would be impossible to word legislation more unequivocally than that.

From the viewpoint of this clear declaration, every other reference to marriage must be interpreted. It is legal procedure to interpret an obscure or less clear statement by the light of a clear, specific and unequivocal statement. Hence St. Paul, who certainly knew the mind of Christ in the matter, spoke as follows on this subject. It was an important issue in the very infancy of the Church. "But to them that are married, not I, but the Lord commandeth, that the wife depart not from her husband" (1 Cor. vii. 10). "A woman is bound by the law as long as her husband liveth, but if her husband die, she is at liberty" (1 Cor. viii. 39). "For the woman that hath an husband, whilst her husband liveth is bound to the law. But if her husband be dead, she is loosed from the law of her husband. Therefore whilst her husband liveth, she shall be called an adulteress if she be with another man" (Rom. vii. 2-3). That was the way St. Paul the Apostle regarded divorce followed by re-marriage. If the Apostles were wrong in this matter, the Church was wrong, and if the Church was wrong, Christ's guarantee was false, and consequently, both He and His religion should be rejected.

However, some contend that the following words of Christ give authorization of divorce and re-marriage on the ground specified: "And I say to you that whosoever shall put away his wife, except it be for fornication, and shall marry another, committeth adultery" (Matt. xix. 9). This statement was in answer to the Pharisees' question: "Is it lawful for a man to put away his wife for every cause?" The Gospel says that they asked him this question tempting Him. The Jews had multiplied the reasons for putting away one's wife. The Pharisees asked if it was lawful to do so for all these reasons. The putting away of one's wife had gotten to be a crying abuse. It was against this abuse that Christ spoke, saying that a man should not put away his wife for every cause, but for fornication only. That answered their question. The words "except for fornication" refer to putting away one's wife. They do not give justification for re-marriage. Christ was not speaking of a man putting away his wife to marry another, which He had already expressly forbidden: "Whosoever shall put away his wife and marry another, committeth adultery against her. And if the wife shall put away her husband, and be married to another, she committeth adultery" (Mark x. 11-12).

In view of Christ's absolute condemnation of re-marriage after separation, the passage in question can have but one meaning. It was the answer to the Pharisees' question which referred to separation only. St. Paul so understood it and so proclaimed it. The Catholic Church has always so understood it. It was so understood by all Christians for fifteen hundred years, until the so-called Reformers reformed the doctrine of Christ Himself and granted the first divorce with re-marriage. Let it be said once for all that if the Church of Christ was wrong in this matter, the Christian religion collapses, for its basis is the guarantee of Christ that it should never teach error.

This much has been said in order to lay a foundation for what follows regarding marriage and divorce. If the Catholic doctrine on this matter were given without the foregoing explanation, it might seem arbitrary or debatable. After what has been said, we know that the Church's legislation on marriage is Christ's. Details of ceremony and other incidental things pertaining to the marriage rite, Christ left to His Church, divinely guided, but the essential nature of marriage as a sacrament is just what Christ proclaimed. With this clear understanding we now approach some questions which arise concerning marriage.

Just as the State legislates how a contract shall be drawn up to be valid, so the Church specifies what constitutes a valid marriage, for marriage is a contract. If a man sign a civil contract fraudulently, the courts decide, not to break the contract, but that it was not a contract at all, because a contract that is not valid is no contract. If one sign a civil contract as a minor, under threat of violence, or through essential fraud, or against existing laws, the contract is null and void.

So with marriage. The Church declares beforehand what constitutes the valid marriage contract. If a marriage be performed without complying with the specified conditions, the Church does not recognize the marriage. The Church in such cases does not undo a marriage, but states that there was no marriage. Whenever, therefore, you hear of a Catholic marriage being set aside, it means that in that case there was no marriage from the beginning. Whenever you hear of a Catholic marrying a divorced person, it means that the party divorced previously was not a Christian or else not rightly married. Even the Pope himself could not annul, with right to re-marry, a valid and consummated marriage. He could not do it for his dearest friend, not for a member of his own family, nor to save a whole nation. So much for the indissolubility of marriage. The nullity of some Catholic marriages has been declared, but always because they were not validly performed. It can be said definitely and explicitly that there is no such thing as divorce and re-marriage in the Catholic Church. The Church stands on that ground.

In another chapter I shall give some interesting and instructive information on what constitutes a valid and consummated marriage, and on the reasons why presumed marriages are declared null and void, thus permitting re-marriage to the parties. I shall also explain the Pauline privilege, which constitutes the only exception for the re-marriage of non-Christians to Christians. This chapter has laid the foundation on which Christian marriage rests.

It has been made evident, I trust, that Christian marriage is Christ's own institution, that His Church is simply carrying out His mind in the matter, and that as long as the world lasts she will not change her position with regard to it, because she cannot misrepresent Him. None but a divine Church could be so firm in a matter where weak human nature is concerned. Every other Church but Christ's yields to human passion and weakness. She, like Him, is the light of the world. She, like Him, holds up to mankind the right standard of living. She, like Him, will be opposed because of the truths she teaches. Men would have proclaimed Him the Messias had He agreed with them and given them what they wanted. But He came to make known God's will to mankind, knowing that it was by doing God's will, not our own, that we may become partakers of the divine nature.

The mistake which many make nowadays is to maintain that man is supreme and owes no allegiance or submission to any one above. But man is a creature. The Creator who made him is his Sovereign. Man owes his Sovereign respect and submission, which are shown by keeping His commandments. If a man owes submission to civil government, much more does he owe it to the King of kings and to the Lord of all creation. For man, therefore, to make his own marriage code after God has once proclaimed it, is to take the law into his own hands. No government would allow that.

Much less will God allow it. Catholics firmly believe that God speaks by His Church. That is why they respect and reverence and obey her. Her position on marriage is God's. In the final reckoning, it is God's standard, not man's, that matters.

CHAPTER XXIV

THE CHURCH AND DIVORCE

IT is a matter of gratification to Catholics to observe that many who are not of the Catholic faith are beginning to recognize that her position on marriage and divorce is the only right one.

Recently a Protestant organization has been formed in order to stem the tide of evil resulting from the moral cancer of divorce. The New York Times, July 6, 1925, published the following news item:

"The Sanctity of Marriage Association launched a movement yesterday to bar absolutely the marriage of divorced persons in the Protestant Episcopal Church. The Sanctity of Marriage Association is headed by the Rev. Dr. Milo H. Gates, vicar of the Chapel of the Intercession, Trinity Parish, and its Executive Committee includes, among others, Bishop William T. Manning, Bishop Frederick Burgess of Long Island and Bishop Paul Matthews of New Jersey.

"The proposed law is:

"No minister, knowingly after due inquiry, shall solemnize the marriage of any person who has been or is the husband or the wife of any person living from whom he or she has been divorced for any cause arising after marriage. Nor shall it be lawful for any member of this Church to enter upon a marriage when either of the contracting parties is the husband or the wife of any other person then living from whom he or she has been divorced for any cause arising after marriage.

"The association gives the following reasons why in its judgment the one 'exception' should be repealed:

"Because nowhere in the New Testament is there a single word in support of re-marriage of either party after 'putting away' during the lifetime of the other. Because nowhere either in the Old or the New Testament is there any assumption, much less assertion, of the modern theory that adultery, or any other sin, ipso facto, dissolves a marriage, which is not a mere contract but a state or condition. Because nowhere in the history of the first three centuries, when the Church was suffering persecution and was free from all entanglements with the State, can there be found a single author who interprets the exceptive clauses of St. Matthew about 'putting away' as reason for re-marriage during the life of the other party. Because nowhere since the fourth century, in the whole Western Church, down to the year 1868 was there any canonical allowance for the re-marriage of the so-called 'innocent party.' Because, in accordance with our Lord's pragmatic test, 'by their fruits ye shall know them,' the census reports for the United States, with their forty-eight codes and fifty-two causes for sundering the bond, show the most rapid increase of divorces of any country, pagan or Christian, in the world."

Such a statement, coming from a non-Catholic source, should certainly make Catholics realize the glory of their unchanging creed. Truth never changes. Only error has to rectify itself. What Christ taught was truth and will never change.

In our last chapter the Church's position on marriage was stated. We saw that Christ Himself declared that the marriage bond held until death severed it. The Church's position, let it be repeated, is just what Christ made it. The Church can no more change her teaching in marriage than can the Supreme Court of the United States, as now constituted, change the Constitution. In other words it is divine not human legislation that constitutes the Church's attitude with regard to matrimony. With this recapitulation we now consider the subject of divorce.

It is a matter of experience that some Catholics who have been married have had the marriage set aside and have re-married. How explain this in view of the Catholic doctrine of the indissolubility of marriage?

To understand this we need to know just what constitutes a marriage. It may be said at the outset that among Christians no consummated valid marriage has ever been annulled, and never can be annulled.

It is a question, therefore, of whether or not the marriage was a consummated valid marriage. What constitutes a valid marriage? Christ recalled and declared the nature of marriage, but left to His Church everything else pertaining to it. Government does something similar with regard to its decrees. Congress makes the laws, but leaves to the various representatives of government the application of the laws. The Church, God's representative on earth, proclaims that Christian marriage, by the ordination of God, is a contract which can never be broken until death intervenes. So much for the nature of marriage.

The Church then decrees how this marriage contract is to be executed. If one makes a civil contract, and it is not done legally, it is null and void before the law. The Church decrees beforehand how the marriage contract must be made, and that only persons who are marriageable may become parties to the contract. She states beforehand the form of the marriage ceremony, and the class of people who are marriageable, and declares solemnly that any contract in violation of these decrees is not a valid marriage.

This power of legislating on the formalities of the marriage ceremony was given to the Church by Christ Himself: "Whatsoever you shall bind on earth shall be bound in heaven." Whenever, therefore, you hear of Catholics having their marriage set aside and re-marrying, you will know that there was, in the case in question, no valid previous marriage. Whenever you hear of a Catholic marrying a divorced non-Catholic, you will know that the previous marriage of the non-Catholic was not valid, or that the Pauline privilege was invoked.

Some marriages are evidently invalid. Others are invalid by reason of the violation of conditions established by the Church. For instance—and this has happened—suppose a family gets separated and that after some years a brother meets his sister, not knowing she is his sister. He falls in love with her, and marries her. It is no marriage. Of course, if both parties are in ignorance of their relationship, there is no fault on either side. If, however, either party should learn of the relationship, and continue in the marriage, it would be sinful. Both parties to such a union, on learning their relationship, would be obliged to separate and would be free to marry others of their choice.

It is a matter of experience that marriage among near relatives results most frequently in abnormal or defective families. The Church, being a solicitous mother, has concern for the physical as well as spiritual well-being of her children. She proclaims beforehand that a marriage between those of specified nearness of relationship is no marriage.

If, after the Church's decree that a person is not marriageable, the person proceeds with the marriage contract, it is no marriage at all. The Church regards the parties to it as single. They may go on living in marriage, but they are in the state of mortal sin until they separate. Catholics may defy the Church. They may also defy God. But defiance of authority does not make wrong right.

Another reason which makes a marriage null and void is the physical inability of either party to carry out the nature of the contract. If either party is physically unable to discharge the function which may constitute parenthood the marriage fails in one of its fundamental factors and may be set aside, permitting the party capable of parenthood to re-marry.

Again, the Church has decreed that a Catholic must not be married to a non-baptized person. In certain cases, for good and sufficient cause, the Church may grant an exception. But always the case must be presented to her and unless she grants a dispensation for the marriage, it is null and void.

A contract must be entered into freely. If force or fear be employed in a civil contract, it is null. Under intimidation a person may do almost anything. The Church decrees that both parties to the marriage contract must be free. If it can be established that the marriage was forced by violence or unlawful threats, it is no marriage.

I have specified some of the things which invalidate the marriage contract. What I want to make clear is that marriage is a contract, that God has stated its indissoluble nature, that the conditions for making the contract rest with the Church, that failure to comply with those lawful conditions vitiates the contract, rendering the marriage null and void.

Whenever, therefore, you hear of a so-called Catholic divorce, you will know that it is no divorce at all, but a declaration that there was no marriage from the beginning. Persons who have their marriage set aside may have very good reasons for not letting the public know why it was done. The Church never informs the public except the case be public, and the reasons for the divorce have been made known by the parties to the divorce. So much for a valid marriage.

What constitutes a consummated marriage? A marriage is consummated when it has been followed by that sexual relationship whose natural outcome is parenthood. In other words, the verbal contract has been ratified by deed. A valid Christian marriage, thus confirmed, cannot be nullified by any power on earth.

Sometimes we hear of a marriage being set aside by reason of the Pauline privilege. Now what do we mean by the Pauline privilege? It is so called from the Apostle St. Paul, who first enunciated it. Marriage by nature's law is indissoluble. Only God, the Author of nature, may make an exception. An exception has been made by Him through the Apostle. St. Paul, divinely directed, proclaimed that a convert to the Christian faith was not obliged to live, in marriage, with a pagan or non-Christian person, if the non-Christian party was a menace to the faith. If the non-Christian husband or wife be willing to live in peace with the Christian, well and good, the marriage is indissoluble. But if the non-Christian refuses to abide with the Christian without detriment to the faith, the Christian party may depart and re-marry. This is the only exception to the indissolubility of marriage. It is an exception made by divine authority.

In order to make use of it, one must comply very exactly with the conditions specified, and have, moreover, the official authorization of the Church. The non-Christian party in this case has it in his own power to continue the marriage union, as all he or she has to do is to agree not to molest the Christian party in the lawful practice of religion. With this single exception, divinely authorized, no consummated valid marriage may be dissolved with right to re-marry.

Altogether there are some twelve reasons for the declaration of the nullity of a Christian marriage. I have specified some of them. Others are immature age, marriage without witnesses, marriage without the presence of a priest, marriage to one in Holy Orders, marriage to one consecrated to God by solemn vow, marriage to one's god-parents, that is to sponsors at baptism, marriage between persons who, in order to marry, have murdered husband or wife, marriage between those of whom one has been taken by violence or intrigue and put into the power of the other. Any marriage under the conditions enumerated is no marriage at all.

The civil government specifies what constitutes a valid contract, so does the Church. The civil government does not make a contract valid. A contract is binding by natural law, but the civil government lays down the conditions that make a contract valid.

Marriage by nature's law is indissoluble. The Church merely specifies what constitutes a marriage. Once the marriage has been performed in accordance with the legislation of the Church, and has been consummated, there is no power on earth which can dissolve it. The Church's position, therefore, with regard to marriage is that by nature's law it is indissoluble. A Christian consummated marriage is absolutely indissoluble. Marriage among pagans or among non-Christians is also indissoluble by natural law, to which there is the one exception, by divine authorization, namely the Pauline privilege.

Having stated the nature of marriage, as God ordained it, we may profitably make some observations on marriage and some of its more salient aspects. In the first place, marriage is the most important contract that man or woman can make. Marriage is the most essential factor in the welfare of society. Because it is so essential to society, nothing that may safeguard it should be disregarded. Civil governments have recognized this in all ages of the world. Any compromise with the sacredness and stability of the marriage bond has resulted disastrously to people and to government.

The family is the foundational unit of the state. If this union be weakened, the state will fall, and crush in its fall those whom it should protect. With regard to the family itself, the loosening of the marriage tie results in evils which eventually far outweigh the hardships which may be alleged for severing the bond. Let us look at the matter calmly and without prejudice.

When a man and woman marry, they enter into a contract. The consequence of this contract is, ordinarily, a family. Children are not like furniture, nor like instinct-guided animals. Children, up to the age of maturity, require careful guidance and supervision.

If death remove father or mother, that is God's affair. But if man deprives children of father or mother, it is a terrible responsibility. If the marriage tie is dissolved, it means that either father or mother is virtually lost to children.

In business contracts, in government contracts, in army enlistment, and in every other civil matter, the parties to a contract are held to it, regardless of hardship or disillusionment. A clerk in a store does not always find things congenial or satisfactory, but nevertheless continues at work. And that for a few dollars a week. The manager or floor-walker or patrons may not be at all compatible, but the clerk does not for that reason give up his position. Children are more than dollars. A young man may enlist in the army or navy and find, after he has signed, that his companions or superior officers or the work is not compatible. But he is held to his enlistment nevertheless.

The marriage bond is more binding than enlistment.

A builder may contract for a piece of work and find unexpected hardship in carrying it out, but that does not free him from the contract. He might have to deal with uncongenial people and put up with all sorts of embarrassments and difficulties, but he surmounts them. If he knew that he could break the contract and make another, his difficulties might seem unsurmountable, but because he knows the contract binds, he meets and overcomes obstacles.

It is so with marriage. Before this modern leprosy of divorce became prevalent, people had their difficulties in married life just as they have now. But because divorce was unheard of, they made up their differences and lived on if not happily at least satisfactorily. Let us be reasonable in this matter and regard it with the same common sense we do other things.

Some people think that marriage opens a career of perpetual

honeymoon. They forget that love is a powerful emotion and that emotion is something transient. After the emotion of love subsides, husband and wife become normal and see each other as they are, not as love, which is blind, pictured each to the other.

A young couple may fancy that their marriage is going to be something different from what they have seen of married life in their own home. In their own home the family group was just human. Father and mother, brother and sister, each had their own characters, temperaments and defects as well as virtues. Familiarity engenders candor, which in turn manifests itself in plain speech and frank conduct. Every human being is selfish more or less. Selfishness, temperament, and a thousand other things soon enter into the marriage relationship, causing, as we know, friction and sometimes serious disruption. Every family has experienced this more or less.

Now a young couple starting out with the idea that marriage is over a path of roses, soon find that there are many thorns among the roses. If the marriage bond is not permanent these thorns will cause bad blood between husband and wife because with the idea of separation as a remedy the thorn pricks will be magnified into serious wounds. But if the bond may not be severed both man and woman will try to avoid the thorns as much as possible, or if pricked by them make light of them.

For sixteen centuries after Christ human nature was the same as now. Incompatibility was as much a menace then as now. But man and wife realized that Christ had raised marriage to the dignity of a sacrament for the very purpose of conferring grace to surmount incompatibility and all the other -ilities. If it were not tragic it would be laughable to see the reasons assigned for divorce in many cases. If these reasons were assigned for breaking a civil contract, the party would be ridiculed out of court.

In every walk of life, business or professional, we have to put up with continual annoyances. It is the law of life. It cannot be escaped. Life is a warfare, married life included. And yet people will rush to a divorce court because married life has the hardships which every career and department of life abounds in.

When God decreed that marriage was indissoluble, it was because

He, the Author of nature, knew the weakness, the selfishness and fickleness of human nature. In former years people were content and happy with all their marriage ills. Now with divorce as an eliminator of wedded evils people are a thousand times more miserable.

Marriage is a gamble. A second marriage is as much a gamble as the first. Some have tried marriage five or six times, only to find that there were five or six divorces necessary. It is true that there are extreme cases where separation is advisable. But not divorce with re-marriage. Often people, after a separation, enter into themselves and find where they were wrong. They come together again, realizing that each must be considerate of the other, and thus their marriage runs on smoothly.

It cannot be said too plainly that marriage does not change one's nature. What one is before marriage that one will be after marriage. For this reason the Church advises her children to proceed carefully in this matter. Nowadays young people rush into marriage without the consideration that they would exercise in buying a house or an automobile. Then they wonder that they are not suited to each other! They are caught by some superficial or artificial attraction, and without knowing the real person at all take a partner for life. They blame marriage or the Church for what they themselves are responsible.

If one makes an unfortunate contract in business or in any department of civil life, one must stand by it. The Church of God requires the same reverence for the marriage contract.

In conclusion let me sum up.

Marriage, even among pagans, is by nature's law indissoluble. The sole exception is the Pauline privilege. Christ raised marriage to the dignity of a sacrament, which gives grace to fulfil its duties and abide by its consequences. Christians who are true to their religion will receive the grace necessary to meet all the eventualities of married life.

That divorce is not a remedy for married ills is proved by the fact that there were never so many and great ills in marriage as at present, with divorce rampant. Thinking people the world over are in admiration of the Catholic Church for her stand on matrimony. In some individual cases the indissolubility of marriage works hardship. That is a Christian trial, just as death, disease, poverty and other ills. Christ came not to remove the cross but to help us carry it. Married life has its cross as single life has. The sacramental grace gives the strength to Christians who practice their religion, to carry the cross and to win a crown. The happiest families are not those which shirk marriage responsibilities, but those which meet them in the spirit of faith. Nothing so unites a family and makes its members so devoted to one another as the mutual bearing of its hardships, and mutual consideration.

Married life calls for the exercise of virtue as well as does single life. Divorce proclaims that separation and re-marriage must take the place of the Christian virtues of patience and forbearance.

If the history of mankind teaches any lesson unmistakably it is that divorce is the moral cancer of society, of the family and of the individual. After all, man cannot improve on God.

CHAPTER XXV

MARRIAGE AND ANNULMENT

WHEN the Roman-Rota declared that the Marlborough-Vanderbilt marriage was null and void because of coercion, unusual interest and considerable misunderstanding were created.

The marriage ceremony took place some thirty years ago, and was the social event of the year in which it occurred, 1895. What caused so much interest in the matter was that the annulment was declared by an ecclesiastical court of a Church to which neither party to the marriage belonged. Other factors in the case which drew attention to it were the duration of the marriage, over thirty years; the apparent confirmation of the marriage contract by its continuance; the birth of two children, who have now reached maturity; the reunion of the parties after a separation of twelve years, from 1907-1919, and finally the evidence brought out in the divorce proceedings in 1920, which appears to show that the former unwilling party to the original contract had at last given free consent to the union.

We shall take up each of these points and consider them with reference to the annulment. Before doing so, it may be well to define and explain certain terms which refer to the matter.

Annulment is not divorce. Divorce is the dissolution of the marriage bond. Annulment is the declaration that no such bond existed. The Catholic Church in the case of a consummated Christian marriage, has never granted a divorce with right to re-marry. It has declared many annulments of marriages. Every time a civil court sets aside a contract by declaring it null and void, it pronounces an annulment. The civil court does not break a contract by annulling it but simply affirms that the agreement in question was no contract at all.

For a contract to be valid it must first of all be according to natural justice. Any bond which by its nature is unjust cannot be made just by law, whether civil or ecclesiastic. Besides the natural justice which is essential to a contract, there are other things which may enter into it, and which may affect its validity.

The State specifies certain conditions which must be complied with for the legal validity of a contract. Every lawyer is familiar with this phase of the matter. A man may have a just claim to a piece of property, but before he can sell it he must comply with the requirements of the law for the transfer of real estate. These requirements differ in different times and places. If a citizen gets title to a piece of property and the deed of transfer be legally defective, his title is in jeopardy. Marriage is a contract. Christ elevated the Christian marriage contract to the dignity of a sacrament but it remains essentially a contract. By the marriage ceremony the contracting parties mutually dispose of what is of most consequence to each, namely their own persons. The very nature of a contract requires that what one disposes of must be one's own, and that one must be free to dispose of it or to retain it. Many other things may and do enter into the validity of the marriage contract, but if either of these two factors be absent, there can be no contract.

Another point, and this is the most important thing to understand with regard to the Marlborough case. If a person be ignorant of the invalidity of a contract, he cannot take measures to validate it. In order freely to rectify what was not right a person must not be bound. He must be free to do what is necessary to validate what is invalid. But if a person believes himself already bound by a contract he is not free to act. Ignorance of invalidity thus prevents one from validating. A person who regards himself already bound may act altogether differently from what he would do if he knew he was not bound. This must be kept well in mind in the present case. Having premised the above we may now proceed with the main issue.

And in the first place, with regard to the declaration of annulment by the ecclesiastical court of another Church, we wish to say that the parties appealed to the Catholic Church for reasons of their own. The marriage was between two Christians. The Catholic Church when called upon by Christians to settle a matter of conscience is not free to refuse. It is no interference or intrusion on her part when the initiative is taken by Christians of any other denomination whatsoever. If the Catholic Church had regard for her own peace, and for what the general public would think of her in this matter, she would have said to the appellants, in the words of the London Tablet: "Please go away. You are rich and well known people. If we declare your so-called marriage null and void, the Catholic Church will be sneered at, and we shall suffer a set-back in our propagandist activities. We must think of Number One. Good morning."

But because the Catholic Church is governed not by expediency but by principle, she took up what was to her most obnoxious, and in the event gave the decision which she knew would bring down upon her the hostile criticism of those who are ever seeking an occasion to vilify her. One prominent prelate had the effrontery to call her an alien Church, forgetting that what is universal cannot be alien. The Catholic Church alone is universal. The meaning of the word Catholic is universal. The Catholic Church is the only corporate religious society that is universal. Every other religion is national or racial or local. There is but one religion in the world to-day that knows no bounds of race, nationality or locality, and that is the Catholic. To denounce the Church of Christ as alien is to proclaim Christ an alien.

The next point to consider is of more weight, the duration of the union, some thirty odd years. It would seem that this should be a serious reason for the maintenance of the bond and for its validity. But time, of itself, does not rectify what was wrong from the first. Unless the continuance of the union was the consequence of renewal of consent freely given, the element of time is not material. But does not the birth of the children imply free consent? Does not the period of twelve years of cohabitation imply free consent? Does not the reunion after twelve years of separation imply free consent? To this we refer the reader to what we said previously on this very point. Free consent cannot be given if one is ignorant that one is free to give it. A person who does not know that he is not bound by a contract will do many things he would not do if he knew he was not bound. Believing that he is inevitably bound he will unwillingly do what he thinks he must do. That this was the condition of mind in the Marlborough case seems evident from the fact that the situation gradually became unbearable, resulting in separation. The reunion twelve years after the separation may have been for any one of many reasons of policy, none of which would necessarily imply renewal of real marriage life. Finally there are the letters which were given in evidence in the court proceedings of 1920, which, with other evidence, resulted in the granting of a divorce. These letters of 1919 express a desire of reunion on the part of the one who was coerced in the original contract. But unless by reunion the appellant meant conjugal cohabitation, and unless at the time of the writing of the letter, the previously coerced party knew that she was not bound by the original contract, the letter would have no bearing on the matter for the reasons previously stated when we considered the question of free consent. At the basis of the whole matter is the factor of free consent. This free consent requirement is not something which has been devised for the occasion by the Catholic Church, but an element which by the very nature of a contract is essential to it. A lack of free consent would invalidate a marriage even if the Catholic Church never existed. Natural justice and natural law demand that a person be free in executing a contract. In any civilized country, if a person were coerced into signing a civil contract, as Consuelo Vanderbilt was coerced in her marriage contract, the courts would nullify it. Free consent does not and cannot exist if one is ignorant that one is not bound. Evidently the Roman Rota had before it most convincing evidence that Consuelo did not know of the invalidity of her marriage during the years she lived as the Duchess of Marlborough. Perhaps it was only after she had confided the details of her marriage to some Catholic friend, or possibly to her present husband, that her eyes were opened to the fact that she was never really married to the Duke. It may have been that as soon as she realized the status of that deplorable union she took steps to have it declared null and void. Why she appealed for annulment to the Catholic Church rather than to her own is her personal affair. But to the Catholic Church she appealed, and the Catholic Church did not shirk a disagreeable duty. The decision of the English Diocesan Court was confirmed by the Roman Rota, and the case is now closed, unless one of the parties concerned appeals for revision. If new evidence of essential bearing on the case should be forthcoming, or if material testimony of the witnesses should be found false, the case could be appealed. Just as the civil courts of justice have various tribunals of appeal so has the ecclesiastical. In civil procedure there are the common courts, the court of appeals and finally the Supreme Court. The Diocesan Court has given judgment in the Marlborough case, and this judgment has been confirmed by the Roman Tribunal of the Rota. In cases of marriage litigation, the Catholic Church takes for granted that a marriage is valid. The burden of proof for its invalidity rests with the appellant. Consequently the Marlborough-Vanderbilt union was held as valid until positive proof to the contrary was presented. When the case was before the Roman Rota it was in the hands of the most learned and competent body of judges in the whole ecclesiastical world. The Tribunal of the Rota consists of ten members, presided over by a Dean. Every member of it must be a doctor of theology and canon law. All take the oath of fidelity to their office and also the oath of secrecy. These ten members of the Rota are called auditors, because their duty is to hear the case in question and to decide it on the evidence presented. Except in matters of very great importance, the Rota assigns a case to a committee of three of its members. A marriage case is ordinarily a matter for such a commission of three. A majority vote, that is, two out of three, decides a case. If an appeal be made against the decision, the case is assigned to a second commission of three, composed of different members from those which constituted the former body. If the second decision be appealed and the appeal be sustained, the case goes before a third commission of the Rota, consisting of the three remaining members. After this final judgment of the Rota, the case may still further be appealed, to the Pope himself, if circumstances warrant it. The Pope's decision in the matter is final, just as a decision by the United States Supreme Court is final. If the appeal be made to the Pope, he assigns the case to a special commission of Cardinals, and when their findings are presented to him he makes final adjudication.

It may not be uninteresting to give a few particulars of the mode of procedure in cases submitted to the Rota. Each appellant may present his case in person or by an advocate. However, all the testimony must be in writing, and duly attested. No oral information is allowed. Oratory has no place in these deliberations. The door is closed to sentiment and to everything but the facts of the case. After all the evidence is presented the auditors carefully consider the case, each one at his own leisure, and privately. Each auditor in due time gives his decision in writing. They meet for final discussion after they have given their respective decisions, each one being free to change his decision if it seems the right thing to do. The judgment reached is signed by all those who were on the commission. It is doubtful if a more wise or competent tribunal of justice exists in the entire world than the Roman Rota. This was the court that decided the Marlborough case. We may be sure that it had evidence for its verdict. It may or it may not publish to the world all the evidence which was placed before it. It simply stated its verdict and gave the reason for it, coercion. The court is sworn to secrecy. It may well be that the appellants gave testimony in proof of coercion, and in explanation of the continuance of the union, which concerns themselves only, and which the world is not entitled to know. Our civil courts often give sealed verdicts on matters which are not the public's business. Of one thing we may be sure, that the Rota realized that a verdict of annulment in the Marlborough case would raise a storm of criticism by those of other denominations, and also by all those who are ever on the alert to challenge the divine institution of the Catholic Church. We may be sure that the Rota was more skeptical of the evidence in the case than any of the critics who assail her verdict. The evidence must have been positively compulsory to induce the Rota's decision in a matter where those of another creed were concerned, and with regard to persons of the prominence and distinction of the appellants. The Rota knew before giving its decision that the verdict would be misconstrued into a concession to wealth and nobility, that it would be assailed as impertinent interference with another creed, and that demagogues would even misconstrue it into disloyalty to civil authority. But the Church which upheld the marriage bond in the case of England's powerful monarch, did not hesitate to declare that there was no bond of marriage in the case of a distinguished nobleman of that same realm. The Roman Rota, we may rest assured, has decided the case on its merits as presented. If it was falsely presented it was not the fault of the Court but of the appellants. The judgment stands, unless, as in our own civil courts, an appeal be granted for sufficient cause.

It may seem to some people that to annul a marriage because of the absence of free consent is to open the door to laxity. But it must be remembered that the existence of coercion must be proved beyond a shadow of doubt. The testimony of the coerced party must be established by unquestionable corroboration.

In the Marlborough case it is hard to conceive that the witnesses would testify to the facts as given unless they were so. The nature of the testimony was such as to reflect no credit on most of those concerned. It may be objected that this decision opens the way to a flood of annulments, because a person may plead lack of free consent if he desires to break the marriage bond. A designing person may do anything. A person who would deliberately enter upon marriage with intent to make it invalid would not care whether the Church declared the marriage valid or invalid. If one does not reverence Almighty God, when taking an oath, one will not care for the decree of the Church with regard to that oath.

This annulment, far from letting down the bars of Christian marriage, makes stronger than ever the barrier to divorce. The Church which has annulled the marriage bond of Marlborough's invalid marriage suffered the loss of England to the faith rather than break the bond of the valid marriage of her King.

CHAPTER XXVI

MARRIAGE AND SEPARATION

SOME people have the idea that because the Catholic Church is opposed to divorce she obliges married people to live together regardless of any or every obstacle to harmonious companionship. This is not so. It is true, that before the Church advises separation of husband and wife (without, of course, the right to re-marry) she endeavors to have them use every means of removing the obstacle to amicable living.

But there are circumstances in which reconciliation or good-will toward each other, seems altogether hopeless, and where living together means living in hatred, scandal, and sin. In these cases it is advisable to consult a prudent priest and be guided by his judgment.

The Church allows separation as the lesser of two evils. Often, however, when a prudent priest is consulted, he will be able to discover the root of the trouble and by wise counsel and direction remedy the evil.

Most marriage trouble in our day comes about from hasty marriages. Moreover, many of the young people, especially in cities, are altogether unqualified for the duties and exigencies of married life. As young women and young men pass you on the street, and you notice their frivolousness and license you wonder what sort of parents they can become. Young women are almost disguised by artificial devices to beautify themselves, and young men seem to disregard all the proprieties in their association with them.

These are the young folks who are to become husband and wife, father and mother. Is it any wonder that in so many cases marriage, after the first few months, settles down to a condition of mere tolerance? Love seems to have departed. Rather it was really never there. It was just sex attraction of the animal sort, which is fickle and selfish. Hence, after marriage, when familiarity discloses the artifices of courtship, and each knows the other for what she or he is, misunderstandings begin.

If at this period there is not a bond of good-companionship between husband and wife they are in bad case. The very purpose of courtship is to learn if man and woman are companionable. They who are not suited to be good friends cannot be good lovers over a long period. While the passion of love exists, it is easy to see only virtues in each other. Even faults are construed into virtues at times. Hence, after the honeymoon, unless husband and wife are naturally companionable, they will drift apart, or get to actually dislike or even hate each other.

A gentleman once said to me, "Why is it that your Church, being so strict about divorce, is not stricter about people getting married?" I told him that he would never ask that question if he had ever tried to get married to a Catholic. I then showed him that the Church takes such precautions with marriage that some criticize her for making it too difficult. She takes all this care and makes her children take it because marriage is the most consequential contract a human being can make. However, in spite of all her pains and precaution, people do at times make unfortunate marriages.

What is to be done in such cases? Divorce in the real sense is out of the question. But separation is another matter. However, before this is advisable, every means of adjusting differences should be exhausted. It is an historical fact that before the so-called Reformation, Christians everywhere lived together satisfactorily in the married state. They had their ups and downs, their differences, their quarrels, but they also had the realization that marriage was for better or worse until death.

Hence there was no such thing as incompatibility. Incompatibility is a modern matrimonial ailment, due to the fact that it may open the door to a new alliance. When courting, and up to the marriage day, both parties were very compatible. It is true that in the intimate nature of married life, one's defects stand out in a particularly annoying manner. But married life, just as every other career of life, calls for patience and self-restraint. It is the price of peace. In every profession and business people must continually put up with what annoys them or else fail. Christ made matrimony a sacrament for the very reason that husband and wife need grace in order to bear the burdens of wedded life.

One's point of view is a special factor in marriage welfare. If one realizes that marriage is bound to have its trials, as has every walk of life, one will not be surprised or rebellious when they come. But if one fancies that marriage is a lifelong romance, and that the wedding day marks the end of family trouble, one will surely get a sad awakening from this pleasant dream. For dream it is. Not that marriage has not its desirable side. I do not wish to disparage this holy state in any way. But there are many who paint the alluring side only.

I am desirous of portraying marriage in its entirety, its shadows as well as its lights. And the surest way to have marriage bright is to realize that it has its shadows. Once a person knows that marriage is going to be just what husband and wife make it, a great step has been taken toward making it a success.

Marriage is a partnership. Neither husband nor wife alone can make it a success. Cooperation is necessary. Both must be tolerant and considerate and solicitous for each other's welfare. The best investment husband and wife can make is for each to live mainly for the other. In that way both will be really living for themselves. When, however, either husband or wife starts in to live mainly for one's self, it will only be a question of time when antagonism or downright hatred will ensue.

Selfishness is the bane of married life. Once man or wife considers only personal interests, friction is bound to develop. The wife who lives for everybody and everything but her home, should not be surprised to find that soon she has no home. The husband whose main interests are everything except his fireside, must not expect to have devoted wife and children.

It is the curse of modern life that so many persons pursue their own course without consideration for others, especially those near and dear to them. Many wives sacrifice home duties to social activities. Many husbands make the club or outside pleasure their chief object in life. The result is that home and mutual love lose their hold, and once this occurs, the way is open to incompatibility and other marriage ailments.

It is true that some wives are shrews and some husbands beasts. In marrying, husband and wife thought each other ideal. There is no guarantee that if husband and wife should separate and remarry, the new marriage would be different from the former.

Children have rights as well as parents. For father or mother to deprive children of their rights rather than bear patiently the crosses of married life is to inflict injustice on their offspring. Hence it is that the Church seeks by every means possible to hold the family together. She says to the father: you alone are not to be considered. You are not a separate unit. You are not yourself only, but yourself as father and husband. In your triple capacity as man, father and husband, you must not act as if you were man only, with your own personal interests to consider, but with your responsibilities as husband and father. Face your home difficulties as you do your business ones.

You do not surmount your business troubles by running away from them, but by meeting them as a man with patience, tact, and fortitude. Do the same at home. The family is a more important business than anything outside. In this way from the beginning the Church has spoken to the father, and held together the family.

To the mother she says: you are not merely a woman, but a wife and mother. Your husband may not be what you would like him to be, but perhaps you, too, are not what he would like you to be. You must be patient with him. He is the mainstay of the family. He has his defects as you have. For the sake of the family you must bear with him, as he must bear with many things in his work all day long, as he toils to support his home. What you cannot change or correct in him, bear with patiently, it will more than repay you. Be considerate with him and he will be so with you. Even if he should not be, at least do your part for home, peace, and family welfare.

By thus counselling husband and wife, and reminding them that they will be held to a strict account by Almighty God for the discharge of their duties and obligations, the Church has shown the world that the remedy for marriage ills is not divorce but devotion to duty.

If however, in spite of everything, the marriage situation becomes intolerable, as it does sometimes, the Church advises separation rather than to live in sin, for sin it is to live in animosity and at cross-purposes. But separation is advisable only as the very last resort, and with every precaution for the well-being of the children.

Sometimes a woman is burdened with a brutal, good-for-nothing husband, who really stands in the way of the family welfare. A prudent priest will be the best adviser in such a case. Again, a good, deserving man finds that his wife neglects the home, neglects herself, has time and energy for everything except the home, or is constantly nagging, or disagreeable or resentful or unbearable. A man with such a wife is in sad case. He comes home tired or worried, only to find that home is more intolerable than the shop or the office.

Constant bickering or sour silence makes a home a hades rather than a haven. In these circumstances a prudent priest will prove to be a wise counsellor. If separation is advised, it is in hopes that it will eventually result in both parties coming together again and living amicably.

There is only one cause which justifies absolute or permanent separation, and that is unfaithfulness to the marriage vow. It was of permanent separation that Christ spoke when He said that a man should not leave his wife except for adultery. That justifies permanent separation if the faithful party insist on it. Every time, however, that the Church advises separation it is in hopes that it may bring husband and wife to a better understanding sooner or later.

The widespread irreligion of our day, which proclaims that man is his own master, and that this life is all that he need be concerned with, tends to make people seek merely their own gratification or present advantage. It does away with the cross, and declares that this life is not the way, but the goal. It tends to make selfish people more selfish, with the result that many live with an eye merely to their own enjoyment. Such a policy is fatal to peace whether in the family or elsewhere.

And that is why divorce is rampant. In two States last year fifty per cent of the marriages resulted in divorce. Think of it! In these States one-half of the most sacred contracts among mankind were broken! It is getting back to paganism. It is making satyrs and fauns of men and women.

The idea of self-control or of Christian restraint seems to have taken flight. And what is the result? With divorce multiplied, matrimony grows continually more and more burdensome and unbearable, until we have reached the stage where, instead of its being the most respected and comforting and helpful state of life, it has degenerated with many into merely legitimatized concubinage.

Marriage is the ordinary state of life for Christian adults. If entered into in the right Christian spirit, and lived in accordance with Christian principles, it will give mankind the maximum of happiness and of real welfare. But like everything else it may be abused, and when it is, it is not the fault of marriage if things turn out badly, but of those who fail in their marriage duty.

It is hard to conceive of any greater earthly happiness than that of a good Christian family. They may have their crosses, which is inevitable, but they also have the affection and sympathy and mutual support which make sorrow to lose its sting, and joy to be intensified. God made marriage indissoluble in order that human fickleness should not disrupt the home.

CHAPTER XXVII

BIRTH-CONTROL

THE press and the lecture platform not infrequently discuss the subject of birth-control. It is also a matter of discussion among people who are interested in social problems. It is a vital question. It means much to the individual, to the family, to society, to the nation.

Man is not a solitary being. He is not alone in the world. His fellow beings, known as society, surround him and influence him. Man owes much to society at large. For it is society in various ways which gives man his comforts, his opportunities, his pleasures and his maintenance. Hence the individual as a member of society must always consider himself not merely as a separate unit but as part of a corporate organization. For the sake of society at large the individual must often sacrifice personal advantages. To give an every-day example, an individual, if he should consider himself only, would drive an auto at a speed to suit himself. As a member of society he must regulate his speed so as not to harm others.

In return for the benefits which come to the individual from society he must recognize his obligations to society. Society in the form of government provides facilities and protection for the individual. The individual on his part must realize that he owes something to government. All this is commonplace, but it is introduced in order to lay a foundation for what follows.

Man as a member of society cannot be a law to himself. He is subject to the laws of the State. Every law for public welfare bears hard on the individual at times. If a law could be set aside because of its hardship in specified cases there would be no law or order. There is no law on the statute books which does not entail individual suffering occasionally or frequently. If law permitted exemption because of individual hardship there would soon be no law. If a person pleads hardship for the violation of a law his plea is not considered by the court. It is a hardship in certain cases to pay taxes, but they must be paid. It is a hardship to obey the draft, but when country summons the hardship must be endured. It is hardship for a mother to have her child torn from her by the laws of quarantine, but the separation must be borne to save others from an infectious disease. And so with a thousand things in daily life. Self must be subordinated. The general welfare must take precedence over the personal. So much for State law. There is another law, a law which exists independent of human legislation.

Man is not only a subject of the State; he is also a subject of the Creator. Man is not his own maker. Man is a creature, and as such subject to the Creator. The Creator legislates for mankind just as the State legislates for its subjects. God's laws are written on the heart of man in a general way and are known as the voice of conscience, bidding him to do right and avoid wrong. By the Ten Commandments God proclaims His law more formally. By His Church He makes known His will in detail. If Jesus Christ is God, and if He established a Church, and declared that it was His voice in the world, then this Church is God speaking to mankind.

As Catholics we believe in the Church as we believe in Almighty God. God cannot be partly true and partly false. God is Truth and truth has no part with error. Consequently, for us Catholics, the teaching of the Church is the teaching of Almighty God. God has said it: "He who hears you hears Me." Once we realize that the Church is the voice of God we hearken to her as we would to God Himself. That is the meaning of being a Catholic. If that is not our attitude we are not Catholics, no matter what we profess.

What does the Church of God say with regard to birth-control? First of all what is birth-control? Birth-control may have two meanings. We may control the birth of children either by taking positive measures to prevent nature fulfilling her functions, or by abstaining from the act which ordinarily results in child-birth. Birth-control may therefore be brought about either by interference with nature's course or by self-control.

Birth-control which is effected by interfering with nature's course is a thwarting of nature's processes in a matter which is vital to the human race, and as such is a serious transgression of nature's course. The Church of God proclaims such birth-control a mortal sin. For a Catholic that ends it. If a Catholic wants to take the law into his own hands he may, just as he may steal or commit adultery or murder. But by so doing he is branding himself with deadly sin.

Having stated the position of the Church with regard to birth-control, and the duty of Catholics in the matter, I shall now consider some aspects of this subject. Advocates of birth-control give various plausible reasons for their cause. Let me say at the outset that every reason they advance would result in the abolition of every law of State or society. The reasons given to justify birth-control may be classified as concerning either health or poverty. There is, of course, a good deal of talk about the physical well-being of the race. But most of those who indulge in birth-control are little concerned about the race. Birth-controllers are mainly concerned with themselves. A proof is that it is not the poor generally nor the less robust who practice this vice, but the rich and the strong. There is a great deal of camouflage about this matter, but the fact is that for the most part selfishness is back of it all. Not that at times the observance of God's law does not require heroic virtue. It does. But God's law at times calls for heroic virtue. Christ distinctly declares: "What doth it profit a man if he gain the whole world and suffer the loss of his own soul?" Again He says: "He who loses his life for My sake shall find it." Christ's religion is not an excursion, but a warfare. The kingdom of heaven suffers violence and only the violent conquer. Not those who do violence to others, but to their own evil inclinations. Christ frequently proclaimed that His followers must deny themselves. He set the example. Advocates of birth-control have the wrong outlook on life. Christ came to give us life, not this present life, which is a living death, for we begin to die as soon as we are born, but life which lasts forever, the very life of blessedness which is God's. The purpose of Christ's religion is not to make us live long nor to be physically sound, nor to be wealthy, but to live in such a way that in the end we may share His everlasting life of bliss.

Religion is being distorted into a sort of hygienic cult. Philanthropy and physical well-being are being substituted for doing God's will. If God's law demands sacrifices, if it entails hardships, it is set aside as being in the way. Liberty is taken with God's law that never would be attempted with State law.

But to return to the main reasons advanced for birth-control. Let us take poverty. As a rule poor people never complain of large families. A few days ago I entered a poor tenement home where there were nine children. I said to the mother, "You have a large and happy family." She replied, as tears came to her eyes, "I buried one a few months ago, Father. God's will be done, but oh, how I miss the darling!" I asked her how she managed to care for them all. "Oh, we go ahead; it's a struggle, but we always get along. We can't have everything we want in this life." A happier family I never saw. The father was a laboring man. The eldest two children had begun to work and were proud that they were helping to support the family.

Do I mean by citing this example to imply that conditions like the above are ideal? By no means. Life is not ideal. But I do mean that for the most part they who advocate and practice birth-control do not do so because of poverty. If people who give poverty as their reason for this practise would curtail some of their ambitions they would find that there are other remedies besides birth-control for proper living. Suppose a man should give poverty as a reason for theft or blackmail or any other crime! If one is poor one does not steal, but adapts himself to reduced circumstances. The fact is that they who practice birth-control mostly want to use it as a help to live beyond their means, or to enjoy sexual privileges without sexual obligations. Large families are as a rule as prosperous as small families with the same income. God's way is always the best.

The second main reason advanced for birth-control is health. I answer this with one brief sentence. There are more human wrecks from the practise of birth-control than from almost any other cause. Tampering with nature's functions is bad policy even from a human standpoint. I have known of more cases of broken health and broken lives from the practise of birth-control than from almost any other mal-practise. But I say that even if health were gained by this evil, it would be no more right to do it than it would be to lie or steal in order to have health. God's Church, His voice on earth, proclaims this vice a deadly sin. The Church may be defied as God may be defied. But that does not justify wrong-doing. Birth-control destroyed the mightiest empire this world has known. Most of the Roman emperors were obliged to adopt successors to the throne. They had no children. Soon they had no soldiers. The wages of sin is death, not only for the individual but for the State also. In some countries where birth-control was advocated as an economic measure, they are now paying out from the public treasury huge sums in order to encourage parents to bring up families without interference with nature's functions. In our own country there are countless invalids and innumerable desolate firesides because of the practise of birth-control.

Some people think that the Church is old-fashioned, not abreast of the times, a good thing for the ignorant and poor, but out of date for the enlightened and successful. The world said the same of Christ. But Christ is to judge the world.

CHAPTER XXVIII

SOCIALISM

NOT infrequently workmen have asked me why the Church is opposed to Socialism. My reply has been that the Church is not opposed to Socialism as such, but to the brand which is current to-day. Socialism is nothing new. But the kind of Socialism in the world to-day is new. The Church in the past has encouraged Socialism of the right kind in every way. But the Socialism of to-day is such that no Catholic can join its ranks without renouncing his faith. Socialism is materialism. It denies the hereafter.

Some people think that labor-unionism and Socialism are much the same. They are not. Time and again Socialist leaders have tried to get the approbation or affiliation of labor-unionism, but without success. In connection with Socialism there are some who ask why is the Church opposed to the betterment of the people, which is the aim of Socialism? She is not. About all the real good which the people at large now enjoy is the outcome of her teaching and practise. Catholics have no fault to find with the object the Socialists have in view, but with their measures to attain their object. Catholics recognize the evils which afflict the people just as thoroughly as Socialists do. Catholics are not blind to the grievances between capital and labor. But Catholics know that God's commandments bind not only capital but labor also. Catholics know that injustice is not remedied by injustice. Catholics know that there are certain natural rights of man which may not be violated. Catholics know that inequalities exist in life, that this world is not the end of man, that poverty cannot be legislated out of existence, that life is not a picnic but probation.

Catholics are not opposed to moral Socialism, but to immoral Socialism. Any Socialism which respects God and His law will find

Catholic support. But the Socialism of to-day respects neither God nor His law. A few years ago Socialism promised a remedy for human ills if it could only have an opportunity of putting its principles in practise. It has had the opportunity, and the condition of Russia to-day is the result. There, Socialism is enthroned and it respects neither God nor man. It may be said in passing that the triumph of Socialism has been the strongest argument against it. Many persons who had championed Socialism before the Russian debacle have turned aside from it altogether, or adopted new ideas with regard to it, which makes their Socialism an entirely different thing from what it was before.

Socialism as commonly understood violates man's inherent rights. Moreover, it attempts to equalize the absolutely unequalable. Its very basis is that man is simply a higher animal than the beast of the field, and that there is nothing in life but material interests. It is glorified materialism. In Russia it has been carried to its logical conclusion. There it is deified, and men and women have been animalized. Women have been made common property like goats or sheep. Men have been turned into machines. Life is held cheap. Children are reared like cattle. In a word, Socialism triumphant is the absolute denial of the spiritual. It makes of man a mere endurance machine, and holds out to him an earthly paradise which is a mirage pure and simple. The triumph of Socialism is its death-knell. Already its former advocates have so modified their Socialism that it is in reality quite a different thing.

However, the basis of Socialism is materialism. That is why Catholicism is opposed to it, and must be opposed to it. No Catholic can be a Socialist. By the very fact of his being a Socialist, he has denied his faith in Christ. Of course there may be men who think they can retain the faith and also be Socialists, but such men are only amateur Catholics or amateur Socialists. There are some men in the Socialistic ranks who see in the organization nothing but a welfare society or group. These are men who do not do their own thinking, and who, moreover, have not the good sense to be directed by those who think right.

The Catholic Church has the interest of the poor at heart at least as much as any other organization on earth. The Church has also the only right and just remedy for the social abuses which abound. It is because modern irreligious governments have tied her hands that she has not been able to apply the remedy. In the days when the Church was unhampered there was no such thing as a poorhouse. Christian charity cared for the poor. There was no such thing as monopoly. Christian justice prevented that. There will always be poverty in the world. Christ foretold it. There will always be wars. Christ foretold that also. There will always be injustice and disease and death. The remedy is not to abolish these various ills, which are unabolishable, but to meet them in the right way and remedy them as far as they may be remedied. Socialism would remedy the ills of life by doing away with them. As well try to do away with a man's shadow when the sun shines on him.

The Church recognizes all the ills that Socialism portrays and denounces, but instead of trying to banish the unbanishable, she endeavors to take the sting out of pain and sorrow and hardship. This she does by supplying a remedy wherever possible or a motive for enduring when there is no remedy. Her past is proof that her way is the right way. In former days when luxuries were fewer and work more laborious, England was known as "Merrie England." It was because of the Catholic faith and practise of her people. She is far from Merrie England now, with all her wealth. Not by bread alone does man live. Possessions do not bring content, but faith does. Last year in the United States eighty-seven millionaires committed suicide. This means that these men who had everything that material possessions could give, found life so intolerable that they could not endure it. Money unlocks every door except that of peace. There was never so much material wealth in the world as to-day, and never so much discontent. Unrest is the label on the world now. The happiest people I have met are those who have very little, just enough to live on, but who are rich in knowing that they are children of God, and happy in realizing that they are on the way to their Father's home in heaven. Hardships they have, and other afflictions, but they know that Christ had His. And they know that life is a warfare, and that on a battlefield one must expect hardships. Knowing that they must give an account of their stewardship, they are not only just to their fellowman, but also charitable. In this way they make life's pilgrimage easier for themselves and for others.

Justice and charity, among high and low, are the remedy for the ills which we all deplore, as far as they are remediable. Legislation will not abolish man's selfishness. Confiscation of others' goods will not give title to them. But the spirit of Christ will make the poor man resigned, and the rich man considerate. A poor man can be as haughty and despotic as a rich man. A rich man can be as simple and humble as a poor man. Both can be just and charitable. And justice and charity are the remedy for the ills of life, as far as there can be a remedy. Christ tells the rich that they are His stewards, and the poor that they are His brethren. It was this that made "Merrie England" and it is this that will make a merry world, as far as this place of probation can be made merry. For there are unavoidable ills after all. We may as well look at life as it is, not as we would have it. Death comes to all. Death is preceded by disease or accident. We lose loved ones. All cannot be rich. Neither can all be young, nor fair, nor famous. To close our eyes to these things and cry out that this world is our heaven is simply to fool ourselves and others. No, life is probation. Death is not the end but the real starting point. We mortals are designed to be immortal. Christ has said it. He knows.

The realization of our destiny will enable us to walk the path of life not only in justice and charity but cheerfully, no matter what our burden, knowing that we are going home, to a home where there is no sorrow nor pain, no parting nor grief, but where all is light and joy and life that knows no end. "They who shall be accounted worthy to obtain life with Me can die no more, for they are as angels and are the children of God" (Luke xx. 36). That assurance of Christ gives an outlook on life which is the real panacea for its ills. Christian faith and hope, with Christian fulfilment of duty solve life's problem. We may as well face the fact that life at best is a succession of uncertainties. For many it is a steep and stony path. Socialism cannot change the nature of man. God who made us knows best how to direct us. By His Church He tells us that life is the way, not the end, that we have not here a lasting city. Socialism proclaims the contrary. We must choose between Catholicism and Socialism.

Catholicism gave the world Christian civilization. Catholicism will give all who live up to it peace here and eternal felicity hereafter. Christ, our Model and Leader, does not promise to free us from burdens but to help us bear them. They who follow after Him in this life will share in His blessed life forever. "To as many as receive Him He gives the power to become the sons of God." That divine promise is the best panacea for life's vicissitudes. For after all what matters the roughness of the path if it leads to the abode of God? Socialism is a mirage. Christianity is an achievement. Socialism leads to a desert—behold Russia. Catholicism conducts to paradise. "Come, ye blessed of My Father, and possess the kingdom prepared for you from the foundation of the world."

CHAPTER XXIX

PAROCHIAL SCHOOLS

RECENTLY Dr. Charles Gray Shaw, head of the Department of Philosophy of New York University, spoke as follows: "Religious development is just as essential as is intellectual. Any one who thinks otherwise is a moron. We have altogether too many intellectual or artistic or musical geniuses who are religious morons . . . Religion and education should go hand in hand to achieve the final goal of a life better fitted for success. I find the greatest men in the greatest fields devoutly religious . . . Religion is necessary and should find a place in every educational institution, from the primary school to the university, throughout the land." Thus speaks a distinguished educator.

The alarming misconduct, not to say lawlessness, which now characterizes our young people, is causing thoughtful people of all denominations to reflect on the lack of religion in our educational system.

Catholics are often asked why they are opposed to public schools. They are not opposed to them as such, but because they are deficient in what Catholics consider the most essential element of education, namely, religious training.

If people of various denominations are persuaded that education without religion is the right and satisfactory education, the public schools may do for them. Catholics, however, are convinced, and are confirmed in their conviction by experience, that education without religion results detrimentally.

It is not that public school education necessarily antagonizes religion, but that it ignores it. You may deprive a child of life not only by poison but also by lack of nourishment. The great proof that education without religion gradually causes the decay of virtue is found in the present day status of the youth of the land.

Everywhere it is being deplored that the rising generation is alarmingly irreligious and lawless.

Recently Judge Ben B. Lindsey of the Denver Juvenile Court has given out data which tends to show that our high school boys and girls are, in large numbers, indulging in immorality. Virtually the prevailing code of morals is, "Don't be found out." That is the only wrong. Being caught is the great sin, the rest does not matter. Judge Lindsey states that many of our young people have banished all idea of religion and of future chastisement for sin. As a result impurity and dissipation are indulged in regardless of everything but appearances. Religion being virtually dead in these young folks, their conduct and principles are those of clever pagans or high grade animals. Let me give a few of his findings.

He is careful to say that he understates rather than exaggerates conditions. The first item in his testimony of high school students is "That of all the youth who go to parties, attend dances, and ride together in automobiles, more than ninety per cent indulge in hugging and kissing . . . I have purposely picked my witnesses from representative Denver homes of reasonable wealth and considerable culture; homes where the entrance of such views as these are completely revolutionary, or would be so if they were suspected . . . At least fifty per cent of those who begin with hugging and kissing do not restrict themselves to that, but go further, and indulge in other sex liberties which, by all the conventions, are outrageously improper . . . These familiarities, quite apart from the obvious danger that they will lead to other things, are responsible for much nervous trouble among young girls and for the prevalence of certain physical ailments which are peculiar to them. Of this fact most parents and teachers are ignorant. The conclusion I draw that fifty per cent of the original ninety per cent indulge in half-way sex intimacies that wreck the health and morals alike is that here is an example of false and illogical thinking . . . Fifteen to twenty-five per cent of those who begin with hugging and kissing eventually 'go the limit.'

"To most persons reasonably well acquainted with girls and boys of high school age, that estimate will doubtless appear excessive.

I can only say that the estimates come from high school students, and that they are the most conservative estimates I have received from that source. If I should name the figures I get from a majority of my informants they would merely excite incredulity and hostility" (Physical Culture, Jan. 1925).

Probably there is no one in the United States more conversant with real conditions among our young people than Judge Lindsey. He is not a theorist. He has facts for his deductions. He has been instrumental in saving hundreds of young people from a life of vice and misery. The young people of his city confide in him because, no matter what their guilt, his aim is to help, not to punish them. During the years 1920 and 1921 the Juvenile Court of Denver dealt with 769 delinquent girls of high school age. Three-fourths of these girls went to Judge Lindsey of their own accord.

During the year 1924, there were one hundred cases of illegitimate pregnancy before him. Of these he says, "With every one of those girls it was a touch and a go whether to come to me and arrange to have the baby, or to go to an abortionist and arrange not to have it."

If all this does not reveal an alarming state of affairs it is because there is no sense of decency or responsibility. Judge Lindsey declares that these young people have, for the most part, ceased to be influenced by religion.

Can there be any stronger argument for the necessity of religion? Yes, it may be rejoined, but that does not mean that the parochial school is the solution. It is the solution for Catholics. Moreover, it would be the solution for others, too, if they had religion really at heart. To this it may be replied that the school is for education and the Church for religion. Let the Church look after religious instruction, but let the schools do what they are intended for, namely, attend to education.

When it is said that we should let the Church attend to religious instruction it presupposes that children are going to church. A majority of them do not attend church or Sunday-school. In our large cities the vast majority get religious instruction neither at home nor at church nor at Sunday-school. They get no instruction at home because their parents are either too busy or negligent, or perhaps are not qualified to impart their knowledge, if they have any. Most denominations find their churches empty on Sunday, or if they have a moderate attendance it is to listen not to religious instruction or exhortation but to a talk on something that could be heard as well or better from a layman or a public lecture platform.

But I prescind altogether from this phase of the matter, and say that even if children went to church and Sunday-school, the religious day-school is the very best and often the only practical way of bringing up children in the religious spirit. Religion is not a garment to be put on at stated times only. It is, or should be, a part of our very being, something inherent in us, a vital principle which animates our purpose in life and our conduct. Religion on Sunday, with the rest of the week a religious blank, is not calculated to implant in a child the habit of religion. Unless religion be a formed habit of living, as God directs, it will not affect conduct to any great extent. Now a habit is not formed except by repeated acts. The religious mind is not the result of merely hearing pious maxims and good counsels at stated intervals, but of living in a religious environment and cultivating religious practises.

The parochial school, while omitting nothing that makes for the best secular education, affords, besides, congenial environment for the cultivation of religious character. The teachers, the class-room, the devotional practises, the whole trend of the day's work, silently and unobtrusively, yet most effectively, develop in the child a realization that the one great thing in life is to live in such a way as to merit God's approval. Moreover, in a parochial school every opportunity is taken to inculcate, along with the daily lessons in the various branches, lessons in Christian virtue. Without any loss of secular knowledge the child acquires gradually a knowledge of the things of God. Thus religion takes deep root and becomes, as it were, a part of one's very nature. It becomes a matter of daily life and not merely of occasional observance. The religious formation instead of interfering with educational progress actually helps it.

It is a well known fact that in cities where there has been competition between the public and the parochial schools, the parochial have almost universally come out ahead, even in distinctly secular branches. Recently in one of our greatest cities the results of the regents' examinations showed such marked and continued superiority of the parochial schools over the others that the authorities decided not to publish the results any more. This is said in passing and to show that education does not suffer by association with religion.

It cannot be said too emphatically that religion is not merely an occasional matter. Public service on Sunday is man's act of worship to Almighty God. After religion has become a living habit Sunday service helps considerably to maintain it and to give it efficacy. But during the formative period of life, religion, unless it be inculcated by surroundings, as well as precept, will not ordinarily take firm root. The result will be that, like the good seed which fell on the uncultivated soil, it will wither and die when exposed to the elements of worldly life. Unless our youths receive religious instruction in a religious school it is to be feared that their religious education will be almost entirely neglected. Outside the religious school the only way of acquiring religious knowledge is from parents or from the Sunday-school.

Very few parents have the time, inclination, or ability to teach their children. The Sunday-school can impart only the barest outlines of religion, and that in a superficial way which lacks the vital incentive to practice, and gives a poor defence against the temptations of later years.

Environment is the greatest factor of life in its formative period. To pass six days out of seven without any practical reminder of God or the soul or the hereafter is a very poor preparation for the temptations which come from the world, the flesh, and the devil.

Education is not simply a veneer. It is not a mere assemblage of data for display. Education means drawing out or developing one's qualities of mind and heart. A child has a soul as well as a body. It has character as well as intellect. Education means the right development of character, mind, and body. The development of mind and body only, ignoring character, will produce simply a high grade animal. A clever man without moral principles is a menace to society. It is because our schools turn out so many whose education is one-sided that our country is flooded with shrewd criminals.

Education without moral restraint has done more to fill our prisons than almost any other cause. It is doubtful if one can find more clever men anywhere than in some of our penal institutions. In saying this I am aware that Catholics constitute a good percentage of these criminals. But the reason of this is not their Catholic education, but the neglect of it. Of course in some cases home and neighborhood environment offset the best religious training. That is no argument against the parochial school, but against bad surroundings outside the school. We do not condemn the medical profession because its prescriptions fail to cure when the patient failed to follow them.

A home where there is bad example or a neighborhood where vice abounds will mislead almost any young person. Christ foretold this when He warned us against scandalizing the young. Extreme poverty is rich soil for vice. That is why our slums furnish so many culprits.

Religious education is not a panacea. It does not make one immune to the assaults of vicious persons and surroundings. It supplies one with armor but does not safeguard one against rash encounter.

Other things being equal, the parochial school gives the best possible equipment for the warfare of life. After all, the great thing in life is to realize that we are in the presence of God always, that He is the Ruler of the world, that we are His subjects, and that we must answer to Him for our conduct. The purpose of religion is to effect a realization of all this. In the parochial school everything tends to impress upon the child that although he must live in this world he must not live for it. This world is not the goal but starting point of man. It is because this truth is inculcated in our parochial school children by everything associated with the school that our parochial school children, besides being truly religious, are unsurpassed as a body for every civic duty.

There are no more loyal subjects of our nation than graduates of our parochial school. Patriotism is taught them as a duty not only to country but to God. A good Catholic must necessarily be a patriotic citizen. If the United States only knew it our government has its strongest support in the parochial school. And the

Church has no better means of perpetuating her God-given mission than by the religious school. That is why her school system is assailed by those who would attack her. They know that so long as the child is religiously trained they have no hope of destroying her. Hence, whenever religion is assailed the religious school is attacked. That ought to teach us its value.

Catholics make great sacrifices for their religious schools. They do this because Christ, the Son of God, declares that the soul is of more value than the whole world. The world passes away. The soul is immortal. It will last as long as God. Christ so valued it as to sacrifice His life for it. That is why we Catholics make such sacrifices for it. A few generations without Catholic schools would mean empty Catholic churches.

If some of our leading Catholic men who pour out their money and lend their prestige to various secular enterprises would only realize what they could do for God and country and countless souls by endowment and social encouragement of Catholic education, what a blessing would be theirs in time and eternity! Our Religious Orders, men and women, sacrifice their very lives in the cause of religious education. Certainly the rest of us should show at least the encouragement of appreciation.

In conclusion let me quote a non-Catholic writer of distinction, Mr. Charles M. Sheldon, who speaks as follows in the Atlantic Monthly, Oct. 1925: "Education without religion is more than a blunder—it is a falsehood; and if we do not teach religion in the schools, we deserve to suffer as a nation and go the way of all those nations that have thought more of accumulating facts than of making life."

CHAPTER XXX

GOVERNMENT PERSECUTION OF THE CHURCH

I T must be a cause of wonder and grief to Catholics in this country that in some countries there is governmental persecution of the Church. This persecution goes so far at times that it leads to imprisonment, confiscation of goods, exile or death. It is so hostile that it forbids the crucifix to be displayed in any civil establishment, even in the class-rooms of distinctly Catholic districts. What is it that draws the hostility of some governments upon the Catholic Church?

Before we reply it should be stated that we should not be surprised nor alarmed that the Church of Christ meets with persecution. Christ foretold it. His Church is the continuation of His ministry in the world. His Church should not expect to fare better than Himself. He was maligned, opposed, persecuted, and finally put to death. But Easter followed Good Friday. Calvary was not the end, but the beginning. The Resurrection followed the Crucifixion. So in every generation the Church is persecuted. Often her death-knell has been rung, only to find that it was the clarion sound of her resurrection and renewed triumph. The Church, like Christ, has her Calvary. Also, like Christ, she has her victory over death. She is continually being crucified yet she is perpetually gaining in vitality. To-day, after twenty centuries of persecution, she is the most virile and extensive corporate body in the world. Christ, who foretold her trials, also foretold her triumphs. He did not guarantee the bark of Peter against storms, but He did say that He would be always with her. And He has been. Else she had perished long since.

Now to come to the matter in hand, why is it that various governments persecute the Catholic Church? There are several reasons. The main reason is because the Catholic Church is the one institution in the world that cannot be controlled by government. It is true that at various times, in order to avoid greater evil, she has made certain concessions to governments in non-essential matters, but on Christian essentials she never has and never will make compromise with any power on earth. She alone of all Churches stands up fearlessly before the mightiest, and says, as John the Baptist said to Herod, "It is not lawful." She it was, who, in the person of Ambrose, stood before the great Theodosius and refused him entrance to Catholic worship unless he ruled as a Christian emperor. She it was who, alone in all Europe, refused to do the bidding of Europe's master, when the all-conquering Napoleon tried to use the Church for his own ends. So it has ever been. If the people only knew it their greatest friend and protector is the Catholic Church. She is the main barrier between the throne and tyranny. That is why the Russian Revolutionists endeavored to annihilate her. That is why some of the South American governments exile her. They cannot use her. They cannot even keep her silent when they try to carry out their dastardly projects. They fear and hate her. For whether her protests are active or passive they cannot endure the sight of an establishment whose very existence is a condemnation of injustice.

Most of the governments which persecute the Church of Christ are resting on injustice. They do not voice the sentiments of the people, but of a rabid and unscrupulous minority. Government that does not represent the people is not government. The very essence of government is to serve the people at large. These persecuting governments serve only an interested minority. It may be said why do people tolerate such governments? As if the people had any say in the matter. We know how a handful of determined and well organized and unscrupulous men can run things as they like in some governments. Most people prefer to endure rather than fight. The unprincipled minority loves to fight. Fighting is its element. Thus it gains control and sometimes holds control for a long time.

It is well known that in some countries to-day five per cent of the people tyrannize over the other ninety-five per cent. This is no exaggeration. As an instance I may refer to a recent attack on the Church in France. The popular vote was twenty-three to two against the measure, yet it was carried by reason of the skilful manipulation of the legislative body. There were many and large meetings of protest, but to no purpose. The people did everything but rebel. Force alone carried through the unjust and irreligious legislation. They call this liberty, and accuse the Church, the mother of liberty, of being opposed to liberty. Another reason why some governments are opposed to the Catholic Church is because she stands as a barrier to their despotism or rascality. The Church, by refusing to sanction or cooperate with them, even though she does not actively oppose them, incurs their enmity. And having power in their hands they do what Herod and Pilate did to Christ. In some countries where priests and nuns have been persecuted, the people as a body have been so incensed that nothing but fear of the military have kept them from insurrection. It is not a nation ordinarily that persecutes the Church, but unjust and unscrupulous misrepresentatives of a nation. This explains why the Church of Christ is persecuted in some countries.

Another reason is that sometimes, when there is a moral issue involved, it is the duty of the Church to cooperate with the party which stands for morality. But apart from this, the policy of the Church is not to interfere with politics. Unfortunately some Catholics at times fail to observe the Church's attitude in this matter, to the detriment of religion. However, the Church as a body holds aloof from all political entanglements as such. Often, too, evil politicians, looking for a pretext to brush aside the Church to give full play to their nefarious designs, proclaim that the Church is a political antagonist when in reality there are no grounds whatever for the charge. If you look at the policy and morals of those governments which assail the Church, you will find in most cases why they align themselves against her. If they were seeking the true welfare of the people they would welcome, not fear, the Church. In the name of liberty they oppose and persecute the Church. Yet in their procedure against her they violate every prerogative of liberty. In ordinary justice a whole body of people do not suffer for the presumed acts of one or a few. Yet this is what happens in the assaults of these governments on the Church. They infringe on the rights of a whole people because it is alleged that an individual here or there was derelict or antagonistic.

In one of these countries recently the attack on religion was so rabid that the crucifix was forbidden to be displayed even in private establishments. And this country was not Russia where everything religious is hated and destroyed, but in nearby Mexico. You may say, why do the people allow it? Well, in this case the people tried not to allow it. They protested—to no purpose. Finally some of the students of the National University held a meeting of protest. What was Liberty's answer? The government suppressed the National University altogether. In our country, or in any country where there is real liberty, the individuals would have been proceeded against if they were guilty of unlawful conduct. But in the eyes of Mexican liberty it was a crime to stand up and defend liberty. Moreover the punishment for the crime of a few students fell on the whole University! This is one instance of many, and a fair example of why it is that some governments are guilty of persecuting the Church. A handful of godless men can hold a nation by the throat.

But, it may be objected, has not the Church at times been a party to a political issue and rightly drawn down on her head the wrath of government? There may be isolated cases where the local Church has forgotten her proper sphere and incurred the enmity of government. In a world-wide Church there may be here and there mistakes of policy. In such cases right action would demand that the guilty parties be punished, not that the whole Church should be defamed and assailed. It may be said that in general, whenever the Church has taken a stand in matters of State it has been not against a party or government but against un-Christian measures. The Church, like Christ, is the Light of the world. She holds aloft the torch of truth and justice. If error or injustice is disclosed as a result of her light she cannot stand by without protest. That is why certain governments are opposed to her. Let them rule in justice and they will find their greatest support in her. But since they love darkness, their policy is to extinguish the Light.

In some countries, like France, where the great body of the people are Catholics, there exist different political parties. These parties are bound to consist mainly of Catholics, since the people at large are Catholics. Consequently in political movements they are acting as Frenchmen, with the liberty of Frenchmen. They are perhaps opposed to the party in power on political or traditional grounds. But what happens? The successful political party, if it be irreligious, persecutes the Church on the plea that government is being opposed by Catholics. And so they use their power to weaken their opponents by assailing the Church. However, apart from all these motives for persecution, the great fact remains that the Church from the beginning has been everywhere and always persecuted. If it is not for one alleged reason it is for another. Why was Christ persecuted? Even His bitterest enemies could find no fault in Him. They hated Him because His goodness showed their wickedness. His Church teaches the sublimest morality, produces the most heroic virtue in her members, stands for everything good and noble in life, exerts the most powerful civilizing influence, inculcates the highest patriotism, yet is assailed by the world! It is as great a mystery as the opposition to Christ, whom even irreligious men proclaim to be the one perfect being that ever lived. If perfect, why hated and persecuted? Answer that and you have the answer to why it is the world persecutes the Church. The Church proclaims the spiritual, the world worships the material. The Church lives mainly for life eternal. The world knows no life but the present. The Church stands for the spiritual and eternal. The world for the material and temporal. There is bound to be opposition between the two.

However it is at times perplexing and humiliating for Catholics to be asked why their Church is opposed at times by some Catholic governments. It is understandable that non-Catholic governments should be in opposition to the Church, but that a Catholic government should be arrayed against her is something that seems inexplicable. When, moreover, the population of the country is almost entirely Catholic, the amazement grows that governmental hostility should be possible. If it be answered that the government does not reflect the attitude of the nation, but is only the animus of a powerful clique, the mystery still remains that a Catholic people should tolerate a government which assails their religion.

Let me begin the explanation of this matter by saying that the worst enemy of the Catholic Church is a bad Catholic. Any one who turns against his own is a bitter opponent. It is unnatural for one to assail one's own. Hence it is that those who turn against any organization or society become its deadliest foes. We see this even in the domestic circle. No enmity is so intense and extreme as that of a person who has turned against his own family.

Now so-called Catholic governments which are hostile to the Catholic Church are inspired by a hatred that is almost diabolical. They stop at nothing. They confiscate church property, imprison, put to death or expel the clergy. They frame unjust laws and then appeal to those laws as justification for their unjustifiable procedure. In the name of liberty and justice they outrage every principle of liberty and justice.

Sometimes a nominal Catholic government will charge the Church with political disloyalty or treason. But always this charge is either a fabrication or else implicates individuals only. These individuals, if guilty, should be proceeded against individually and in accordance with the laws. These individuals, if guilty of any wrong-doing, do not represent the Church, which is opposed to everything wrong. The Church is the greatest upholder of lawful government in the world. Mark Hanna, who was the political adviser of President McKinley, went on record as stating that the two greatest supports of government in the United States were the Catholic Church and the United States Supreme Court. Mark Hanna was not a Catholic. Such a statement coming from such a source should stop the mouths of those who declare that political disloyalty is the cause of governmental persecution of the Catholic Church. It may be true that in some places, at some time, Catholics have opposed government. Not as Catholics, but as citizens. There have been patriotic but misguided citizens always and everywhere. In our own country we see them. If they violate the laws they are proceeded against legally. There are hundreds of organizations in our own country, some of whose members from time to time oppose authority. Our government does not, for that, outlaw and persecute these organizations. Those charged with infringement of the law are dealt with by the law in lawful fashion. Catholics in the United States are the same as those everywhere else. We know that the Church inculcates loyalty to government by every possible means. If, as Catholics, we have a grievance we proceed lawfully to have it remedied. If that cannot be done we submit and bear patiently what cannot be lawfully rectified. But in those Catholic countries where government persecutes the Church, it is either because they charge against the Church the conduct of an individual, or because they attempt to carry out measures which are unjust and they find that the Church is in their way. No just government ever found the Catholic Church opposed to just measures. The Church exclaims with the Apostles, "We must obey God rather than man." Whenever man's laws are against God's law the Church stands for God. The Church never opposes government. But it is the opponent of injustice. Consequently, when men with unjust designs get in power they become by the very fact hostile to the Church.

It may as well be said plainly that generally those governments which persecute the Church are made up of those who for one reason or another hate the Church. It is hard to understand why any one should have hated Christ, but He was hated unto calumny and death. His Church may not hope to fare better than Himself. Nominal Catholics are the bane of Catholicity. Some nominal Catholic governments are, like Julian the Apostate, mortal enemies of the Crucified.

But why does a Catholic population tolerate a government which assails their faith? If true liberty, such as exists in our own country, prevailed in these countries such governments would not be tolerated.

A clever, determined, and irreligious group get control of the machinery of government, with absolute power over finance and army, and nothing short of a revolution can dislodge them. Most people prefer to tolerate injustice rather than incur the awful consequences of revolution. Moreover, the intrenched government prevents any organized movement which would tend to check their sway. That is why, generally, Catholic countries submit to government which assails religion. As an example of how a devoted Catholic people may be dominated by a government persecuting the

Church, I quote the following description of a Catholic event which occurred some time ago in Mexico. To appreciate this occurrence it is necessary to know that the Mexican Government is one of the most hostile governments on earth toward the Catholic Church.

"The ancient Mexican cathedral, the largest church in America, was beautifully decorated with curtains of damask in white and red, the colors of the Congress. A magnificent ostensorium, expressly manufactured for the occasion in the city of Puebla, enclosed the Consecrated Host. This huge monstrance, six feet high, weighed 864 pounds, consisting of 12 pounds of 20-carat gold and the rest pure silver, embellished with a hundred or more diamonds, emeralds and rubies, and was valued at $60,000. The decoration of the cathedral, including the installation of new electrical fixtures, cost more than $90,000. These expenses, including the expense of the Congress, were raised by public subscription in a very few days.

"The Congress opened in the cathedral, and inside the church were gathered more than 12,000 who had been admitted by special ticket; while outside, in the great public square, were gathered more than 100,000 persons who could not gain admission. Twenty-two archbishops and bishops, three of them Americans, were present at the ceremony.

"Nor is this all. Mexico City, with a population of 1,000,000, has over one hundred churches and chapels. In every church, the Blessed Sacrament was exposed during the entire week of the Congress. People of all classes, eager to manifest their love for Christ, received holy communion daily; on a single day more than 60,000 children—both boys and girls garbed in white—received the Blessed Sacrament. The total communions distributed in Mexico City during this week numbered over 3,000,000. Every Catholic in the city made several visits to the Blessed Sacrament, and there was a constant stream of people going about from church to church day and night, engaged in adoration of the Holy Eucharist. Masses were celebrated, in every church, simultaneously with the cathedral Mass, and every church was crowded to the doors. It was like a great religious fair or pilgrimage, continuing for a week. Never before has a similar manifestation of faith in Christ Our Lord been seen in America, as the American bishops present can testify."

Explain that if you can. Why does a Catholic people of such devoted attachment to the faith submit to a government bitterly persecuting the Church? The people are helpless.

It is much the same in France. France, a Catholic country, is controlled by a government diabolically hostile to the Catholic Church. The government cannot say that Catholics are disloyal. Foch is a Catholic; the thousands of priests who came from the farthest corners of the earth to suffer and die for their country's welfare were Catholics; the thousands of nuns who saved more thousands of lives and who, many of them, lost their own in serving a government which had exiled them, were Catholics. Why, then, does the government persecute the Church and try to drive again into exile these heroic priests and nuns who came from afar to do and die for their country in need? It is diabolical. Let me conclude with the following letter addressed to the French Premier by a priest war-hero. This letter was written November 14, 1924. It shows better than anything else that the spirit back of Church persecution is diabolical. At the same time it makes us admire the holy Roman Catholic Church which can produce such patriotic and heroic sons as this letter gives evidence of.

The author of this letter is an officer of the Legion of Honor and was decorated nine times on the field of battle. One of the citations drawn up by his commanding officers declared that "he has exposed his life many times in order to save those of others."

After reminding M. Herriot of the fact that he caused the passage of an amnesty law permitting the return to France of insurrectionists, deserters, and traitors, Father Doncoeur shows the sorrow he felt in 1902 when he was forced to take a train for Belgium because the law expelled Jesuits and members of all Religious Orders:

"I lived twelve years in exile from the age of twenty-two until the age of thirty-four, the best part of my man's life. I forgive you for it. But on August 2, 1914, I was on my knees before my Superior: 'To-morrow it is war,' I said, 'and my place is on the firing-line.' And my Superior kissed me and gave me his blessing. On crazy trains, without mobilization orders (I was a reforme) and without military booklet, I followed the guns to Verdun. On Aug. 20 at dawn, before the renewal of fighting, I went out to look for the wounded of the 115th and advanced beyond the outposts when, suddenly, I was surrounded by the crackling of twenty rifles; and I saw my comrade stretched, full-length, on the ground beside me, with his head crushed. The German post was thirty steps away. I felt at that moment my heart was protecting my whole country. Never did I breathe the air of France with such pride, nor tread her soil with such assurance.

"I do not understand how I was not killed at that time nor twenty times since. I was thrice wounded. I still have in my body a fragment of shell received in the Somme . . . and after being demobilized I committed the crime of staying at home . . . . And now you show me the door!

"You must be joking, M. Herriot.

"But one does not joke over these things.

"Never, during fifty months, did you come to seek me out either at Tracy-le-Cal, or at the Fort of Vaux, or at Tahure. I did not see you anywhere, talking about your 'laws on Religious Orders,' and yet you dare to produce them to-day!

"Can you think of such a thing?

"Neither I, nor any other man, nor any woman will take the road to Belgium again.

"Never!

"You may do as you please, you may take our houses, you may open your prisons—there are many places in them left empty by those whom you know—so be it.

"But leave as we did in 1902? Never.

"To-day we have more blood in our veins, and then, you see, as soldiers of Verdun we were in the right place to learn how to hold our ground! We were not afraid of bullets, or gas or the bravest soldiers of the Guard. We shall not be afraid of political slackers.

"And now I shall tell you why we shall not leave. Dispossession does not frighten us. We own neither roof nor field. Jesus Christ awaits us everywhere and suffices unto the end of the world.

"But we shall not leave because we do not want a Belgian, or an Englishman, or an American, or a Chinaman, or a German, to meet us far from home some day, and ask us certain questions, to which we would be forced to reply with downcast head: 'France has driven us out.'

"For the honor of France—do you understand this word as I do? —for the honor of France we shall never again say such a thing to a foreigner. Therefore, we shall stay, every one of us. We swear it on the graves of our dead.

"Paul Doncoeur, S.J."

A religion which inspires loyalty and courage like that is the foe of no just government. Mercier in Belgium, and Foch in France are proof that the Catholic Church is the true support of the State and the best school of patriotism.

CHAPTER XXXI

CATHOLICS AND CONDUCT

SOMETIMES we are asked how it is that Catholics who declare that theirs is the true, and the only true religion, nevertheless conform to a standard of conduct lower than that of those who have no religion at all. Of course, those who ask such a question judge all Catholics by the one or few whom they know, and who perhaps are the kind that we ourselves condemn.

Evil is prominent, goodness is hidden. A Catholic who does wrong attracts attention, but the thousands who are upright and honorable are unnoticed. The public at large gets its ideas mainly by observation. People are too busy or too much disinclined to examine into the nature of things, preferring to judge by results. Hence nothing succeeds like success. If a man fails in an undertaking he is a failure, that is all. And yet one who fails may be a bigger success than one who succeeds, if all the circumstances were known. All that people see ordinarily are results. One reason for the popularity of moving pictures is that they spare the spectators mental effort. Picture magazines are popular for the same reason. The eye gets results with less effort than the mind. Hence it was that Christ was so particular about good example. A good deed requires no effort to recognize it. A bad deed needs no branding to condemn it.

A man's principles are not in evidence, but his conduct is. Therefore it is that action speaks so loudly and emphatically. Christ recognized this when He said, "By their fruits you shall know them." One of the finest tributes paid to the religion of Jesus Christ is that people are shocked if a Christian does wrong. The world expects only good conduct from those who are followers of Christ. It is because some Catholics, at least Catholics in name, fail to be Catholic in conduct that at times the Catholic religion has been brought into disfavor if not into disrepute. If Catholics in public and professional and business life lived up to their religion, there is no doubt at all that many, very many would look differently at the Church and in consequence be influenced to embrace our faith.

If a man is a practical Catholic he will be a good man, a good citizen, a good father, a good husband. If a public man is a practical Catholic he will be a credit morally to his office. If a professional man is a practical Catholic, he will be honorable in his career, no matter what the inducements may be to the contrary. The standards of the Catholic religion are the highest on earth. The pity of it is that some so-called Catholics drag the standard down into the dust. One Catholic in a prominent position can do more by wrong conduct to harm the Church than a thousand or ten thousand good men can do by their virtue to repair the harm. Men of good-will outside the Church have, not infrequently, been kept from looking into her claims because of the bad example of some of her nominal subjects.

If people of no religion or of different religion from ours misconduct themselves, the blame and burden rest on themselves. But somehow if a Catholic is delinquent in public or private it reflects on his faith. To be sure this is a great compliment to our faith. It shows that only what is right and good is expected of us. But, at the same time, it does harm to our religion, since with many it signifies that our faith is one thing in principle and another in practise. It must be borne in mind that very few people make a difference between a person and his creed. Of course, that is not fair to the creed, but it does not, nevertheless, prevent many from identifying the individual with his religion. Hence, Christ declared woe to them that cause scandal. He also foretold that scandals would come in His Church. There were scandals in the first Catholic congregation, although Christ was the Pastor and the Apostles were the members.

Religion will, of itself, make no one good. Christ Himself did not make Judas good. Religion directs and helps, but man must do his part. The best physician in the world cannot cure a patient if his prescriptions are not followed. The surest guide cannot assure a traveler safety if his directions are disregarded. Christ is the Light of the world and His Church holds that Light aloft. But she does not and cannot oblige people to walk by It. Some prefer darkness to light. It has always been so. Darkness favors certain deeds.

The majority of the people of our country are fair-minded. Prejudice and bigotry make some of them unfair and unjust to us. Often that is not their fault. Education and environment count for a great deal. But not infrequently Catholics, nominal Catholics, give color to the false idea such people have of our religion. It is a dreadful responsibility we have, no doubt, that of portraying our faith to the world, but it is also a wonderful privilege. Christ says, "He who confesses Me before men him will I confess before My Father in heaven." They whose lives reflect the Catholic faith are confessing Christ unto mankind. But there is another side also. "He who denies Me before men him will I deny before My Father in heaven." Catholics whose lives are a scandal are certainly denying Christ before man, for as Catholics they are the representatives of Him and His Church.

The Church is not a building nor a book nor anything that can be seen as a visible object, but a congregation of the people who constitute it, under God's guidance. Hence the only thing visible to people ordinarily are the individuals who compose the Church and the deeds they perform. They get their notion of the Church not so much from her teaching as from her practise. It is the conduct of her members which, ordinarily, shows her practise. If Catholics, therefore, do not manifest in their lives her high standards people will judge of her accordingly.

It is true that it is not easy to live up to our faith, especially in our day when pagan standards prevail. Dishonesty is so prevalent in public and private life that it demands courage and sacrifice to be a Catholic of the true kind. And yet what is our religion for if it is not to give us courage and the spirit of sacrifice? Why should not that man have the spirit of sacrifice who has received his Lord in holy communion? Is it fair to take all and give nothing? Christ gave us Himself on the cross and gives us Himself entirely in holy communion. He made the greatest possible sacrifice for us. Should not we be prepared to make sacrifices for Him? The martyrs sacrificed their comfort, their possessions, their lives for Him. During the first three centuries of Christianity it is estimated that eleven millions of martyrs sacrificed their lives in torment for Christ. Our forefathers suffered confiscation of goods, exile and death for the faith. We certainly should be ready to make the sacrifices which ordinary duty demands.

Our faith, if it means anything, is of more value, if we live up to it, than the whole world. The world passes away. Our faith gives us everlasting life and blessedness. That is certainly worth making sacrifices for. Sir Thomas More was called on by his king to do what conscience would not allow. His answer was, "My Lord King, if I had two souls I would gladly give one for my king, but as I have but one, it belongs to God, and I must use it in His service." A few days later the noblest man in England was led to the block and the axe that severed his head from his body sent Sir Thomas More to the eternal King to be crowned with immortal glory. Sir Thomas More was a statesman, the most renowned not only in England but in Europe. With him it was not a question of profit or advantage but of right. No sacrifice was too great for his Lord and Saviour, who had sacrificed life on the cross for him. Would that men like Sir Thomas More, rather than cheap, ward politicians, were the standard for the public men of to-day.

Unfortunately, some public men, calling themselves Catholic, instead of holding aloft the Catholic ideal, present to the world a spectacle to make real Catholics mourn. In business, too, and in the professions, some Catholics, instead of being a credit, are a disgrace to their religion. The public generally associates a Catholic with integrity, and Catholics as a body justify this opinion. But there are some who seem to forget by their conduct that they are Catholics, and who cause their brethren in the faith to blush for the sad display they make of their religion. The Catholic standard of conduct should make a man the very best possible citizen, the most honest in business and the most honorable in the professions.

There is no higher standard conceivable and no motive more powerful than the Catholic. The pity of it is that some who parade as Catholics belie the lofty ideals of faith and lay aside its motives for those of the worldling, and not the decent worldling at that. At times we see those nominally of the faith acting in a way which disgusts the average man of the world, who, if he has no religion, at least has some regard for common honesty and the proprieties of life. If *nominal* Catholics could only be labelled, so that the Church would not suffer for their *unfaithfulness* not only to her, but to ordinary standards of decency, it would be a blessing. But God Himself permits the tares to grow along with the wheat for His own good reasons. He permitted a Judas among the Twelve. God forces no man to do right. Man has free will.

In this country to-day the Church has a wonderful opportunity of bringing people to the knowledge of the true faith if only her children will try to be loyal to her standards. Too often we suffer as a body for the delinquency of an individual. This imposes on each one of us a duty to be true to the faith which has made saints, patriots, and heroes in every age of Christianity.

CHAPTER XXXII

CATHOLICS AND CULTURE

A REMARK that I once heard made a deep impression on me. It was made by a very refined clergyman, one of the most influential priests of his day, the Rev. Neil Norbert McKinnon, S.J. He was pastor of one of the great churches of New York, St. Ignatius Loyola. The remark was occasioned by a funeral service at which he had just officiated. The deceased was a man of distinction in the financial world, and at his funeral was a large attendance of men and women socially prominent, and most of them non-Catholics.

On his way from the church to the rectory Father McKinnon heard one of his good, simple parishioners say to another: "Isn't it strange that all those big bugs are wrong and we are right?" Afterwards he said to me, commenting on what he had heard: "In this country, one of the obstacles to the conversion of Protestants is their worship of respectability."

I have often reflected on that remark. Time and again I have seen it verified. I recall that an aristocratic and very well educated man in Boston came to me to protest that his son had disgraced the family by becoming a Catholic. The man was very indignant, and among other things said: "Do you think that my cook and coachman are right and that I am wrong? Must my son's religion be that of laborers and chambermaids, rather than of cultured and professional people?"

What he said is what a great many of his social class think. It is also at times a temptation to the faith of Catholics. For it does seem strange that the bankers and great merchants and distinguished lawyers and doctors should as a class be wrong and that their servants and others of inferior cultural status should as a class be right.

As Father McKinnon said: "The worship of respectability is a great obstacle to the conversion of Protestants in this country."

To the gentleman who protested to me that his son's becoming a Catholic had disgraced his family I said, very quietly and calmly, for I made allowance for his state of mind: "My dear sir, I appreciate your position and I sympathize with you. If you will bear with me a while, I shall try to give you another view of the matter."

As he seemed disposed to hear me, I told him briefly that if he went to France or Belgium or Spain or other continental countries, he would find that nearly everybody who was anybody was a Catholic. In fact if he went far enough back his own ancestors were Catholic. Oxford and Cambridge were once Catholic universities. England's rulers in the days of England's glory were Catholic. English aristocracy at its highest was Catholic. European civilization was mainly Catholic. European art was almost entirely Catholic. It was the Catholic Church which took in hand the Huns and Vandals and other devastating races which threatened to overthrow civilization, and made them the modern nations of Europe, now so much admired for their progress and culture.

In this country, in some parts, it is true that Catholics, as a class, suffer in comparison with Protestants from a cultural standpoint. This is due to the fact that culture presupposes leisure. A day laborer has neither time nor opportunity for acquiring culture. Catholics, as a class, have had to struggle for their livelihood, so that until very recently they have not had the leisure which culture of a certain conventional type presupposes. They, for the most part, came to this country after it was mostly in the possession of Protestants, who owned not only the land, but the factories and banks and industry generally. Coming here poor and without influence, and deprived of education by penal laws in their native land, they naturally became laborers and servants.

It was not the wealthy and cultured from other countries who came to our shores, but the poor and the oppressed. Exile sent them to us deprived of almost everything but their faith. It was mainly because they were true to their faith that they were reduced to a condition so deplorable that they came here to better themselves. They lost their goods and opportunity at home rather than forsake their religion. Settling in this country, of course they were cooks and butlers and laborers. But, to their credit be it said, no body of people in the history of the world has advanced so fast and so far in cultural development as these immigrants from Catholic countries.

Without education themselves, these early immigrants made every sacrifice in order that their children might have it, until to-day in every profession and business they are worthily represented. No other class of people in our country has so many institutions of higher education nor so many privately supported secondary schools as the descendants of those immigrants who came here without anything but a stout heart and a firm faith.

In a generation or two more non-Catholics will not be able to point to their Catholic fellow-citizens as ignorant or lacking in culture. It is only too true that until very recently Catholics as a class in certain parts of our country, were the hewers of wood and makers of brick and toilers generally. But our aristocratic and cultured critics were no better than that in the early days of their occupancy. They should not forget that. Unfortunately they do. They also forget that all the culture bequeathed to them in literature, art, and architecture, was what the Catholic Church preserved to them from the cataclysms of the period following the fall of the Roman empire, or what Catholic genius produced in the ages of faith.

However, this is only a personal retort, an undesirable argument. I have mentioned it because we should know that Catholic culture needs no apology other than a statement of facts. What *supposedly* cultured people now cast up against Catholics is what the cultured Romans objected to in the Apostles. I designedly said supposedly cultured, because a cultured person is a gentleman, and a gentleman never inflicts pain. A gentleman never embarrasses an inferior by humiliating comparisons, explicit or implied.

The *cultured* Romans were no doubt shocked by the preachers of the Gospel. How could they, noble Romans, be wrong, and these peasants right? But the peasants were right, as we know. Christianity is the answer.

Herod and his court laughed Christ to scorn and paraded Him

as a fool through the streets of Jerusalem. Yet Christ was Truth itself, and Herod was not only wrong, but vicious. Christ did not come to give us worldly honor, or success or wealth, or conventional culture, but the Truth, the Truth that makes us the children of God, if only we live by the Truth.

He came to give us eternal life, a share in His own glorious life. All of us, cultured and ignorant, rich and poor, are the objects of His love. The only aristocracy that God recognizes is that of virtue. The Scribes and Pharisees were the great people of Israel in His day. Yet these He called whitened sepulchres. They were fair to behold, but full of deceit and hypocrisy, the "better than thou" kind. Christ flayed them.

Culture is a most desirable thing, but not if it despise the clean of heart and those of good-will for no other reason than that they are poor or lack culture. Christ loved the poor. He foretold that the poor should always be found in His Church. To despise the Catholic Church because of her poor is to despise Truth itself. Herod and Nero were rich. Christ was poor. Herod and Nero were powerful. Christ was weak. Herod and Nero were wrong. Christ was right. Christ was Truth.

His Church is as true as Himself, for He said it. His Church is the Catholic Church. As He Himself was opposed by the world, we should not be surprised that His Church is. We do not look for better treatment than He had. At the same time we should endeavor to be true followers of our Model and Leader. Too often it is un-Christian conduct rather than poverty or lack of culture that repels our non-Catholic countrymen.

CHAPTER XXXIII

THE ROSARY

A SHORT time ago the New York Times reported the discourse of a Protestant clergyman at a large meeting of ministers, in which he advocated the Catholic devotion of the Rosary. Some Protestant Churches now have what they call the Mass, and, moreover, venerate the cross, and observe Lent, and practice other devotions which formerly they rejected as idolatrous.

By degrees the old Catholic devotions are gaining the admiration of non-Catholics, and furthermore, are finding their way into their churches. That a Protestant minister should regard favorably the devotion of the Rosary is, however, quite surprising. The Rosary is a distinctly Catholic devotion. Moreover, it glorifies the Blessed Virgin, whom most Protestant sects from their very origin have entirely ignored. For us Catholics it is a gratification, and a strengthening of our faith, to see various practises of our religion winning esteem and adoption by those who formerly condemned them. It will soon come to the point where the various sects will have to return to the faith of their forefathers or else abandon the Christian religion altogther. It is becoming more evident every day that a choice must be made between the Catholic Church or no Church. The various denominations which began with the Reformers have drifted so far away from the creed of their founders that many of them are now little more than philanthropic or social organizations.

Religion is a bond between man and God. Religion must speak with the authority of God Himself, or it has no power to influence the generality of mankind. It is because the non-Catholic churches fail to speak with the certainty and authority of God that they are by degrees meeting the fate of every human institution. The Catholic Church is divine, and speaks as God's representative. These reflections come to mind in connection with the present condition of non-Catholic Churches which are drifting by degrees toward the abyss of unbelief. The Catholic Church, on the other hand, is the continuation of Christ's ministry in the world.

Christ loved and reverenced His Mother. The Catholic Church, in imitation of her divine Founder, also loves and reverences the Mother of God. One of the first things the so-called Reformers did was to put the blessed Virgin Mary out of doors. They had no place for her in their system. Having begun by ignoring Christ's Mother we should not be surprised that the latest Protestantism is now discarding Christ, stripping Him of divinity and reducing Him to the level of a merely exalted man. Devotion to the Mother of God has characterized the true Church always. This devotion has assumed different practical manifestations in accordance with different conditions and needs of the faithful.

At present we shall consider that devotion to Mary, known as the Rosary. The Rosary is a form of prayer by which we repeat, in honor of Mary, the salutation of the Angel Gabriel to her, and implore her intercession. The complete Rosary consists of fifteen decades. Decade means ten. The Rosary therefore means the recitation, fifteen times, of ten Angelical Salutations. Before each ten the Our Father is said, and before the first ten the Apostles' Creed, the Our Father and three Angelical Salutations. As the Angelical Salutation begins with the words, "Hail Mary," it is called ordinarily the "Hail Mary." The Rosary, therefore, in its entirety consists of the Apostles' Creed, the Our Father and three Hail Marys, followed by fifteen decades, consisting of one Our Father and ten Hail Marys each. This is merely the outward form of the Rosary. A word now as to the inward significance and the spirit and manner of reciting the Rosary. The Rosary is sometimes called the beads. This is because the Rosary is a string of prayers, the word bead, in old English, meaning prayer. Presently we shall consider the origin of the mechanical device called the Rosary beads. But first let us look into the significance and spirit of this devotion.

It begins by making the sign of the cross, recalling our redemption by Christ's death on the cross. The Apostles' Creed is the first prayer. It brings to mind the chief points of the religion established by Christ. The Creed is followed by one Our Father and three Hail Marys, which symbolize one God in three Persons, the Father, Son, and Holy Ghost. Then begins the recitation of the fifteen decades, each of one Our Father, ten Hail Marys and the Glory be to the Father, etc. Each decade commemorates a mystery of the life of Christ, the whole fifteen decades recalling the chief events of our redemption. While reciting a decade the mystery associated with that decade is meditated upon. It will thus be seen that the right recitation of the Rosary is a brief meditation in the truths of salvation. Of course there is danger of the Rosary becoming a mechanical repetition—that is not the fault of the devotion but of the individual. The Our Father or any prayer may become mere lip-service, but that is not the fault of the prayer. It is because of the danger that constant repetition of the Hail Mary might degenerate into a merely mechanical prayer that meditation on the mysteries of faith is an important feature of the Rosary. The mysteries of Christ's life are divided into three groups of five each, the Joyful, the Sorrowful, and the Glorious. The Joyful Mysteries are 1. The Annunciation. 2. The Visitation. 3. The Nativity. 4. The Presentation. 5. The Finding in the Temple. The Sorrowful Mysteries are 1. The Agony in Gethsemane. 2. The Scourging. 3. The Crowning with Thorns. 4. The Carrying of the Cross. 5. The Crucifixion. The Glorious Mysteries are 1. The Resurrection. 2. The Ascension. 3. The Descent of the Holy Ghost. 4. The Assumption. 5. The Coronation in Heaven.

It will thus be seen that the Rosary is an epitome, or brief record of the life of Christ. The right recitation of the Rosary recalls the great truths of salvation and implores the powerful aid of God's Mother, while at the same time specially honoring her by repeating in her honor the words of the Angel who, as messenger of the Blessed Trinity, saluted her "Hail, full of grace, the Lord is with thee, blessed art thou among women."

By Rosary or the beads is also meant the mechanical device which is used in telling or reciting the various prayers. The Rosary could be recited by keeping count on one's fingers or mentally or in any other way. Custom and convenience and church tradition and sanction have given us the present material form of the Rosary, which consists of a string or chain of beads, separated into decades. For convenience sake, the beads are made into a form of five decades only. Ordinarily when we speak of the beads, five decades only are meant. If one wishes to say the fifteen decades one may say the five decade Rosary three times. Unless fifteen decades are distinctly mentioned, all references to the recitation of the beads mean five decades only. In some Religious Orders, the Rosary consists of a large Rosary of fifteen decades, and this Rosary is worn as part of the religious habit.

Generally speaking, however, the Rosary or beads are the five decade beads in ordinary use. Having stated what the Rosary is, in its inward and outward form, we may now with interest and profit consider its origin, both as regards its prayers and the material device for numbering them. It is clear that any form of prayer which consists of a definite number of repetitions must have some way of numbering them.

At an early date among the Monastic Orders it was customary to offer up for the repose of the souls of deceased brethren, not only the holy sacrifice of the Mass, but also the recitation of the 150 psalms or a part of them. In the year 800 A. D. St. Gall ordained that for each deceased brother all the priests should say one Mass and also fifty psalms. Another Monastic Order prescribed that each monk is to sing fifty psalms twice and each priest is to say two Masses and each deacon to read two Passions for the souls of certain benefactors. In the course of time, as lay-brothers became distinct from the choir monks, and in consequence of being illiterate were unable to participate in the choir and the recitation of the psalms, they were directed to say, instead, so many Our Fathers, or *Pater Nosters*. (The Latin for Our Father is *Pater Noster,* and the Latin for Hail Mary is *Ave Maria*.)

We read in the "Ancient Customs of the Monastery of Cluny," that when the death of any brother at a distance was announced, every priest was to offer Mass and every non-priest was either to say fifty psalms or to repeat fifty times the *Pater Noster*. Among the Knights Templars, those who could not attend choir were obliged to say instead fifty-seven *Pater Nosters*. On the death of one of the brethren they were obliged to say one hundred *Pater Nosters* every day for a week. To count these prayers accurately it was customary to use discs of bone or some other substance threaded on a string. Hence we read in the will of the Countess Godiva, A. D. 1075, that she left to a certain monastery, "the circlet of precious stones which she had threaded on a cord, in order that by fingering them one after another she might count her prayers exactly." These circlets were known in the middle ages as *"Pater Nosters."* Their use was so general that the making of them gave employment to quite a few craftsmen who formed important guilds in various countries. Paternoster Row in London, the location at that time of these guilds in England, still bears witness to this craft. The "Hail Mary" at first consisted of a salutation only, the words of the Angel Gabriel to the Blessed Virgin: "Hail Mary, full of grace, the Lord is with thee, blessed art thou among women." The pious faithful repeated these words frequently as a salute to the Mother of God. As we know, a salute is often repeated to manifest the honor it conveys. In the firing of military salutes or the giving of cheers the honor is measured by numbers or continuance. So many guns are fired for a prince, so many for a king and so on.

As the recitation of the Psalms, divided into fifties, was a favorite form of devotion for religious and learned persons, so those who were simple or who had not leisure for long prayers, showed their devotion to the Blessed Virgin by the repetition of fifty, or a hundred, or a hundred and fifty salutations in her honor. In this way the practise of reciting fifty or more *Ave Marias* in honor of our blessed Lady became quite common. This occasioned the employment of some device in order to keep count of the prayers, and resulted in that chaplet which we now call the Rosary, a string of beads threaded with wire and divided into sections of ten, with one large bead for the Our Father between each section of ten small beads for the Hail Marys.

As repetition is apt to become a routine affair, the pious custom was introduced of associating a mystery of Our Lord's life with each decade of the Rosary, and meditating on that mystery while reciting the decade. The Rosary thus became known as Our Lady's Psalter, and was a favorite form of devotion among all classes.

In the days, before printing was invented, and when books were very few and outside the reach of the multitude, the Rosary was a particularly acceptable and helpful manner of prayer. As said before, it is an epitome of our religion, and besides helping those who are qualified mainly for vocal prayer, it also furnished those who practice mental prayer subject matter for sublimest contemplation. The Rosary is thus in a special manner the prayer of the people, both simple and learned. Those who find fault with its many repetitions fail to understand the wealth of devotion which it inspires in those who recite it properly, and the wonderful consolation and strength it gives to those who are faithful to it. The last thing that a good Catholic would want to be deprived of is his beads. High and low, rich and poor, learned and ignorant, young and old, tell their beads with true filial love for her in whose honor they say them, and with confidence in help from her to whom they send up their petitions. The world is familiar with that incident of the World War, when, in its darkest hour, a soldier entered a wayside chapel to pray, and there saw a figure bent in prayer at the foot of the altar, telling his beads fervently. Closer inspection showed that the man was none other than Marshal Foch, Generalissimo of the Allied Forces. Pasteur, the greatest scientist of modern times, perhaps of all times, began his day's work only after reciting the Rosary, and on his death-bed he held in one hand the crucifix and in the other the Rosary.

Rosary means a garland of roses. A legend has it that Our Lady was seen to take rose-buds from the lips of a young monk when he was reciting Hail Marys, and to weave them into a garland which she placed on her head. A mother never tires of hearing her child tell its love for her. Our blessed Mother hears no more grateful sound from earth than that of her devoted children who repeat in prayer the words of the Angel who saluted her, in God's name, as full of grace, and the Mother of God: "Hail Mary, full of grace, the Lord is with thee, blessed art thou among women." Having thus saluted her, it is with confidence that her children continue:

"Holy Mary, Mother of God, pray for us sinners, now, and at the hour of our death! Amen."

Mary was not only God's Mother but she is our Mother also. When the Second Person of the Blessed Trinity became man it was as the Son of Mary that He became one of us. Jesus Christ who is one person in two natures was born of Mary. As our mother is truly our mother although she gives us our bodies only, and not our souls, so is Mary truly the Mother of the person Jesus Christ who is God and man, and who was born of her. As God He existed always; as God-Man He was born of one of His own creatures, the blessed Maid of Nazareth. Before leaving this world He gave her to us as our Mother. He wants us to honor her as His Mother and our Mother. The best way to honor her is to live in such a way as to be pleasing to her Son. Devotion to her, and especially the devout recitation of the Rosary, is a wonderful help to live as God wants us to live. If we live as God wants us to we shall one day see Him face to face, and with Him His blessed Mother, our Mother. With them we shall form a heavenly family, sharing in the very life of God, forever.

Pray for us, O holy Mother of God, that we may be made worthy of the promises of Christ!

CHAPTER XXXIV

FASTING AND OTHER SUCH THINGS

CATHOLICS are often asked if fasting and mortification and other forms of self denial (*agere contra*) are not contrary to nature. They certainly are. So is Prohibition. They are furthermore asked if it is right to be required by their Church to refuse nature various gratifications. Why not, it is objected, why not satisfy nature's demands with regard to food, pleasure, and other such things? Why are instincts implanted in nature if not to be satisfied? Our appetites should be a guide and should be followed not thwarted, it is asserted. Instinct guides animals, they argue, why should not man's impulses and inclinations guide him? Each one of us, if candid, can answer these questions for himself. We know and we realize that unless reason curbs instinct in man, he will rush to ruin. Self-restraint is the law of life. Man is animal plus. Man has reason to preside over his natural tendencies and activities. In animals, instinct is sole guide. In man reason is ruler. If man followed instinct he would kill for revenge, eat and drink what he liked, disregard chastity, and plunder another man's possessions.

Instinct, at times, urges man to gratify these and other impulses, which, if yielded to, would lead to dreadful consequences. Any one who knows life realizes that instincts require the curb of reason. Self-control is the very law of life. Self-mastery is the secret of well-being. If one eats only what one likes, one will become a confirmed invalid. If one satisfies a craving for strong drink, one will end a drunkard. If a person indulges certain sexual instincts he will find himself a human wreck. Always man finds it necessary to curb natural tendencies or to suffer dreadful consequences. Man alone of all living creatures is thus in conflict with himself. Man alone experiences a rebellion within himself. Man's animal and rational nature are at odds. It is useless to argue against fact. The fact is that man finds his lower nature at variance with his higher. This has led Chesterton to say that if revelation did not teach the dogma of original sin, man would have to invent it or something similar in order to explain human nature. Man rebelled against God, and in consequence man's animal nature is in rebellion against his rational nature. We all know this, we feel it daily.

If we gratify our passions against reason's protest, we pay dearly for it. Nearly all the misery of mankind is due directly or indirectly to yielding to passion against the dictates of reason. Under passion a man is ordinarily unreasonable. Under passion a man does what frequently causes him years or a lifetime of regret. Hence a man aims at directing himself by reason. Likes and dislikes do not govern his actions. We observe this in every career of life. A merchant does not conduct his business as pleasure dictates, but as business experience has taught him.

Often a business man, if he consulted his feelings, would rest at home or take a holiday or close shop early or do one of many things which nature craved. But he refuses to indulge himself because he knows that to gratify his inclination would result detrimentally. Restraint must be practiced by every human being who would escape evil consequences. In society people must continually practice restraint or lose social standing. A man who acted on instinct in his social relations would soon find himself ignored.

It is the same with regard to the various professions. Lawyers, doctors, and teachers must constantly subordinate their feelings to professional demands. Life is just one constant exercise of self-restraint or the experience of misery in consequence. It is self-mastery or self-slavery. If reason does not rule passion will ruin. Man must be master of his animal nature or it will run away with him. In the long run it costs man less to curb passion than to pay the tax it levies. The toll on uncontrolled instinct is very heavy. Only a child or a simpleton can fail to realize that man cannot afford to be led by instinct. Hence self-mastery becomes vital to well-being. Without self-mastery man becomes the plaything of his inclinations, the slave of animal desires, virtually an animal without the animal's instinctive guidance. He who is servant to his body is not master but slave. Christ came to make us free with the freedom of the children of God. He came to make us masters of ourselves instead of slaves of passion. Hence He proclaimed self-denial as the way to freedom. For no man is free who is chained by desire or governed by the body's clamor.

Christ proclaimed that self-denial was to characterize His followers. "He who will be My disciple let him deny himself." Christ bids us to do for eternal life what we must do for this passing earthly life if we would not wreck it. He bids us to do for fellowship with Him what we must do for fellowship in society. He commands us to exercise for immortal well-being that control which is necessary for mortal welfare. He orders us to do for an eternal crown what we must do for success in temporal matters.

The Church, in His Name and by His authority, proclaims the necessity of self-denial. Self-denial is simply self-mastery. It is an indication that we rule the animal that is in us, that we hold the reins and are not run away with. Self-denial in the religious sense is mastery of self in accordance with Christ's counsels and for love of Him. Christ for love of us denied Himself what was most congenial to human nature. He denied Himself food when hungry, rest when weary, comfort when fatigued. Having joy set before Him He chose sorrow. Willingly He went to His passion and death, enduring pain and shame for love of us, to redeem us, and to set us an example. He bids His followers do for themselves a little of what He did for them. Realizing that love shows itself in suffering and sacrifice, He proved His love for us by pain and privation, and in return He wants us to show our love for Him, not by what we say but by what we do and endure. Christ does not take pleasure in our suffering or privation. But He does take pleasure in what they signify, namely, respect or reverence or love. If a child, for love of its mother, does without something it likes, the mother is pleased, not with the privation, but with the love that was its motive. If a son, in order to lighten his father's work, abstains from an afternoon of pleasure and helps his father, the father does not rejoice in the privation of pleasure suffered by his son, but he does heartily rejoice at the affection of which the sacrifice of the day's pleasure gives proof.

And so with us, when we practice self-denial, God is pleased, not that we deprive ourselves of what we like, or endure what we dislike, but because it is done as an act of obedience or reverence or love for Him. The Church specifies certain periods of penance, such as Lent and Advent, and certain practises of self-denial, such as fasting and the withdrawal from various forms of entertainment. She does this in order to help us to carry out Christ's precept of self-denial, and to furnish us with the opportunity of doing penance for our sins.

We are children of holy Mother Church. Frequently children need to be told what is good for them and given the opportunity of doing what is for their welfare. In like manner we children of the faith need to be reminded from time to time that we must do penance. Hence the Church appoints certain definite periods of the year as penitential seasons, and reminds us of the necessity of self-denial in one form or other. Christian self-denial means first of all that we must keep away from the occasions of sin. No matter what pleasure or profit certain things might give us, we must deny them to ourselves if they lead us into the path of sin. People ordinarily do not sin because they want to sin, but because they want some gratification which they obtain by sin. Everyone who wants to save his soul must practice self-denial to the extent of avoiding what is sinful. If any pleasure or gain must be obtained by violating one of God's commands it must be rejected, no matter how ardently we crave it.

Everybody would be virtuous if everybody could have whatever desire and passion called for. If we had no unruly inclinations to curb we should all be saints. Life would not then be a warfare but a pleasure trip. It would be going to heaven in a Pullman. But life is a pilgrimage. It is a way of the cross, and the sooner and better we realize it, the cross will be lighter and the way easier. It is not they who take up their cross after Christ and carry it for His sake who find life hard, but rather they who try to refuse the cross. Carrying it with Christ makes it light and even sweet, for we know that it is the means of enabling us to share in His glory.

Trying to reject it not only makes it heavier, but in rejecting it, and the self-denial it implies, man gives rein to his passions, with the result that he takes the path of sin, whose wages is death.

The most miserable people one can find in this world are they who have put no curb on their desires, who have denied themselves nothing that inclination called for, who have gratified every demand of nature. Hospitals, and insane asylums and prisons number only too many who have ruined themselves by self-indulgence. The world is strewn with human wreckage, the result of yielding to nature's base inclinations. Scripture says that man is prone to evil from his youth. Unless, therefore, he restrains his evil passions by the reins of reason he will find that they will rush him headlong to ruin. Experience, therefore, dictates and confirms the Catholic doctrine of self-denial. Man must practice this virtue with regard to what is sinful or lose his soul. Not only his soul but his earthly peace and welfare.

But self-denial does not stop at what is sinful. That degree is necessary for salvation. Christ counsels self-denial as a most effective means of sanctification. And it is this degree of self-denial that we ordinarily mean when we use the term. Self-denial in this sense means doing without what we like, or doing what we dislike, even where there is no question of sin in the matter in question. It is an act of mortification whereby we deprive ourselves of pleasure, or inflict pain on ourselves for the love of God. This degree of self-denial is always a voluntary matter. When the Church commands us to fast or to practice any other act of penance it is not a matter of choice with us. Once the Church authoritatively commands it is sinful not to comply, unless conditions justify our non-compliance.

But he who limits himself to what is obligatory in self-denial will find ordinarily that it is barely sufficient for a virtuous life. If one really wants to be virtuous, one will find that Christ's counsel of voluntary self-denial is one of the most effective means. A marksman must aim higher than his objective if he hopes to score. Unless we aim at more than barely keeping the commandments of God and Church it is to be feared that we shall not succeed in avoiding sin. But if by voluntary self-denial we refrain from what is permissible, we are not likely to indulge in what is sinful. Hence it is that self-denial is a basic virtue with the saints and with all religious orders. St. Ignatius wisely says that in proportion as we practice self-denial do we make ourselves dear to Christ and merit His assistance to live more and more worthy of Him. In every department of life we must deny ourselves or meet with disaster.

Christ bids us deny ourselves in order that we may more securely attain eternal welfare. The Church, His voice on earth, proclaims certain periods and kinds of self-denial in order to help us fulfil the will of the Master.

CHAPTER XXXV

EVOLUTION

SOME people have the notion that Christianity and science are at odds. A false Christianity may be at odds with science, or a false science may be at odds with Christianity. But true Christianity and true science cannot be opposed. Wherever there is opposition of science to Christianity it is because a false champion of either is defending or expounding his case.

The reason why true science and Christianity cannot be in opposition is because they both emanate from the same source. God is the Author of nature and the Founder of Christianity. As God cannot contradict Himself, science cannot contradict Christianity. Science is the revelation of God in nature. Christianity is the revelation of God in religion. It is the same God who made nature and revealed Christian truth. Hence there can never be real antagonism between true science and the true religion.

Science is experimental. It is changing continually. What it teaches to-day it discards to-morrow. In the process of change science assumes various temporary forms. Some of these forms may be opposed to Christianity. In fact some of them are opposed to former accepted teaching of science itself. In the past eighty years, for instance, the theory of evolution has undergone three distinct changes. As each theory was born it claimed to be final and true, sounding the death-knell of previously accepted theories. When Darwinism was in its early stages it spoke with finality. It was a dogma of science. It was infallible. Now no first class scientist accepts Darwinism, as we shall see presently.

Darwinism is not evolution, but only a phase of evolution now discarded by the foremost evolutionists. Evolution in its general acceptance means the theory which holds the change of one species of plant or animal into another distinct species. It is only a scientific theory, not a fact. Darwinism is an attempt to explain how this change takes place. His doctrine of the survival of the fittest is his theory of how the theory of evolution operates. Evolution itself is, I repeat, only a theory, it is not a fact. Most people take it for granted that evolution is an established fact. In some museums of natural history you will find types of man's evolution from ape to civilized man. All such exhibitions are scientific imaginings. In the whole history of evolution there is not a single proven case of transition from one species to another different species.

Scientists have been searching the world over for the missing link, but it has never been found, as the foremost scientists readily admit. Some people swear by any pronouncement labelled science. They accept a so-called scientific statement without question, simply because they are hypnotized by the term science.

I am not belittling science. Far from it. It is man's greatest natural achievement and the promise of his greatest earthly advancement. But the pronouncements of science are not infallible. True science knows its limitations. The great scientists are humble and conservative. They know the difference between theory and fact. They distrust themselves and their findings.

Some of my readers may feel that I am too positive in this matter. In order to confirm what I say it is sufficient to state that many scientific dogmas of one generation are exploded the next. As an example take the matter of spontaneous generation. Up to the time of Pasteur this was a scientific dogma. Now it is absolutely relegated to the realm of discarded theories. Another scientific dogma, lately discarded, is that the atom was the ultimate constituent of matter. Until recently this was an unquestioned and fundamental doctrine of physical science. To-day it has given way to a new dogma, that of electrons.

Evolution the past century has passed through three distinct phases, that of Lamarck, followed by that of Darwin, which in turn has given way to present-day evolution, embracing a number of various theories, of which the most notable is that of Mendel. A fact never changes. Evolution is constantly changing. It is, therefore, a theory only. As a scientific theory it is not opposed to

Christianity. By scientific theory I mean one that adduces evidence for its conclusions. That scientific evolution is not opposed to Christianity, let me quote one of the greatest living scientists, who is also a Catholic priest. Wasmann has written over thirty volumes on Evolution, and is one of the foremost authorities in the world on biology. "Human knowledge and the Christian faith are not opposed to each other. Both are streams flowing from one original source, from one and the same infinite, eternal and divine wisdom. This wisdom cannot contradict itself, although it may address us now in one, now in another language. Hence I am firmly convinced that there can be no real contradiction between Christianity and science. I appreciate fully the zeal with which scientists are carrying on their investigations into the primitive history of the human race; and provided they do so in accordance with scientific procedure, I have no reason at all for protesting. Whatever science reveals I shall accept without reservation, but the case is entirely different with phantoms of the imagination set forth as facts. If we assume that God is the Creator of all things and that the world created by Him has evolved independently and automatically, we have actually a greater idea of God than if we regard Him as constantly interfering with the working of the laws of nature. Let us imagine two billiard players, each having a hundred balls to direct. The one needs a hundred strokes in order to accomplish his end, the other with one stroke sets all the balls in motion as he wills. The latter is undoubtedly the more skilful player . . .

"St. Thomas stated long ago that the force of any cause was the greater the further its action extended. God does not interfere directly in the natural order where He can act through natural causes. This is by no means a new principle, but a very old one, and it shows us that the theory of Evolution, as a scientific hypothesis, is perfectly compatible with the Christian theory of the origin of things. According to this view, the evolution of the organic world is but a little line in the millions of pages contained in the Book of the Evolution of the whole universe, on the title page of which still stands written in indelible letters, 'In the beginning, God created heaven and earth.' "

Thus speaks a great scientist, who is also a devoted clergyman. Wasmann's works are found in every scientific library of the world. He is recognized as a foremost scientist by scientists. But long before Wasmann, Catholic scholars and theologians held a theory of evolution. It was not precisely the same as present day evolution, but nevertheless a very decided form of evolution. Centuries ago St. Augustine, St. Basil and St. Gregory wrote long and learned treatises on this subject. St. Augustine, in particular, advocated the theory of the formation of the present species of animals and plants from certain previous seminal forms, just as the oak is evolved from the acorn.

Scientific evolution is not opposed to Christianity. But unscientific evolution may or may not be opposed. It does not matter. In order to show that there is no opposition between true science and religion, I quote a recent proclamation on Science and Religion, given at Washington, D. C., May 26, 1923.

"We, the undersigned, deeply regret that in recent controversies there has been a tendency to present science and religion as irreconcilable and antagonistic domains of thought, for, in fact, they meet distinct human needs, and in the rounding out of human life they supplement rather than displace or oppose each other.

"The purpose of science is to develop, without prejudice or preconception of any kind, a knowledge of the facts, the laws and the processes of nature. The even more important task of religion, on the other hand, is to develop the consciences, the ideals and the aspirations of mankind. Each of these two activities represents a deep and vital function of the soul of man, and both are necessary for the life, the progress and the happiness of the human race.

"It is a sublime conception of God which is furnished by science, and one wholly consonant with the highest ideals of religion, when it represents Him as revealing Himself through countless ages in the development of the earth as an abode for man and in the age-long inbreathing of life into its constituent matter, culminating in man with his spiritual nature and all his Godlike powers."

Signed by forty distinguished Americans, including the following: Charles D. Walcott, President of the National Academy of Sciences; President Angell, Yale; President Burton, University of

Chicago; Dr. William J. Mayo; Fairfield Osborn, President of the American Museum of Natural History; Professor M. Pupin, Columbia; Professor George D. Birkhoff, Harvard; Director Noyes, California Institute of Technology; Professor William W. Campbell, Director of Lick Observatory.

Whenever there is apparent conflict between science and religion it is due to the fact that the scientist is operating in a field outside his proper sphere.

Science has to do with what may be seen, weighed, or measured. Its activities are concerned with observation of things and deducing conclusions from evidence. Anything beyond that is theory or guess. Here is where certain advocates of evolution leave their field of experimentation for that of speculation, and in so doing go astray. Without having data they attempt to explain the origin of things. And as the wish is father to the thought, they explain the origin of the world without God. But so eminent a scientist as Sir Oliver Lodge says: "Science knows nothing about the origin of matter" (Lit. Rev. Feb. 23, 1924).

Science, knowing nothing about the origin of matter, can only theorize or guess. Yet many so-called scientists are not content with their guess, but boldly proclaim materialism. They announce that there is no God, that matter is its own origin, and thus assail Christianity. They oppose a theory to a fact—materialism to Christianity. It would be well if they listened to the celebrated scientist, Alfred Russel Wallace, co-discoverer with Darwin of Natural Selection. In "The World of Life" pp. 403, 423, he makes open profession that materialism is untenable.

"Man is the one being who can appreciate the infinite variety and beauty of the world, the one being who can utilize in any adequate manner the myriad products of its mechanics and its chemistry. Man is the only being capable, in some degree, of comprehending and apprehending the foreordained method of a supreme mind. That is surely the glory and distinction of man—that he is continually and steadily advancing in the knowledge of the vastness and mystery of the universe in which he lives. We are forced to the assumption of an infinite God by the fact that our earth has developed life and mind and ourselves."

Evolution has turned the heads of not a few, even among scientists. The reason it has led them astray is because they are unscientific scientists. Professor William Bateson, one of the greatest authorities on evolution, speaks as follows:

"Every theory of evolution must be such as to accord with facts of physics and chemistry, a primary necessity to which our predecessors paid small heed. Of the physics and chemistry of life we know next to nothing. Living things are found by a simple experiment to have powers undreamed of, and who knows what may be behind? My predecessor, Sir Oliver Lodge, said last year that in physics the age is one of rapid progress and profound scepticism. In at least as high a degree this is true of biology, and as a chief characteristic of modern evolutionary thought we must confess also to a deep but irksome humility in presence of great vital problems."

Thus speaks this distinguished scientist. Instead of looking upon evolution as the final answer, he considers that science is bewildered in the presence of these great vital problems. And yet in newspapers and magazines and in many colleges it is proclaimed that evolution is a fact. And most of these upholders maintain that materialistic evolution is the only evolution. They would do away with God, with free will, with conscience, and with the hereafter. And all on a guess! If Christianity did not present an austere code of morals these people would not be so desirous of opposing science to religion.

Real thinkers, far from finding antagonism between scientific evolution and God, see in it a proof of an all-wise Providence. I cite W. H. Lecky, who is not a Catholic.

"It is perhaps not too much to say that the more fully this conception of universal evolution is grasped, the more firmly a scientific doctrine of Providence will be established, and the stronger will be the presumption of a future progress."

Materialistic evolution will never be proven. In the words of Bolingbroke:

"Since there must have been something from eternity, because there is something now, the eternal Being must be an intelligent Being because there is intelligence now; for no man will venture to assert that non-entity can produce entity, or non-intelligence, intelligence. And such a Being must exist necessarily, whether things have been always as they are, or whether they have been made in time: because it is no more easy to conceive an infinite than a finite progression of effects without a cause."

Scientists of the highest rank, no matter what their religious creed, are Catholics in this at least, that they firmly believe in God.

Lord Kelvin declares: "Nature declares that there is one ever-acting Creator and Ruler."

Lamarck, father of organic evolutionism, states:

"Nature being subject to law cannot, therefore, be God. She is the wondrous product of His almighty will. Thus the will of God is everywhere expressed by the laws of nature, since these laws originate from Him."

And Sir Isaac Newton:

"The existence of a Being endowed with intelligence and wisdom is a necessary inference from a study of celestial mechanics."

Theories will come and theories will go, but Christianity will last forever. God has proclaimed it.

In conclusion let me cite the words of Horace Walpole to the Earl of Stafford:

"How many theories have I lived to see established and confuted! We are poor silly animals, we live for an instant upon a particle of a boundless universe, and are much like a butterfly that should argue about the nature of the seasons, and of what creates their vicissitudes, and does not exist itself to see one revolution of them."

Catholics have the word of God for their faith. Heaven and earth may pass away, but not God's word. Christianity has nothing to fear from science. For the past two thousand years the Catholic Church has been the best supporter of science. But she has been the foe of false science as she has been the foe of false everything else. In the transitional or experimental stages of science the Church acts conservatively. But there is no truer friend of true science than the Catholic Church. Pasteur, the greatest scientist of modern times, was a devout Catholic. Mendel, the founder of Mendelism, the science of genetics, was a monk. Wasmann, one of the greatest living biologists, is a Catholic priest. Fabre, the world's foremost authority on entomology was a most ardent Catholic. Away, then, with this talk of science being incompatible with revealed religion. Science is the revelation of God's work. Religion is the revelation of God's word. The two can never be at variance.

CHAPTER XXXVI

DARWINISM

DARWINISM is not evolution. Darwinism is a theory of evolution. Darwinism is a theory only. It is not a fact. Many people believe it is an established, scientific fact. It is not. That is flat, but nevertheless it is the verdict of the foremost scientists of the world to-day, as we shall see presently.

Most people who pronounce on Darwinism know little about it except from what they get second hand or tenth hand. Their knowledge rests on a superficial magazine article or on a dogmatic pronouncement of a text-book. Darwinism is readily believed because people follow a lead. They take so-called scientific statements on the slightest pretext, flattering themselves that in accepting a scientific statement they appear learned. It is always thus. What is new and high-sounding and also at variance with accepted beliefs has a charm for some people. But let us first lay a solid foundation.

I give here the statements of scientists who are recognized as such by scientists. Not one of these men is a Catholic. I purposely give non-Catholic authorities in order that the reader may not think that I am presenting only one side of the matter.

Rudolf Virchow, a renowned scientist of the twentieth century, founder of cellular pathology and distinguished in anthropology, states:

"Natural science, so long as it remains science, works only with really existing objects. A hypothesis may be discussed, but its significance can be established only by producing actual proofs in its favor, either by experiments or direct observation. This, Darwinism has not succeeded in doing. In vain have its adherents sought for connecting links which should connect man with the monkey. Not a single one has been found. This so-called pro-anthropus which is supposed to represent this connecting link has

253

not appeared. No true scientist claims to have seen him." (Address at the Twentieth Congress of the German Anthropological Association.)

"At present it would be impossible to find any working naturalist who supposes that Darwinism is competent to explain all the phenomena of species formation." (Professor Romanes, Journal of Linnean Society, Vol. XIX.)

"The Darwinian theory of descent has not a single fact to confirm it in the realm of nature. It is not the result of scientific research, but purely the product of the imagination." (Professor Fleischmann, Die Darwinsche Theorie.)

"In the first decade of the twentieth century it has become apparent that the days of Darwinism are numbered. Among its latest opponents are such savants as Eimer, Gustav Wolf, DeVries, Hoocke, Von Wellstein, Fleischmann, Reinke, and many others." (Hartmann, Annalen der Naturphilosophie, Vol. II, 1903.)

"We go to Darwin for his incomparable collection of facts, we would fain emulate his scholarship, his width and his power of exposition, but to us he speaks no more with philosophic authority. We read his scheme of evolution as we would those of Lucretius or Lamarck, delighting in their simplicity and their courage." (Bateson, Presidential Address to British Association.)

"When we descend to details we can prove that not one species has changed." (Darwin, Life and Letters, Vol. I, p. 210.)

"I for one can conscientiously declare that I never feel surprised at any one sticking to the belief of immutability." (Darwin, Ibid., p. 211.)

"In my most extreme fluctuations I have never been an atheist in the sense of denying the existence of God." (Darwin, Ibid., p. 274.)

"In no department of natural science has the attempt to draw general conclusions from an aggregate of facts been so much influenced by subjective opinions of the individual scientists as in the primitive history of mankind. On this subject it has frequently happened that views based on a few facts have been regarded as definitely obtained scientific results, by those who have not studied the matter closely, because these views have been enunciated with a peculiar assurance." (Prof. Schwalbe, Primitive History of Man.)

"Palaeontology tells us nothing on the subject; it knows no ancestors of man." (Prof. Branco, Lecture on "Fossil Man," Fifth Zoological Congress.)

"Darwinism is a fiction, a poetical accumulation of probabilities without proof, and of attractive explanations without demonstration." (Charles Robin, Dictionnaire Encyclopedique des Sciences Medicales.)

"It is established that natural selection (Darwinism) cannot have originated any species." (Prof. Vines, Presidential Address to the Linnean Society, 1902.)

How it is that any one in the face of that scientific testimony can proclaim Darwinism to be a scientific fact is a mystery. If an opponent of evolution should make those statements he would be ridiculed. But all these men are upholders of evolution as a scientific theory. By that I mean that they do not consider evolution demonstrated but that they find it a more or less satisfactory working theory. But as Bateson says, scientists find themselves bewildered in the face of the problem of evolution.

But some of our superficial Darwinians are not bewildered. They are cocksure. To read some magazine articles or listen to some lectures of college professors, or to view the exhibits in some of our natural history museums, one would think that there was no problem at all with regard to evolution or Darwinism, that it was all settled. The more people know about anything the less dictatorial they become on that subject. That is why real scientists tread the ground carefully. As proof of this read Darwin's statements above. He with all his knowledge and evidence and insight hesitated. Not so his followers. They plunge.

Having demonstrated the shaky foundation on which Darwinism rests let me make a few observations on the theory in its relation to Christianity. Darwinism is an attempt to explain how one species of plant or animal changed into another altogether distinct and different species. Darwinism, therefore, takes for granted that evolution is a fact, namely, that the various species we see in the world to-day are transitions from preceding different species. In the first place evolution is not a fact. There is no scientific proof of evolution. A variation of a species is not an essentially different species. In the second place, even if evolution were a fact, Darwinism does not and cannot explain it. The foremost scientists of the world are now agreed that Darwin's theory of natural selection does not work.

Let me substantiate this statement by citing scientists. I begin with Dreisch:

"It must be certain from the very beginning of analysis that Natural Selection, as defined here, can only eliminate what cannot survive, what cannot stand the environment, in the broadest sense, but that Natural Selection is never able to create diversities." (Science and Philosophy of the Organism, Vol. I, p. 262.)

Professor Romanes says:

"At present it would be impossible to find any working naturalist who supposes that Survival of the Fittest is competent to explain all the phenomena of species formation." (Journal of the Linnean Society, Vol. XIX.)

In conclusion I quote Bateson, who in his presidential address, 1914, to the British Association of Scientists virtually sounded the death-knell of Darwinism:

"Darwin speaks no more with philosophic authority: we read his scheme of evolution as we would those of Lucretius or Lamarck."

The above are the pronouncements of scientists. Yet to-day in many of our school text-books students are taught that in accordance with Darwinism man has descended from the monkey. Why is such false education tolerated? So-called learned professors will lecture to admiring students on Darwinism as a fact of science. If you call in question their infallibility they will give you a look of pity.

It is absolutely a gratuitous doctrine that man is descended from the monkey. On this subject hear Reinke:

"The only statement consistent with her dignity that science can make is to say that she knows nothing about the origin of man." (Modern Biology, p. 480.)

In his address to the Twentieth Century Congress of the German Anthropological Association, Rudolf Virchow said:

"A hypothesis may be discussed, but its significance can be established only by producing actual proofs in its favor, either by experiment or direct observation. This Darwinism has not succeeded in doing. In vain have its adherents sought for connecting links which should connect man with the monkey. Not a single one has been found."

That is about as flat as it can be put, yet we poor benighted Catholics are to be pitied because we do not throw overboard our religion for every wind of doctrine that blows with a scientific sound!

Darwinism would not be such a pet unless it gratified man's desire to be an irresponsible agent. Man would like to be a law to himself. If materialistic evolution were true man would be merely a resultant of material forces, obliged to act on material impulses, and consequently actuated by forces over which he had no control, thus making him a sort of animal automaton, without any moral responsibility. A very congenial way to go through life! No soul, no conscience, no judgment, no hereafter! And that is what evolution is leading to. That is one reason why it appeals to the unthinking crowd. It is only necessary to look into our popular magazines or to gaze at theatrical bill-boards, or to see the present modes of dancing and dress in order to realize how well evolution is doing its work on the masses.

Christianity teaches that man is the image of God: that he will live as long as God: that this life is not the goal but starting point of man: that Christ came to put us on the highway to eternal life: that we must walk the way of His commandments which leads to life with Him, or turn aside and take the broad way of our own will, which leads away from Him to everlasting death. Christianity is true. Darwinism is false. Christianity is God's word. Darwinism is man's guess, and a wrong guess at that. Eternity is too vital to hesitate between these two.

CHAPTER XXXVII

FREEMASONRY

IT is well known that the Catholic Church is opposed to Freemasonry. Indeed it is excommunication for a Catholic to be a Freemason. Freemasons know this. Parkinson, an illustrious Mason says: "The two systems of Romanism and Freemasonry are not only incompatible, but they are radically opposed to each other" (Freemason's Chronicle, 1884, II, 17). This is so well understood that we are not surprised to know that Masons as a body do not want Catholics in their ranks. "We won't make a man a Freemason until we know that he isn't a Catholic" (Freemason's Chronicle, 1890, II, 347).

Freemasonry is a very widespread organization, and it may well be that in certain localities and among certain groups these sentiments toward Catholicism and Catholics do not prevail. However, all that I shall say with regard to Freemasonry characterizes the order as it shows itself in its constitutions and as it has manifested itself in its activities. I have met Freemasons who have assured me that there was nothing in their organization which was in any way opposed to the Catholic Church. These were sincere men, and doubtless spoke from personal knowledge. Some of these men were high up in the order and respected it greatly. These men were converts to the Catholic faith. They left Freemasonry because they understood that they could not be Catholics and Freemasons.

In considering Freemasonry, we must keep in mind the distinction between the order and the individual. One may be opposed to the Republican or Democratic party and yet esteem the individual members of the party. In considering Freemasonry we have in mind the order as an order, its essential and practical attitude toward the Catholic Church. In the first place it is necessary to say that very few of the rank and file of Freemasonry are acquainted with the real purpose of the order. This may sound strange, considering that Freemasons are for the most part men of superior intelligence. It seems so strange that I feel I must give authority for the statement. "Brethren high in rank and office, are often unacquainted with the elementary principles of the science of Freemasonry" (Oliver, Theocratic Philosophy, 355). "Masons may be fifty years masters of the Chair and yet not learn the secret of the Brotherhood" (Oliver, Hist. Landmarks, I, 11, 21). There is no higher authority on Freemasonry than Oliver, himself a Freemason.

The fact that the real purpose and aim of the order is so little known to the generality of Masons explains why it is that Masons themselves, in all sincerity, will declare that the purpose of the order is mainly fraternal and philanthropic. However, we shall see for ourselves, by the clearest evidence, what the real purpose of the order is. The Catholic Church is the greatest encourager on earth of fraternalism and philanthropy. She is also the best informed organization in the world. Unless, in fact, Freemasonry was opposed to what she fundamentally stands for, she never would be opposed to it as she is. In point of fact Catholic Freemasonry existed for centuries as a benevolent and fraternal organization before the birth of the present non-Catholic Masonry. Catholic Freemasonry took its origin from the guilds of the middle ages. Stonemasons had their guilds as well as other crafts. Each local group had its own guild. Certain skilled masons used to travel from place to place wherever there was a Gothic cathedral in course of erection. These masons in coming to a new place had to be acknowledged by the local guild before they could practice their craft. For this purpose they carried with them certificates that they were qualified masons and free to work in any place. Hence they were called freemasons, not being restricted to a local guild. These freemasons formed a guild of their own, with a code of signs and passwords. All talk about the antiquity of Freemasonry is myth, pure and simple. Freemasonry, as it exists to-day, began with the foundation of the Grand Lodge of England, June 24, 1717. In the beginning it was just a social organization. By degrees it developed into its present form and purpose. Modern Freemasonry is not a continuation of the Catholic freemason guilds which preceded it. The Catholic guilds were formed by craftsmen who, as said previously, went from one city or country to another, wherever a Gothic cathedral was being erected, in order to help in its construction. On the decline of Gothic architecture Catholic Freemasonry ceased to exist, or rather was absorbed by local guilds. Freemasonry as it now exists is absolutely a non-Catholic foundation of the beginning of the eighteenth century. It was introduced into the United States about the year 1730, and subsequently into France, Germany, Italy, and Europe generally.

Why is the Catholic Church opposed to Freemasonry? The shortest and best answer is because Freemasonry is opposed to the Catholic Church. Even to some Freemasons this statement will come as a shock. But we must remember what was said previously by authoritative men of the order, that the rank and file of Masonry are ignorant of its real significance. Moreover, Masonry in this country and in England has not openly adopted the measures against the Catholic Church which have been employed by Freemasonry in France, Italy, and other Continental countries. In fact, English and American Freemasonry have endeavored to deny connection with the revolutionary and anti-religious Freemasonry of Continental Europe. But only they attempt to do this who are not initiated in the real inner purposes of the order. In proof of this let me say, that when the English public was shocked at the anarchistic and irreligious activities of Continental Freemasonry, and disclaimed fraternity with these societies, it called forth a protest from authoritative Masonic sources. In the Official Bulletin, 1885, VII, 29, we find the following reprimand of English Freemasonry for its denial of union with Continental, by no less a personage than Pike himself, who of all men should know the nature of the fraternity. "When the journal in London which speaks of the Freemasonry of the Grand Lodges of England, deprecatingly protested that the English Freemasonry was innocent of the charges preferred by the Papal Bull, and that it did not sympathize with the loose opinions and extravagant utterances of part of the Continental Freemasonry, *it was very justly and very conclusively checkmated* by the Romish organs, with the reply, 'It is idle for you to protest, you are Freemasons. You give them countenance, encouragement, and support, and you are jointly responsible with them and cannot shirk that responsibility.'" These are hard and plain words to be applied to the order by one who held highest position in it.

In further confirmation let me quote from the Cyclopedia of Fraternities, p. XV. "Few who are well informed on the subject will deny that the Masonic fraternity is directly or indirectly the parent organization of all modern secret societies, good, bad and indifferent." The activities of Continental Masonry became so revolutionary that they occasioned the following communication from the Registrator of the London Grand Lodge to the Grand Lodge of Massachusetts. "We feel that we in England are better apart from such people. Indeed Freemasonry is in such bad odor on the Continent of Europe, by reason of its being exploited by Socialists and Anarchists that we may have to break off relations with more of the Grand Bodies who have forsaken our landmarks" (New Age, New York, 1909, I, 177).

Although apparently condemning the outrages of Continental Masonry, the real guiding spirits of English-speaking Freemasonry are working hand in hand with their Continental brethren. The Grand Commander of the Mother Supreme Council of the World, A. Pike, in a letter Dec. 28, 1886, to the Italian Grand Commander says: "The Papacy has been for a thousand years the torturer of humanity, the most shameless imposture in its pretence to spiritual power of all ages . . . In presence of this spiritual cobra, this deadly, treacherous, murderous enemy, the most formidable power in the world, the unity of Italian Masonry is of absolute and supreme necessity . . . The Freemasonry of the world will rejoice to see accomplished and consummated the unity of the Italian Freemasonry" (Official Bulletin, Sept. 1887, 173).

In further proof that Masonry is unified the world over, let me quote a Past Grand Master, Clifford: "The absolute oneness of the craft is a glorious thought. Neither boundaries of States, nor vast oceans separate the Masonic fraternity. Everywhere it is one. There is no universal church, but there is a universal fraternity, Freemasonry" (Freemason's Chronicle, 1906, II, 132).

Individual Masons and local fraternities may be sincere in disclaiming association with the dreadful doings of the order in other lands, but it is because they do not know what is going on among those who control the activities of their order. Having demonstrated, from official and public sources, the brotherhood which exists among Freemasons the world over, let us see why the Catholic Church is opposed to the order, and excommunicates those of her subjects who join it. I shall make no charges of my own against Freemasonry, but shall let it speak for itself. Senator Delpech, President of the Grand Orient, in an address Sept. 20, 1902, said: "The triumph of the Galilean (Jesus Christ) has lasted twenty centuries. But now He dies in His turn. The mysterious voice, announcing the death of Pan (to Julian the Apostate), to-day announces the death of the impostor God. Brother Masons, we rejoice to state that we are not without our share in this overthrow of the false prophets. The Romish Church, founded on the Galilean myth, began to decay rapidly from the very day on which the Masonic association was established" (Compte-rendu Gr. Or. de France, 1902, 381). That is plain language and plain opposition to Christianity. Italian Masonry is even more radical than the French, and proclaims that it is supported by the Freemasonry of the world, and especially by the Masonic centers at Paris, Berlin, London, Madrid, Calcutta and Washington ("Riv." 1842-291; Gruber, "Mazzini" 215).

In our own country official Freemasonry's attitude toward Catholicism is seen in the following declaration: "Popery and priestcraft are so openly allied that they may be called the same. Nothing that can be named is more repugnant to Masonry, nothing to be more carefully guarded against, and this has always been well understood by all skillful masters" (Freemason's Chronicle, 1887, I. 35). In the countries where the Catholic Church has been persecuted it is well known that it was in great part the work of Masons. From the official documents of French Masonry it is manifest that all the anti-clerical measures passed in the French Parliament were decreed beforehand in the Masonic lodges, and executed under the direction of the Grand Orient. Massé, the official orator of the Assembly of 1898, declared that: "It is the supreme duty of Freemasonry to interfere each day more and more in political and profane struggles. Success (in the anti-clerical combat) is in large measure due to Freemasonry. If the Bloc has been established, this is owing to Freemasonry and to the discipline learned in the lodges. For a long time Freemasonry has simply been the Republic in disguise. We are each year the funeral bell, announcing the death of a cabinet that has not done its duty, but has betrayed the Republic. We need vigilance and, above all, mutual confidence if we are to accomplish our work, as yet unfinished. This work, you know, the anti-clerical combat, is going on. *The Republic must rid itself of the religious congregations,* sweeping them off by a vigorous stroke; the system of half measures is everywhere dangerous, the adversary must be crushed with a single blow" (Compte-rendu Grand Orient, 1903; Nourisson, "Les Jacobins" 266-271). If that is not opposition to Christianity nothing is. The President of the 1902 Assembly said with regard to the French elections of that year, "We would have been defeated by our well organized opponents, if Freemasonry had not spread over the whole country" (Compte-rendu, 1902-153). From these declarations it is evident that Freemasonry is an active and irreconcilable opponent of Catholicism.

In some countries, our own, for instance, and England, where public opinion does not countenance irreligion, Freemasonry does not disclose its attitude toward Christianity. But in very truth, the essence of Freemasonry is opposition to revealed religion. If its main assaults are against Catholicism it is because the Catholic Church is the main bulwark of Christianity. Freemasonry employs the symbols and the terminology of religion in order the better to carry out its purpose. As said previously, American and English Masons among the rank and file are unacquainted with the real purpose of the order. They even praise Freemasonry as an upholder of religion, and quote their ritual to prove it. But the religion which Freemasonry upholds is the religion which ignores the revelation of Jesus Christ, and assails the doctrines which His divinely instituted Church proclaims. "The two systems of Romanism and Freemasonry are not only incompatible, but they are radically opposed to each other" (Freemason's Chronicle, 1884,

II, 17). Hence Voltaire, who spent his life fighting Christianity, was welcomed into the ranks of Freemasonry by solemn initiation, Feb. 7, 1778, and received the Masonic garb from no less a personage than the famous Helvetius (Handbuch, 3rd ed., II. 517).

This was at a time when Voltaire was employing all his resources to destroy the Church of Christ. Continental Freemasonry is unquestionably anti-Christian. This is so evident that English and American Masons have endeavored to repudiate connection with the French and Italian fraternities. But those who are in the secret of Masonic activities and aims, know, and have declared that the aims of the order are the same the world over, expediency dictating that they be camouflaged in certain places and under certain conditions. As said before, the individual Mason may or may not know the secret purpose of the order. Most of the members, even those in advanced degrees, look upon the order as simply fraternal and philanthropic. In our characterization of the order we specify the order only, and its essential aims, not the individuals who compose it, most of whom would never join it if they knew its real nature.

In the United States, in many places, Freemasons and Catholics fraternize in society, business, and sport. In certain localities Freemasonry has actually joined hands with Catholic organizations for social and other undertakings. In point of fact Freemasonry has officially praised one of the foremost organizations of the Catholic Church in the United States. The following statement concerning the Knights of Columbus speaks for itself: "The ceremonial of the order teaches a high and noble patriotism, instills a love of country, inculcates a reverence for law and order, urges the conscientious and unselfish performance of civic duty, and holds up the Constitution of our country as the richest and most precious possession of a Knight of the Order" (Committee of Masons, Report on the Knights of Columbus).

This tribute to a distinctively Catholic fraternity was doubtless given in good faith, and with good intention, on the part of those who issued the report. This is perfectly compatible with the real opposition of the order, as an order, to the Catholic Church. Let us recall the words of Oliver, a Freemason himself, and one of its highest authorities: "Masons may be fifty years Masters of the Chair and yet not learn the secret of the Brotherhood" (Oliver, Hist. Landmarks, I, 11, 21). Moreover, when English-speaking Masonry was appalled at the anarchistic and anti-religious activities of Continental Masonry, and protested against it, Pike, a Mason in highest office in the United States, declared officially that English-speaking Masonry could not repudiate or disown the European aims and activities of the order, since the aims of Freemasonry were the same the world over.

In time of war the soldiers in the ranks, and often commissioned officers, know little or nothing of the plans and purposes of their superior officers. They have no personal hostility to the soldiers of the enemy army, often fraternizing with them when occasion offers. Notwithstanding this, the two armies are opposed to each other, and the men in the ranks, without knowing the mind of the commanding general, are executing his commands and carrying out his purposes. It is against the enemy, as an organized opposition, and not against individual soldiers, that war is declared and fought. A government would condemn a subject as guilty of treason if he went over to the enemy ranks. This is what the Catholic Church does if one of her subjects joins the Freemasons. She knows, not from hearsay, but from official documents, and from actual hostilities, that Freemasonry, as an institution, is unequivocally and essentially opposed to her. She stands for revealed religion. Freemasonry ignores revelation, and in European countries openly employs all its resources to crush the one Church which upholds in its entirety the religion of Jesus Christ. The Catholic Church would be a coward, and a traitor to her trust if she did not oppose Freemasonry, and excommunicate any of her subjects who joined its ranks. In the words of a high Masonic authority quoted previously, "The two systems of Romanism and Freemasonry are not only incompatible, but they are radically opposed to each other" (Parkinson, Freemason's Chronicle, 1884, II, 17).

Recently two facts have made it evident that Masonry in the United States is subtly engaged in warfare on the Catholic Church. It is known that the Oregon School law was directed against parochial schools. This law was instigated by the Scottish Rite

Masons of the Southern Jurisdiction, and sponsored by P. S. Malcolm, sovereign grand inspector general in Oregon for the Scottish Rite Masons.

Very recently a society calling itself the "American Prohibition Protestant Patriotic Protective Alliance" which has for its real object warfare on Catholicism, gave out the following statement:

"Regularly, beginning with the fall, when the active work of laying the foundation will start, the plans, policies, purposes and special utterances of the 'American Prohibition Protestant Patriotic Protective Alliance' will find expression through The Fellowship Forum, published in Washington.

"This publication, which has grown 'from an idea to a million in four years,' is already the world's greatest Protestant interfraternal newspaper, and probably has more circulation than any dozen to fifteen of the leading journals of as many of the largest Protestant denominations. It prints the news of all the leading Protestant fraternal orders, but is not owned or officially controlled by any of them. Its control is vested in individuals all of whom are thirty-third degree Masons" (New York Times, June 25, 1925).

Notwithstanding this open declaration, there are some frivolous Catholics who see no harm in Freemasonry, and criticize the Church for condemning her subjects for joining it. As well say there is no harm in a soldier joining the enemy ranks in time of war. Freemasonry is at war with Catholicism. If these same persons assumed such an attitude toward the enemy of their country they would be set down as traitors. Our government knows who and what her enemies are. So does the Catholic Church know her opponents. In Italy and France she beholds spiritual devastation from Freemasonry more destructive and deplorable than the material damage wrought by the World War in these countries. And official Masonry proclaims unity of aim of Freemasonry throughout the world. In some countries it has subordinated the public welfare to its own aims. It has been active in bringing about legislation not only hostile to religion but to the State also. In Italy, Freemasonry was gradually supplanting the government. As proof I quote the following from her greatest statesman and staunchest patriot. "It is an outrage that the highest functionaries of state should frequent the lodges, inform the lodges, take orders from the lodges. It is inadmissible; it must end" (Mussolini, in Italian Parliament). If the Catholic Church were not opposed to Freemasonry, the most surprised organization in the world would be Freemasonry itself.

Imagine what a disloyal organization the Catholic Church would be if she were not opposed to a society whose spokesmen thus characterized her founder: "The triumph of the Galilean (Jesus Christ) has lasted twenty centuries. But now He dies in His turn. The Roman Church, founded on the Galilean myth, began to decay rapidly from the very day on which the Masonic association was established" (Compte-rendu Gr. Or. de France, 1902, 381).

Is it surprising, in view of this declaration, that American Masonry has officially stated, "We won't make a man a Freemason until we know that he isn't a Catholic" (Freemason's Chronicle, 1890, II, 347). A Catholic should consider himself bereft of self-respect to join an organization essentially opposed to his religion, and which, furthermore, proclaims that it does not want him unless he is a renegade to his faith. Let us, as Catholics, trust our Church as much as citizens trust their government. Let us be at least as loyal to our Church as we are to our country. No self-respecting citizen would turn his back on his country and go over to the ranks of his country's professed enemy. Freemasonry, let it be repeated, is the professed enemy of Catholicism. No Catholic with any sense of loyalty or a spark of faith will join the ranks of Freemasonry. Freemasonry offers many social and business inducements to its members. That explains how it recruits an army of followers whom it uses in its own way, often unknown to the many, to carry out its purpose, just as a skilled military board uses an immense army to do its will. No Catholic at heart can even think of giving support to the Church's sworn enemy. The most authentic documents proclaim Masonry to be the uncompromising foe of Catholicism. The Catholic who becomes a Mason has ceased to be a Catholic. Benedict Arnold received many emoluments and high distinction for going over to the enemy. But Benedict Arnold was despised even by those who used him.

Masonry has the trappings of religion, but of a religion which is its own, not Christ's. In order to gain the support of Christian men against Christianity, it employs symbols and a ritual which impress the observer. It needs a great army in order to carry out its purpose. It is closely united throughout the world in its aims. It has shown its hand where it could do so, with the result that it is in open war on religion in most Continental countries, and also in some South American countries.

It seeks to destroy revealed religion, and to establish in its stead a religion of naturalism. Hence its aim is to destroy Catholicism, the one religion in the world which effectually maintains the religion of Jesus Christ. The rank and file of Masonry are for the most part, and especially in this country, ignorant of the real purpose of the organization. The Catholic Church is opposed to Freemasonry as an organization sworn to her destruction. Toward Freemasons, personally, the Church has the kindest regard. Christ, who condemned sin, loved the sinner and gave His life for his salvation. The Church condemns Freemasonry, but would make every sacrifice for the spiritual welfare of the individual Mason. If the Catholic Church were not opposed to Masonry she would be false to Christ. The Catholic who joins Freemasonry is as much a traitor to Christ as was Benedict Arnold to his country. This is plain speech, but true, and no one knows it better than the guiding spirits of Masonry. The religion of Masonry is naturalism. The religion of Christ is supernaturalism. They are as incompatible as darkness and light. Christ is the Light of the world. This Light will shine to the end of the world. Many have tried to extinguish it, but to-day it is brighter than ever. Masonry will pass away, as so many of its predecessors have done. But Christ's Church will endure to the end. He who is God has said it.